William Hanna

The Wars of the Huguenots

William Hanna

The Wars of the Huguenots

ISBN/EAN: 9783337287481

Printed in Europe, USA, Canada, Australia, Japan

Cover: Foto ©Andreas Hilbeck / pixelio.de

More available books at **www.hansebooks.com**

THE WARS

OF

THE HUGUENOTS.

BY

WILLIAM HANNA, D.D.,

AUTHOR OF "THE LIFE OF CHRIST," ETC.

NEW YORK:
ROBERT CARTER & BROTHERS,
530 BROADWAY.
1872.

NOTE.

This volume consists of Lectures which were delivered to the members of the Edinburgh Philosophical Institution. The writer was thus precluded from dwelling upon the more purely religious aspects of the History of Protestantism in France.

EDINBURGH,
November 18, 1871.

CONTENTS.

CHAPTER I.

FRANCIS I. AND HENRY II., 1515–1859.

PAGE.

Early History of the Reformation in France.—Age of persecution.—Character of Francis I.—Extraordinary procession in Paris.—Calvin's "Institutes."—Massacres of Cabrières and Mérindol.—Character of Henry II.—Edict of Chateaubriand.—Affair of the Rue St. Jacques.—Anne du Bourg.—Death of Henry II. . 11

CHAPTER II.

FRANCIS II., 1559–1560.

Duke of Guise and Cardinal of Lorraine.—Antony of Bourbon.—Prince of Condé.—Coligni.—D'Andelot.—Conspiracy of Amboise.—The Assembly of Notables.—Condé condemned.—Death of Francis . , . 38

CHAPTER III.

CHARLES IX., 1560–1563

Meeting of the States-General.—Catherine's letter to the Pope.—Colloquy of Poissy.—Conference at Saverne.—The massacre at Vassy.—Coligni at Chatillon.—Montluc and Des Adrets.—Battle of Dreux.—Death of the Duke of Guise 76

CHAPTER IV.

JEANNE D'ALBRET, QUEEN OF NAVARRE, 1528–1572.

Kingdom of Navarre.—Birth, education and marriage of Jeanne d'Albret.—Birth of Henry IV.—The Queen becomes a Protestant.—Letter to the Cardinal D'Armagnac.—Bull of the Pope.—Plot of Philip II.—Code of Laws.—Conferences at Bayonne.—Glimpses of Prince Henry.—Breaking out of the war.—Battle of St. Denis.—The Queen, Prince Henry, and Condé at Rochelle.—Battle of Jarnac.—The Queen's address to the soldiers.—Battle of Moncontour.—Invasion of Navarre.—Arnay-le-Duc.—Proposed marriage of Prince Henry with Marguerite of Valois, sister of Charles IX.—Illness and death of Jeanne d'Albret.—Her character 110

CHAPTER V.

CHARLES IX., 1570–1572.

Pope Pius V.—Philip II. of Spain.—How the peace of St. Germain-en-Laye was brought about.—Proposal of breach with Spain.—The anti-Spanish policy advocated by the Admiral.—Conduct of Catherine de Medicis and the Duke d'Anjou.—Marriage of Henry of Navarre.—Coligni wounded.—Massacre of St. Bartholomew.—Sieges of Rochelle and Sancerre.—Party of the *Politiques*.—Francis Othman.—Death of Charles IX. 161

CHAPTER VI.

HENRY III., 1574–1589.

Origin of the League.—Henry and his *Mignons*.—Projects of Philip II. of Spain.—Alliance contracted at Joinville.—Treaty of Nemours.—Effect upon Henry of Navarre.—Papal Bull against Henry, and his reply.—Exploit at St. Foy.—Interview with Catherine.—Battle of Coutras.—The day of the Barricades.—The Spanish Armada.—Meeting of the Estates at Blois.—Assassination of the Duke of Guise.—State of Paris.—Interview of the two Henrys at Plessis-les-Tours.—Arrival before Paris.—Death of Henry III. . 208

CHAPTER VII.

HENRY IV., 1589–1593.

Acknowledgment of title.—Arrangement with the Catholic Lords.—Their desertion.—The battle of Arques.—Siege of Paris.—Relief of the city.—Siege of Rouen.—Adventure of the King.—Triumph of Parma.—Abjuration of Henry IV. 249

CHAPTER VIII.

HENRY IV., 1593–1610.

Entrance into Paris.—Attempt at assassinating the King.—Affair of Fontaine Française.—Absolution by the Pope.—Reception at Amiens.—Siege of La Fère.—Submission of Mayenne.—Sully.—Assembly of Notables.—Taking of Amiens.—Recapture of the city.—Close of the civil wars.—Edict of Nantes.—Peace of Vervins.—Death of Marshal Biron.—Ten years of peace.—Their fruitful labors.—Assassination of the King 288

THE WARS OF THE HUGUENOTS.

CHAPTER I.

FRANCIS I. AND HENRY II., 1515-1559.

Early History of the Reformation in France.—Age of persecution.—Character of Francis I.—Extraordinary procession in Paris.—Calvin's "Institutes."—Massacres of Cabrières and Mérindol.—Character of Henry II.—Edict of Chateaubriand.—Affair of the Rue St. Jacques.—Anne du Bourg.—Death of Henry II.

MILMAN has remarked that throughout the world wherever the Teutonic is the groundwork of the language, Protestantism either is or, as in Southern Germany, has been dominant; wherever Latin, Roman Catholicism has retained its ascendancy; or, taking it geographically, that the Reformation gained all the Northern, the Papacy kept all the southern countries of Europe. France lies in the centre between the northern and the southern, the Teutonic and the Celtic tribes; its population so mixed in origin and character that both tendencies were found in it,—that which clung to, and that which recoiled from, Rome. It was natural, therefore, that France should be the country which the great religious movement of the sixteenth century divided and distracted beyond all others. It proved in fact the bloodiest battle-field of the Reformation, in which the opposing forces, when each had marshalled its full strength, were found to be the most nearly matched, and were thrown into the fiercest collision, victory trembling often in the balance, as scarce knowing on which side to fall. Nowhere else did the Reformation give birth to fifteen years of almost uninterrupted and most embittered civil war.

Yet it was not till the year 1559—by which time in Germany, Switzerland, England, Scotland, Denmark, Sweden, all the great battles of the Reformation had been fought, and all its great victories won—that it took any tangible shape in France, or originated any political movement. The first country in Europe in which the new doctrines had been taught, France was the last country in which they were embodied in an ecclesiastical institute, the last in which they proved the occasion of social strife and political division. This may partly have arisen from the weakened condition of the state. France for the time had lost her leadership of European civilization. In the twelfth century she had headed the Crusades; the most brilliant intellectual lights of the thirteenth century shone in her great university; her monarchs had triumphed in the fourteenth century in their contests for supremacy with the Popes; and in the fifteenth century it was she mainly that in the Councils of Pisa, Constance, and Basle, stood out successfully for the rights of the Church at large against the claims of the Roman Pontificate. But her step was not the foremost in the century of the Reformation. It was not within her bounds that the telescope was invented or the art of printing discovered; it was not her ships that first doubled the Cape of Good Hope, and made their way across the Atlantic; it was not her schools or universities that gave to art a Leonardo da Vinci, a Cardan and a Copernicus to science, an Erasmus to general literature.

There were, however, more special reasons why in the great religious movement of the time France walked at first with a slow and lingering footstep. In other countries the Reformation found from the beginning some ecclesiastical or political support to lay its hand upon, by which to help itself forward. None such was found in France. The Church was not groaning there under the same bondage that elsewhere oppressed her; she had already fought for and so far achieved her independence, that no foreign ecclesiastics were intruded into her highest offices, nor were her revenues liable to be diverted at the will of the Pope into Italian channels. Philip the Fair had two centuries before emancipated the monarchy from the hierarchical thraldom. Neither Church nor State had in France the same grounds of quarrel with Rome they had in other lands. There was less material there for the Reformers to work upon. With little to attract either King or Clergy, the Reformation had in its first aspects every thing to repel. The Church saw in it a denial of her authority, a repudiation of her doctrine, a simplification of her worship, an overturn of her proud and ambitious hierarchy. The Royal power was in conflict with two enemies: the feudal independence of the nobles, which it wished to destroy; the growing municipal freedom of the great cities, which it wished to curb. To both enemies of the Crown, the Reformation, itself a child of liberty, promised to lend aid. Absolutism on the Throne looked on it with jealousy and dread. Alone and unbefriended, it had from the beginning to confront in France bitter persecution, a persecution instigated in the first instance exclusively by the clerical body, afterwards by the Clergy and the Monarch acting in willing concert.

For nearly half a century, from 1515 to 1559, during the reigns of Francis I. and Henry II., the history of French Protestantism offers nothing to the eye of the general historian but a series of attempts to crush it by violence. We scarcely wonder, therefore, Mignet should have said, that the religious revolution proclaimed forty years before, by Luther on the banks of the Elbe, by Zuinglius on the lake side of Zurich, was not seriously entered on in France, till about the year 1560.[1] Nevertheless, the forty previous years are as full of interest to our eye as any equal period in the entire history of French Protestantism. They form its age of martyrdom. In no country, the Netherlands alone excepted, did Protestanism furnish so large and so noble an army of martyrs as in France. In Scotland and England, the martyrs of the distinctively Reformation-period were so few, that we can stand by every stake, and grave the name of every one who perished in the flames upon our memory. In the pages of Crespin and elsewhere, are described at large the death-scenes of many hundreds burned alive in France during these forty years.

Besides being fitly described as its age of persecution, these first years of Protestanism in France may also fitly be described as its age of purity. The Reformed had as yet no organization, civil or ecclesiastical; they had no Church, no creed, no fixed form of worship. They had entered into no political alliance with any party in the State. It was a quiet, hidden movement in the hearts of men, thirsting for religious truth, for peace of conscience, for purity of heart and life. They sought each other out, and met to help each other on. But it was in small bands, in closets with closed doors, in the murky lanes of the city, in the lonely hut by the wayside, in the gorge of the mountain, in the

[1] "Memoires Historiques," par M. Mignet: Paris, 1854, p. 255.

heart of the forest, that they met to study the Scriptures together, to praise and pray. They did so at the peril of their lives, and the greatness of the peril guarded the purity of the motive. Ordinarily, they had no educated ministry. Those who—as Luther and Melanchthon in Germany, Knox and others in Scotland, Zuinglius in Switzerland—might have formed the nucleus of a new clerical institute, were either, like Lefevre, Farel, Calvin, forced into exile, or, like Chatelain, Pavanes, and Wolfgang Schuch, burnt at the stake. Left for a time without such guidance, the Reformers had to provide for religious instruction, and for the administration of ordinances among them as best they could. Bernard Palissy, who was one of them, tells us in his own quaint and simple style how they did in his own town of Saintes. "There was in this town," he says, "a certain artisan marvellously poor [it is thus he describes himself], who had so great a desire for the advancement of the gospel, that he demonstrated it, day by day, to another as poor as himself, and with as little learning—for they both knew scarcely any thing. Nevertheless, the first urged upon the other, that if he would employ himself in the making of some kind of exhortation, it would be productive of great good. The man addressed thus, one Sabbath morning assembled nine or ten persons, and read to them some passages from the Old and New Testaments, which he had put down in writing. He explained them, saying that as each one had received from God, he ought to distribute to others. They agreed that six of them should exhort, each once in the six weeks, on Sundays only. That was the beginning of the Reformed Church at Saintes;" that, we have to add, was the beginning of many other churches all over France, and that was the way in which they were often served. In France the Reformation began in the University. The lettered classes were the first to hail the new ideas that it taught. Many of the nobles—their wars with one another now prohibited—gave their leisure hours in their country castles to the reading of the Bible and of Lutheran tracts. But it was among men like Palissy, the skilled artisans of the towns and villages of France, that the Reformation made the greatest and the purest progress. "Above all," says a Catholic historian, " painters, watchmakers, sculptors, goldsmiths, printers, and others who, from their calling, have some mental superiority, were among the first taken in."

To provide all who could read with the Scriptures, and religious books and tracts—the writings especially of Calvin and of Luther, a prodigious activity was employed. The printing-presses of Geneva, Lausanne, Neufchatel, teemed with such productions; nor were there wanting brave men who took and bore them all through France, not a few of whom paid the forfeit of their lives for doing so. Under this simple *régime*, and amid all difficulties and disadvantages, the Reformation made such extraordinary progress, that at the death of Francis I., which took place in 1547, it largely leavened seventeen provinces, and thirty-three of the principal towns in France,—those who had embraced it forming about a sixth of the entire population of the country.

With Francis I. the middle ages ended, and the age of the *renaissance* commenced. The idol of his country, Francis was the living image of the times in which he lived,—times that present to us a strange *mélange* of barbarism and refinement, of chivalry and cruelty, of bloody wars and luxurious fêtes. Francis was a brilliant soldier, but it was as a royal Bayard that he headed his troops in battle; sleeping all night in full armor upon a gun-carriage at Marignano, that he might renew the conflict betimes next day. He was a King to whom the country he ruled was dear; but it was the military glory of France, her place of pre-eminence and power in Europe, that he mainly sought to guard, and elevate, and extend,—type and model, in this respect, of many a successor upon the Gallic throne. As fond of gayety as of glory, he gathered round him so numerous and splendid a court, that we read of 130 pages and 200 ladies, sons and daughters of the chief nobility, being in constant attendance at it. The number of horses required by it was 6000. In that Court he inaugurated the fatal reign of mistresses, so mischievous afterwards to France. But there too he showed himself the munificent patron of art and letters. He failed to bring Erasmus to Paris, but Leonardo da Vinci lived with him as a friend, and died in his monarch's arms.

Neither naturally cruel, nor religiously a bigot, for the first twenty-five years of his reign he was rather favorable than otherwise to the Reformers. Lefèvre, the father of the Reformation in France, was protected by him against the assaults of the Sorbonne, and it was by a prompt and arbitrary exercise of the royal power, that the learned and high-spirited De Berquin was rescued out of the grasp of the Parliament of Paris. Francis enjoyed greatly the classic wit of Erasmus, and the coarser jests of Rabelais pointed against the Romish clergy. He was present at, and loudly applauded, a theatrical representation, in which the Pope and other high dignitaries of the Church were very roughly handled. He lent, for many a year, an open ear to the counsels of his wise and witty and gentle sister, Margaret of Valois, whose mystic piety inclined her to Lutheranism. He allowed her favorite ministers to preach for a time under protection of the Court. She published a little volume which the Sorbonne publicly condemned: the King resented this as an insult, and forced the University of Paris to disown the censure of the Sorbonne. Some monks had a play acted in their presence, in which Margaret, while sitting spinning and reading the Bible, was transfigured into a devil: the King inflicted on them a severe mark of displeasure. A popular orator of the Church proclaimed from one of the Parisian pulpits, that Margaret deserved to be enclosed in a sack and thrown into the Seine: Francis doomed the preacher to that punishment. It was only the intervention of Margaret herself that saved him. So far did Francis go, in manifesting a favorable disposition to the Protestants, that he wrote with his own hand to Melanchthon, earnestly soliciting him to come and settle in Paris.

The battle of Pavia, however, fought and lost in 1525, was in this, as in other respects, a turning-point in the King's history. He was carried a prisoner into Spain. He returned next year to France, soured as well as saddened in spirit, having fresh difficulties to contend with, and a new edge set upon his ambition. He opened his ear to his mother Louisa of Savoy, to the Prelates, to the Parliament of Paris, by all of whom he was assured that the calamities of the country sprung from the growth of heresy, that the Reformers were enemies of the Crown as well as of the Church. The marriage of his son Henry with Catherine de Medicis, the niece of the reigning Pope, and his personal interview with the Pontiff at Marseilles in 1533 drew him into closer relationship with the Holy See. He at last openly declared, that in his realm there should be but one King, one law, one faith. He was heard to say of Lutheranism, that that sect, and others like it, tended more to the overthrow of governments than the good of souls. Still, however, the force of earlier feelings, the sway not yet departed of Margaret's graceful wit and devoted love, and still more, perhaps, the weighty political considerations that in his life-long struggle with Charles V. led him to cultivate the friendship of the Protestant Princes of Germany, might have held him back from taking personally any part in the persecution of the Protestants, had not a rash deed of their own, touching the most sensitive part of his character, turned dislike into bitter hatred.

On the 18th of October 1534, the inhabitants of Paris, on going out into the streets in the morning, found the walls of their houses and the corners of their squares covered with placards denouncing, in the most virulent language, "the horrible, great, and unbearable abuses of the Popish mass." The eye of the King fell upon one of these placards posted on the door of his own cabinet. He felt this as a personal insult, and finding his passion seconded by the anger of the citizens, he gave instant orders to search for and punish, summarily, not only those who had taken part in affixing the offensive placards, but all who acknowledged or favored Lutheranism. The search was made, a number of the guilty found, and the utmost pains were taken to make their punishment impressive to the public eye.

Between eight and nine o'clock on the morning of the 21st January 1535, an extraordinary procession issued from the Church of St. Germain l'Auxerrois in Paris, headed by a company of priests, bearing in coffers upon cushions of velvet the most precious relics of saints and martyrs. For the first time since the funeral-day of St. Louis, the Reliquary of La Sainte-Chapelle exposed its treasures to the public eye. There was the head of St. Louis; a piece of the true Cross; the crown of thorns; the spear-head that had pierced the Saviour's side. Ecclesiastics of every order, Cardinals, Archbishops, Bishops, Abbots, Monks, all clad in their richest robes, followed the relics. The Bishop of Paris bore on high the Holy Sacrament. Then came the King, his head uncovered, and in his hand a large burning torch of virgin wax. Princes of the blood, nobles of all ranks, the high court of Parliament, the foreign ambassadors, the great officers of State, came after the King. The oldest inhabitant of Paris had never seen so imposing a *cortége*, nor such a multitude gathered to gaze on it. Not a house-top but was crowded, not a jutting projection that could support a spectator but was occupied; the windows all filled with faces, the streets all paved with heads. With slow and solemn pace the great procession moved on through the principal streets of the city. Six times it stopped, each time before a temporary altar, decked with its crucifix, its candlesticks and flowers. Beside each altar, had the common custom been obeyed, fair children dressed as angels, emblems of

Heaven's love to man, should have appeared. But now beside each altar there was a pile of blazing fagots, above which there was an iron beam, turning on a pivot, and so movable by pulleys that it could be lifted and lowered at pleasure. To each of these beams a Lutheran had been attached,—the executioner instructed to plunge him occasionally into the scorching flames, so as to prolong his sufferings, and to time these terrible dippings into the fire in such a way that the fastenings which bound the victim should be consumed, and he fall into the flames at the moment when the procession stopped and the King stood before the gibbet. Six times the King thus paused, handing each time his torch to the Cardinal of Lorraine, clasping his hands and prostrating himself in prayer as the heretic was burned.

The tidings of what Paris saw that day were borne over Europe. The Protestant Princes of Germany remonstrated with Francis. He excused himself by saying that "he had been constrained to use this rigor against certain rebels who wished to trouble the State under the pretext of religion"—the one great excuse of despots, which on this occasion called forth a momorable reply. A few months afterwards (August 1535) a volume issued from the press at Basle. Its author's name was not upon the title-page. It opened with a dedicatory epistle to Francis, and bore to be throughout an apology for the Protestants of France, to redeem their faith from the charge of fanaticism, their conduct from the charge of sedition. "This," said its author afterwards, "was what led me to publish it: first, to relieve my brethren from an unjust accusation, and then, as the same sufferings still hung over the heads of many poor faithful ones in France, that foreign nations might be touched with commiseration for their woes, and might open to them a shelter." "If the act," says Michelet, speaking of this volume, "was bold, no less so was the style. The new French language was then an unknown tongue. Yet here, twenty years after Comines, thirty years before Montaigne, we have already the language of Rousseau; his power, if not his charm. But the most formidable attribute of the volume is its penetrating clearness, its brilliance—of steel rather than of silver; a blade which shines, but cuts. One sees that the light comes from within, from the depth of the conscience, from a spirit rigorously convinced, of which logic is the food. One feels that the author gives nothing to appearance; that he labors to find a solid argument upon which he can live, and, if need be, die." The work thus characterized by so capable, at least by so unprejudiced a judge, was Calvin's "Institutes of the Christian Religion." Its diffident and retiring author was then in his twenty-sixth year, and had been seeking, as he himself tells, some hiding-place from the world where he might pursue his studies at leisure. But that book once published, he could be hidden no longer. He was hailed at once by all the Reformers of France not only as the apologist of the martyrs, but as the theologian and legislator of the Church.

The invasion of France in 1536; the temporary reconciliation of the two great European rivals; their four days' interview at Aigues Mortes; the breaking out of the war almost immediately afterwards,—kept the hands of Francis too full to be turned against the Lutherans. From 1536 to 1543, the persecution languished. At last the peace of Crespy set both Charles and Francis free to pursue an object upon which both had now set their hearts, and which they mutually encouraged each other to prosecute—the utter extirpation of heretics in their respective dominions. In France the first blow fell upon an innocent and secluded community.

Well nigh three hundred years before this time a colony of the Vaudois, survivors of the terrible crusade of Innocent III., driven from Dauphiny and Piedmont, had settled in Provence. They occupied a district on the banks of the Durance, in the high lands between Nice and Avignon. They found it bleak and sterile. The industry of successive generations turned it into a garden—olives, vines, almond-trees, clothed their hill-sides, and the breed of their mountain cattle was in demand through all the country round. Their tribute to the King, their dues to their liege lords, were paid with exemplary regularity. There was nothing to expose them to the jealousy of their rulers. But their pure and simple faith rendered them obnoxious to the Roman Catholic population by which they were surrounded. As Louis XII. was passing through Dauphiny, they were denounced to him as heretics. He ordered an inquiry to be instituted into their character and habits, and when the result was before him, he ordered the process against them to be cast into the Rhine, saying, "These people are much better Christians than myself." Tidings of the great religious movement in Germany and Switzerland reached them. Their hearts were stirred. They sent deputies to confer with Œcolampadius in Basle, with Bucer at Strasburg, with Haller at Berne. The report of these deputies led them at once to hail Luther and Zuinglius, and the Reformers in their own land, as of the same faith with themselves. Throwing themselves into the great movement of their age, they felt that their own country has the first claim upon their regard. But what could a small community of peasants in a remote region do? It was told them that a translation of the Bible into the French tongue had just been finished by one of their countrymen, Peter Olivetan, but that a pecuniary difficulty had arisen as to carrying it through the press. They resolved to undertake the cost, raised 1500 golden crowns, and had the first edition of the French Bible published at their expense at Neufchatel. Hundreds of copies passed instantly into

France, and contributed more, perhaps, than any single instrument to the spread of the Reformation. Identified now with the Lutherans, a terrible sentence was pronounced against them by the Parliament of Aix. It decreed " that the villages of Mérindol, Cabriéres, and Les Aigues, and all other places the retreat and receptacle of heretics, should be destroyed,—the houses razed to the ground, the forest-trees cut down, the fruit-trees torn up by the roots, the principal inhabitants executed, and the women and children banished forever out of the land." Francis hesitated long before he consented to sanction this; but at last, in an evil hour in 1545, he gave instructions that the sentence should be executed. The Baron d'Oppède, to whom the execution of it was committed, made his preparations with the utmost secrecy. Six regiments of mercenaries, trained to murder and pillage in the Italian wars, were collected. A company of cavalry was placed under the Baron de la Garde, a captain notorious for his ferocity. These troops, despatched in bands so as to surround the district, were launched upon the unprepared and unsuspecting Vaudois, with no other instructions than to burn and pillage, and kill at random. Taken unawares, the inhabitants of the first village they fell upon, man, woman, and child, were massacred. The light of their burning villages gave warning to the others. In Mérindol, one of the two chief towns, but a single man was found. He was a poor simpleton, and had given himself up to one of the soldiers, to whom he had promised a few crowns for his ransom. D'Oppède heard of it, paid himself the ransom, had the man tied up to a tree and shot. From Cabrières, the other chief town, the bulk of the inhabitants had fled. Sixty men, and about thirty women, remained in it. It was a walled town, and for twenty-four hours held out against the soldiers. Their lives were promised to its defenders, and they gave themselves up unarmed. They were cut to pieces on the spot. The women were shut up in a barn filled with straw, which was set on fire. One soldier, touched with pity, opened for those within a way of escape. But his companions were merciless. Whosoever tried to escape was thrust back by pike and halbert. They all perished in the flames. Night and day the murderous work went on. Within a week or two twenty villages had been destroyed, and four thousand of their inhabitants had been slaughtered. Those whom fire and sword had spared, wandered in the mountains and the woods. There were no fruits for them to gather, for it was yet early spring. Many perished from hunger. The miserable survivors besought D'Oppède to allow them to return to Germany. "We will give up every thing," they said to him, "but the clothes upon our back." Their request was contemptuously denied. "I know what I have to do with you," he replied; I will send every one of you to hell, and make such a havoc of you that your memory will be cut off forever." Numbers fell into their hands. After the mockery of a brief trial, 250 of them were on one occasion executed together. La Garde selected 600 of the finest young men and sent them to the galleys, where the treatment given them was such that in a few weeks 200 of them died. It was but a miserable remnant that, escaping fire, sword, famine, fatigue, the galleys, made their way into the land of the stranger. A houseless, treeless, scorched and barren wilderness was left, where the vines, and the olives, and the almond-trees had flourished, where the homes and the families of the Vaudois had been.

The tale of that wholesale butchery was one that Francis never liked to hear. The image of it haunted his deathbed. He left instructions to his son Henry to inquire into a deed that he felt had sullied his reign, and to punish the perpetrators. Three years after his death, but not at Henry's instance, the matter was brought before the Parliament at Paris. Fifty sittings of that Court were devoted to it. D'Oppède was acquitted. One of his officials was indeed condemned, not for the part he had taken in the massacre, but because it was found that he had filched a portion of the public treasure.

Francis died in 1547. His eldest son having died some years before, his second son, Henry, ascended the throne. Henry had a showy exterior, was expert in all manly exercises, could run, could ride, could chase the deer, could break the lance with the most expert performer in the lists, the best trained knight of the tournament. Nor was he altogether deficient either in talent or in industry. He gave hours each day to the public business of the State. But he had none of the qualities of a great prince. In boyhood, it might be said in childhood, he had given himself up to the empire of Diana of Poitiers; and that empire, one of the most singular that even French history, prolific in such instances, presents, lasted undiminished through life. When under eighteen years of age, he married Catherine de Medicis, but marriage did not shake his early attachment, nor did his wife apparently desire that it should. Diana became the friend and protectress of Catherine, and for more than twenty years that subtle Italian bided quietly her time, consenting murmuringly to occupy her most anomalous position; the mother of the King's children, but in no sense the Queen of France.

Henry was twenty-eight years old when his father died. Diana was twenty years his senior. It was she who in 1547 ascended the throne, and for the twelve years of Henry's reign it was she who ruled; a rule fatal to the Protestants, whom, with a touch of the Herodias spirit, she both hated and feared. One other only shared her influence with the King, the Constable de Montmorency, an early friend of Henry's, disliked by Francis and excluded by him from power, but now recalled to take his place in the Council, and to become the chief adviser of the King. Montmorency, who prided himself on being the descendant of the first Christian Baron of France, was at one with Diana in her dislike of the Protestants, and under their joint instigation, Henry launched at once upon the career of the persecutor.

On the 27th January 1551, an edict against the Lutherans was issued, known by the name of the Edict of Chateaubriand.[1] Not only was the old law of St. Louis dooming all heretics to death, which had all along been acted on, renewed in this edict, but the secular and the ecclesiastical courts were equally empowered to judge in cases of heresy, so that though absolved by the one, the accused might be carried before the other and condemned. All intercession on behalf of the condemned was prohibited. The sentences were to be executed without delay and without appeal. To encourage informers, the third part of the goods of the condemned was to be appropriated to them. Heavy punishments were to be inflicted upon all who introduced into the realm, or were found possessed of, any book in which the new doctrines were inculcated. The entire property of the refugees who had left France to escape the persecution was confiscated to the Crown. To send money or letters to them was forbidden; and finally, every one even suspected

[1] See "Histoire Chronologique de l'Eglise Protestante de France," par Charles Drion, t. i. p. 45. Paris, 1855.

of heresy was obliged to present a certificate of orthodoxy.

The whole machinery of persecution was put into full operation all over France, one spring acting with peculiar potency,—for Diana, Montmorency, and other favorite courtiers it was a profitable employment to persecute, as the confiscated estates found their way into their hands. One step only remained to be taken to place France abreast of Spain: a royal edict was drawn up establishing the Inquisition. Presented to the Parliament of Paris it encountered there an unexpected opposition. Séguier, the President of the Parliament, in communicating to Henry its refusal to register the decree, had the boldness to say to the King (I quote the words as the first indication in France of the true idea of toleration), "We take the liberty to add that since these punishments on account of religion have failed, it seems to us conformable to the rules of equity and right reason to follow here the footsteps of the early Church, which never employed fire and sword to establish or extend itself, but a pure doctrine and an exemplary life. We think, therefore, that your Majesty should exclusively apply yourself to preserve religion by the same means by which it was first established."

The King was forced unwillingly to yield. Other matters besides engrossed him. More fortunate than his father, he had seen, in the early part of his reign, the arms of France and her confederates triumph over those of the empire; the Emperor himself on the edge of being taken prisoner at Innspruck; and the peace of Cambrai established. But the fortune of war had changed. The disastrous battle of St. Quentin—that fatal Flodden Field of France—in which the flower of her chivalry perished, laid her at the feet of Spain. At Paris, the greatest consternation prevailed. They fancied they heard the enemy already at their gates. Superstition took advantage of the national disaster. The priesthood inflamed the spirit of the mob.

Late in the evening of the 4th September 1557, a few weeks after the tidings of the battle of St. Quentin had reached Paris, three or four hundred Lutherans met to partake secretly of the Lord's Supper, in a house in the Rue St. Jacques. The buildings of the Sorbonne stood near. Some members of the college, struck at the sight of so many people from such different quarters going into the same building at so late an hour, suspected the character of the meeting, watched till all had entered, then hurried from house to house, raised the multitude, and set afloat the most frightful tales as to what the Lutherans had met to do. The streets around soon filled with a mob excited to the highest pitch. Piles of stones were heaped together; hasty preparations made for assault. About midnight, the service being over, those engaged in it prepared to depart. The doors were opened. It was the signal for a fiendish shout and a shower of stones.

Torches brandished in the air shone on faces glowing with passion, and showed the streets blocked up with men armed with all kinds of weapons. The doors were shut, and there was a short deliberation. The bravest of the Lutherans, rather than abide the issue of an assault, determined to force a passage. Drawing their swords, they dashed out upon the crowd; it gave way before them; one only of their number fell, whose mutilated body was exposed for days to the outrages of the multitude. About 200 persons, chiefly women, remained within the building. In vain they supplicated mercy. The doors had been already forced, and the work of slaughter was beginning when the city authorities arrived. They seized all found within, and bound them in couples, to carry them to prison. It was through a perfect hail of missiles of all kinds, their clothes all torn, their bodies covered with blood and filth, that the prisoners at last reached the jail. Seven of their number soon perished at the stake; for more of them the same doom was ready, when foreign intervention, which Henry at the time dared not despise, stayed its execution.

The year 1559, a memorable one in the history of Protestantism in France, opened with the inglorious treaty of Cateau-Cambresis, entered into between France and Spain. A secret article, appended to that treaty, concocted by the two great clerical persecutors, the Cardinals of Lorraine and Granville, bound the two monarchs to employ the whole force of their kingdom in the extermination of the heretics. The later history of the Low Countries proved the faithfulness of Philip II. to that engagement. His brother of France showed no want of alertness or vigor in following the same course. The treaty was signed on the 3d April. On the 12th of the same month letters-patent were sent to all the provinces, in which the King said—" I desire nothing more than the total extermination of this sect; to cut its roots up so completely that new ones may never rise again; have no pity then nor compassion, but punish them as they deserve."

The authorities were generally but too ready to carry out the royal instructions. One instance, however, of hesitation appeared. The Parliament of Paris was divided into two sects—the Great Chamber and the Tournelle. The former called for the infliction of death without mercy upon all heretics. The latter, when four young men were convicted before it of holding some of the new opinions, sentenced them not to death but to exile. Such leniency was appalling. It showed something fatally wrong in the court that could extend it. It was whispered that the heretic leaven had infected some of its members. The names of the suspected were privately presented to the King. The Cardinal of Lorraine, who had been telling Henry that the true way for him to cover before God and man all the vices to which he might abandon himself, was to root out the adversaries of the Romish Church, now took upon him to become his monarch's counsellor. "You must lay a snare for these dangerous men; call a Mercuriale; invite them all to speak freely out their sentiments, and then punish them upon their own confession. The burning of half a dozen heretic members of Parliament will be a pleasant sight to the Duke of Alva and the Spanish grandees, who are now in Paris." The King took the Cardinal's advice. A meeting of both Chambers of Parliament was held. Henry himself presided. The amplest encouragement was held out by the King to every one to speak his mind without reserve. The snare succeeded but too well. One member of the house, Anne du Bourg, distinguished himself by the openness and boldness of his remarks. "One sees committed," says he, "every day crimes of all kinds which are left unpunished, while those guilty of no crime are dragged to the stake. It is no light thing to condemn to the flames those who in the midst of them invoke the name of Jesus Christ." The conference at last closed, the King rose to depart, but as he went, and by his order, the Constable advanced, laid his hand upon Du Bourg and four others who had been guilty of the same license of speech, and committed them to the Captain of the Guard to be carried to the Bastile.

A few senators were thus secured to grace the festivities the Court was holding in honor of the two marriages—that of Philip of Spain with Henry's daughter Elizabeth, and that of the young

Dauphin of France with our own Mary of Scotland. Among these festivities was the Tournament, in which the King delighted to exhibit his own skill in arms. The lists were erected in the Rue St. Jacques. Henry had encountered one and another of his nobles, who gracefully yielded to him the palm of victory. To make a last display of his prowess, he insisted on Montgomery, the stout Scottish knight, breaking a lance with him. Montgomery sought to be excused, but the King insisted. They met; grasped by a strong hand, the knight's well-laid and well-aimed lance struck the visor of the King, and was broken by the shock. A splinter of it pierced the eyehole of the visor, and penetrated the brain. A shrill cry of pain was heard, the King sunk down upon his saddle, and a few days afterwards expired (10th July 1559).

CHAPTER II.

FRANCIS II., 1559–1560.

Duke of Guise and Cardinal of Lorraine.—Antony of Bourbon.—Prince of Condé.—Coligni.—D'Andelot.—Conspiracy of Amboise.—The Assembly of Notables.—Condé condemned.—Death of Francis.

It was during the reign of Henry II. that the seeds were sown of all those dissensions by which France was torn asunder for so many years after his death. The Court had become corrupt. "Almost every vice," says Mézeray, "which tends to the ruin of great States reigned in this Court: luxury, immodesty, libertinism, blasphemy, and that impious curiosity which seeks the secrets of futurity in the detestable illusions of magic." The Crown had fallen into contempt. The Princes of the blood and the higher nobility, all power being withdrawn from them to be bestowed upon a few reigning favorites, were alienated. The highest offices of State were shamelessly bought and sold. The fountains of justice, the courts of law, had become tainted with the prevailing venality. The wars with the House of Austria, the lavish expenditure of the Court upon idle shows, the want of any fixed sources of royal income, the expedients that were adopted to meet existing difficulties, had drained the public treasury, plunged the monarchy in debt, and created an inextricable financial confusion. In the midst of all this Henry was cut off. Francis, his eldest son, a youth not sixteen years old, succeeded. The Government of France lay open to the hands that were the first to grasp and that had the power to hold it. Let us cast a glance around upon the leading men who now step upon the stage.

Forty-six years before this time, Claude, fifth son of René, Duke of Lorraine, entered France. He came to take possession of extensive estates in that country, left to him at his father's death, and to establish there a separate branch of his family, as the houses of Mantua and Savoy did in the persons of the Dukes of Nevers and Nemours. Among the captains whom Francis I. gathered round him in his wars, Claude speedily distinguished himself, attaining the rank of a General at an age when many of the bravest scions of the nobility were only passing through military apprenticeship as knights. At the head of a small band of followers he once penetrated the English camp, and left five or six hundred dead behind him as the trophies of his success. During the captivity of Francis in Spain, he surprised 10,000 German *Reiter* in their march to Neufchâteau, and cut them to pieces. He turned his sword next upon 15,000 German communists who had penetrated France, and disposed of them in such a way that not more than a thousand were left to carry home the news of their enterprise. He hastened then to the relief of the terrified inhabitants of Paris, who saw an English army within a few leagues of their ramparts, threw himself into the city, and by saving it forged the first link of that chain that attached the Parisians to his family. When twelve years old, he had seen his mother, Philippa of Gueldres, lay aside riches and honors, part from her seven young children, and not in disappointment or chagrin, but on the impulse of an intense pietism, retire into a cloister. From her he inherited that fanatical attachment to the ancient faith which in his warlike heart turned into a desire to bathe his hands in the blood of heretics. For good or for evil, he linked his fortunes with those of the Papacy, and in doing so marked out for his sons the path they followed. Francis at last gave him a place in the French Peerage, by creating him first Duke of Guise. His fortunate marriage with Antoinette de Bourbon, sister of Charles, first Duke of Vendôme, associated him with the ancient nobility, who nevertheless always looked on him as an intruder within their domain. Despite their jealousy, by his talents and address he won for his family the highest positions in Church and State. His daughter Mary, married to James V. of Scotland, became the mother of Mary Stuart. Six sons grew up around him, sharers of his fanaticism, his ambition, his talents, and his success. Two of them became Dukes, two rose to be Cardinals, one is known to history as the Marquis d'Elbœuf, and another as the Grand Prior. It was the two eldest, Francis who succeeded his father as second Duke of Guise,—and Charles the Cardinal of Lorraine, who played so conspicuous a part in the religious wars of France. Before he died, Francis I. had warned his son Henry against these two young men, whose ambition, he feared, might become dangerous to the monarchy. Henry did not heed the warning. Under his patronage the young Duke of Guise rose to share the command of the French armies with the Constable Montmorency. His gallant and successful defence of Metz against all the forces that Charles V. could muster; his victories at Renti, and above all his capture of Calais—his wresting out of the hands of the English that last relic of their victories in France—covered him with glory, and made him the idol of the people. Skilful, courageous, successful as a soldier, he had little capacity as a politician. What he wanted, his brother amply possessed, and under the Cardinal's guidance, Francis put himself at the head of the ultra-Catholic party. Sincere in his religious belief, but grossly ignorant, he was ready at command to march in any direction, to draw the sword and strike any blow, if only once assured that the double object was to be gained thereby—the Church's interests served, and his own family exalted. There was nothing, however, mean or double in his nature. Choleric, at times brutal in his rage, he had withal that generous nature which knows to pity a fallen enemy and forgive the deepest wrong.

His brother Charles, the Cardinal, was fashioned after a different mould. Invited by the King, at the age of three-and-twenty, to take part in the management of public affairs, he ingratiated himself with Diana of Poitiers, and rose rapidly at Court. He had every qualification for a courtier— an imposing exterior, a graceful address, a fertile and playful wit, a copious and persuasive eloquence. The Italians, the Spaniards, the Germans, the English, the Dutch, all noticed with admiration the fluency and accuracy with which their different languages were spoken by him. The successes and high alliances of his family; the marriage of his sister to the King of Scotland, and then of his niece with the heir-apparent to the French throne, fed that ambition which developed all the vices of his character. He gave himself to the pursuit of power. In that pursuit he displayed the quickest foresight, extraordinary subtlety; the talents, however, rather of the diplomatist than of the statesman; but he displayed at the same time selfishness, meanness, cowardice, cruelty. Insolent and overbearing when things went well, he sank under adversity into the sycophant and flatterer. "Come, tell us," said one of the ladies of honor to whom he had been speaking in a very humble and gracious manner,—" Come, tell us, what great misfortune has befallen you that you are speaking to us in that way?" His cowardice was so notorious, that to cover it he made it the subject of his own pleasantry. He was the chief persecutor of the Huguenots, but he had not the excuse of the fanatic in becoming so. His faith was as versatile as his intellect; now, he could preach the highest doctrines of the Papacy, and again, so that the Lutherans could find nothing to condemn.

Opposed to the Guises stood the Princes of the House of Bourbon. This house, which ascended the French throne in the person of Henry IV., and gave afterwards so many kings to France and Spain and Naples, took its origin from Robert, sixth son of St. Louis (Louis IX.), who married Beatrix the heiress of Bourbon; Bourbon being originally a simple barony, which in 1327 was erected into a duchy in favor of Louis, Robert's eldest son. In the succession to the French throne, this family stood next to the reigning family of the Valois. Jealousies between the two houses had arisen. In the reign of Francis I., the Constable of Bourbon openly revolted. His failure and disgrace excluded, for a time, all members of his family from the higher offices of the State. Under the reign of Francis' successor, they had hoped to be restored to their natural position in the monarchy, but the Court influences were against them. They remained excluded from the government. The Guises had taken a chief part in that exclusion, and had usurped the places that should have been theirs. The Bourbons counted them as their enemies. Subject themselves to a political persecution, they sympathized with those of their fellow-countrymen who were exposed to a religious one, a sympathy not lessened by the circumstance that the Guises headed the persecution.

Antony of Bourbon was now the head of the family. By his marriage with Jeanne d'Albret, daughter of Margaret, the favorite sister of Francis I., he became King of Navarre. Shortly before the death of Henry, Antony had abjured the Roman Catholic religion, and openly professed himself a Protestant. The cause of Protestantism, however, lost more than it gained by the accession of a man so weak and vain and vacillating, yet so ambitious, who, pleased for the time by being hailed as the head of a party, had none of the energy or resolution needful for that post. The crown he wore did not sit firmly upon his head, and it was a crown with but little of a kingdom: half of the old territory of Navarre having been annexed to Spain. Knowing all Antony's weaknesses, and determined to detach him from Protestantism, Philip II. held out the threat, that if he persevered in heading the Huguenots, the half that he still possessed should likewise be annexed. And now, he promised that if he deserted the Huguenots, and united with the Guises for their extermination, he would give back the appropriated half, or, better still, would give him a new kingdom.—that of Sardinia, of whose extent and wealth fabulous accounts were given. Antony yielded, returning into the bosom of the Church, but there was no enlargement of his kingdom.

The attachment to the reformed doctrine of his younger brother, Louis Prince of Condé, was more sincere and steadfast. There was little in that doctrine to attract such a laughter-loving, pleasure-loving, gay, and gallant youth as Condé was. But he was chivalrously honorable; there was depth as well as liveliness in his character, and wayward and wild as his conduct often was, his religious convictions appear to have been genuine and strong. He could never, at least, be induced to renounce them. Bribes of all kinds were held out to tempt him to do so; bribes that, to one so poor, must have been very tempting, but he spurned them indignantly away.

Another family, inferior in rank to the Bourbons, lent to the cause of Protestantism a purer and more efficient aid. The Marquis de Chatillon was the head of a family that for nearly 500 years had been mixed up with all the great political movements of their country. He died in 1522 in the service of Francis I., leaving his widow, a sister of the Constable Montmorency, with three sons, Odet, Gaspard, and Francis. When the eldest of the boys was but sixteen years old, a Cardinal's hat was placed by the Pope at the disposal of the Constable, to be given to one of his nephews. It should naturally have fallen either to Gaspard or to Francis. Both, however, young as they were, showed an invincible repugnance to accept of it. Their elder brother, who was of a gentler nature, was induced to do so. To the Cardinalship, the rich Bishopric of Beauvais was forty years afterwards annexed. Finding himself so well provided for, Odet generously ceded all his patrimonial rights to his younger brothers. Gaspard became thus the head of the family of Chatillon, taking the title of Count of Coligni, from a village in Franche-Comté, an ancient possession of his house.

Coligni was early introduced at Court, under the auspices of his uncle the Constable. That gay court-life had little or no charm for this thoughtful, studious, retiring, and somewhat austere youth. He formed there but a single friendship, that with the young Duke of Guise, but it did not last long. The Duke one day asked Coligni's opinion as to the projected marriage of one of his brothers, with a daughter of the Duchess of Valentinois (Diana of Poitiers). "I would prefer," said Coligni, "an honored name to all the riches a woman could bring into my family." In his twenty-fourth year Coligni entered upon his military career. Distinguishing himself in Flanders, he served as a volunteer in the army of Italy, and displayed such bravery in the bloody fight at Cerisoles that he was knighted on the field. Returning to Paris in 1547, he married a daughter of the illustrious house of Laval. The accession of Henry II. to the throne brought with it fresh addition to his honors. He was appointed Colonel-General of the French infantry. In that office he matured and introduced those military ordinances, of which Brantôme says, that "they were the best and most politic that have ever been made in France, and, I believe, have preserved the lives of a million of persons, for, till then, there was nothing but pillage, brigandage, murders, and quarrels, so that the companies resembled hordes of wild Arabs rather than noble soldiers.

In 1551, Coligni was nominated Governor of Paris and of the Isle de France, and in the following year, created Admiral of France, a military as well as a naval office, next in rank to that of the Constable. Soon afterwards he was invested with the military government of Picardy, and admitted a member of the Privy Council. In 1556, he negotiated a peace with Spain on terms honorable to France. It was but two months after the signature of this treaty, that the intrigues of the Pope and the Guises induced Henry to attack Spain, without even the formality of a declaration of war being issued. Coligni was ordered to commence hostilities. He remonstrated in the most forcible terms against so flagrant a breach of faith, but his remonstrances were overruled. The loss of the battle of St. Quentin was the penalty France paid for her treachery on this occasion. In that disastrous campaign the one redeeming incident was the heroic defence of St. Quentin by Coligni and his younger brother. The town was taken at last by assault, and the Admiral had to yield himself a prisoner of war. He was confined first in the fort of L'Ecluse, and afterwards in the citadel of Ghent. He occupied his leisure hours in reading the Bible, and the writings of the Reformers. .His generous spirit had been already deeply moved by the heroism of the Protestant martyrs. He now discovered the source of that heroism in the simple but sublime truths they had received out of the Holy Scriptures. So deep was the impression made upon his mind, that, when in 1559 he was released from his captivity, he did not return to court. He threw up the government of Picardy and of the Isle de France, and retired to his country seat of Chatillon. His two brothers joined him there. Days and months were given by the three to earnest reading of the Scriptures, and consultations as to the future. The mind of the youngest brother, Francis, better known by his second name D'Andelot, had already been made up. Three years before, he had been confined in the citadel of Milan, had taken the same means to relieve his solitude as his elder brother had done, and with the same result, only his more ardent temperament had carried him somewhat further; for upon his release, which took place the year before the battle of St. Quentin, he announced himself a convert to Protestantism, and in his own country of Brittany openly encouraged it. The Cardinal found himself at first much in the same state of mind with the Admiral. The result of their conferences was, that all three resolved openly to cast in their lot with their persecuted fellow-countrymen. D'Andelot was the first to be exposed to danger.

One evening in the spring of 1557, some students were sauntering along the Pré-aux-Clercs, the fashionable promenade on the banks of the Seine. They sang together, as they walked, the French Psalms of Clement Marot in the harmony of four parts, set by Goudimel. Such kind of singing was new to the ears of the Parisians. They had many listeners, and many assistants too; for, evening after evening as the singing was resumed, the band of singers swelled in numbers, good proof how many voices had been trained in secret to this kind of psalmody. The King of Navarre, who happened to be in Paris at the time, in the fresh impulse of his new-born and short-lived Lutheranism, put himself at its head. Lords and gentlemen, French and foreign (among the latter we notice some Lords of the Congregation from Scotland), joined the ranks and took part in the music. It became for the time the great evening incident of the Parisian day. The clergy took instant and grave alarm. Henry was not at Paris, but they forwarded in haste a representation to him at Amiens, denouncing these reunions as seditious assemblies. A royal order for their suppression immediately appeared.

Among those reported to the King as having taken part in these musical promenades was D'Andelot. In itself it was but a slight offence; but it had been told the King besides, that Protestant books had been found in D'Andelot's luggage, and that Protestant ministers had been openly protected by him in Brittany. He was summoned into the royal presence. The King asked his opinion of the mass. "I look upon it," said the frank and fearless soldier, "as a detestable profanation." The King reminded him of the honors he had heaped upon him, and reproached him with ingratitude. "Sire," said D'Andelot, "the obligation I feel for the honors you have conferred upon me is such that I have not spared either body or goods in your service; but do not think it strange if, after having rendered that service to your Majesty, I study the well-being of my soul. I entreat you that you leave my conscience free, and take my body and goods which are altogether yours."—"But I did not give you that order," said the King, pointing to the collar that he wore, "that you might act as you have done. In accepting it you swore to follow my religion." "Sire," replied D'Andelot, "I did not then know what it was to be a Christian. I should not have accepted it on such conditions had God then touched my heart as He has touched it since." The King could restrain his rage no longer. Seizing the first thing he could grasp,—some say a knife, and some a plate,—he flung it at D'Andelot, missing him, and hitting his own son the Dauphin instead. Ordered out of the royal presence, D'Andelot made his obeisance and withdrew; but at the door of the palace he was arrested and carried prisoner to the citadel of Melun.

The imprisonment of so distinguished a nobleman produced a profound sensation. The Cardinal of Lorraine would have liked to have seen the law at once carried out in all its rigor. The Pope expressed his astonishment afterwards that this was not done; but D'Andelot had many friends at Court who busied themselves incessantly in trying to persuade him to make some concession. Calvin heard of this and wrote to warn him against yielding to such solicitation. All that D'Andelot was asked to do was to allow the mass to be celebrated in his presence; he was neither asked to take part himself in the service, nor to retract his formerly expressed opinion of it. He did so, and purchased thereby his liberty; but so strict were the ideas of religious duty entertained among the Calvinists, that his concession was generally lamented as a dishonorable fall, and Calvin wrote to reproach him with it as such. D'Andelot lived to prove that these injurious suspicions of him were unfounded.

The Protestants hailed with hope the advent of Francis II. to the throne. He was not yet sixteen years old; too young, too feeble, to take the government into his own hands. The Queen-Mother, Catherine de Medicis, though she had not yet declared herself for either, had shown herself ready to take any side. With one exception, that of the Cardinal de Bourbon, the Princes of the blood—into whose hands, had all ordinary precedents been followed, the power should have fallen—had espoused their cause. Visions of a happier future, of the fires of persecution quenched, of liberty of worship established, of the truth triumphing all over France, were floating before their eyes. A few days sufficed to dispel all these visions, and to bring down a deeper darkness than ever upon the future. When Henry received his death-wound, and it became evident that a change of government was at hand, the Constable had despatched a courier to the King of Navarre, urging his immediate presence at Paris. Instead of acting at once upon the counsel given him, the irresolute Antony loitered by the way, and finally stopped altogether at Vendôme. When Henry died, the Constable's hands were for the time tied up, it being part of his official duty to conduct the funeral obsequies of the monarch, and the custom of the times forbidding that for thirty-five days he should meddle with public affairs. The Constable thus set aside, and the Bourbons and the Chatillons being at a distance, the Guises were masters of the position, and lost not a day in occupying it. Their influence over the new boy-king, through their niece Mary Stuart, was unbounded. Catherine they propitiated by the sacrifice of the Duchess of Valentinois. As by the law of France the King attained his majority at the age of thirteen, they were able to act under royal sanction. The late King's seal was demanded and obtained from the Constable; the Cardinal was placed at the head of the Finance, the Duke at the head of the War Department. When the Deputies of the Parliament of Paris presented themselves to congratulate the young Prince upon his accession, they were informed by him that, with the approbation of the Queen-mother, he had committed the entire charge of the government to his two uncles. Released from his funeral duties, the Constable appeared at Court; he was informed that the King had no further need of his services, and he retired. Condé was appointed ambassador to the Low Countries, an office unsuited to his position, which he rightly interpreted as only another way of banishing him from the Court.

Action so prompt and decisive, such an instant and entire exclusion from the government of all the natural and hereditary counsellors of the Crown, excited the keenest indignation and discontent. Condé, Coligni, D'Andelot, the Prince of Porcian, the Count of Rochefoucault, the Vidàm of Chartres, and others, hastened to Vendôme, where Navarre was still resting on his way to Paris. The bolder spirits, such as Condé and D'Andelot, were for instant recourse to arms; the wiser, as Coligni, resisted the proposal. It was at last resolved that the King of Navarre should at once proceed to Paris, and claim and insist upon his rights. But all vigor went out of him by the way. Instead of resenting the studied affronts put upon him, on reaching the metropolis he meanly submitted. The Guises knew well with whom they had to deal. A letter from Philip of Spain was put into his hands, threatening an invasion of Navarre; and so terrified was Antony that he accepted the inglorious office of conducting the Princess Elizabeth to Spain, in the hope that in a personal interview with Philip —an interview that was never granted him—he might move that monarch from his purpose.

Meanwhile, the Guises, intoxicated with success, advanced in their career. Montmorency was stripped of the office of Grand Master (originally that of the Mayor of the Palace), which was assumed by the Duke. The government of Picardy, which the Admiral had resigned, in the expectation that it would be given to Condé, was bestowed on a creature of the Lorraines. The Cardinal, with nothing in the public treasury, found himself besieged by old servants of the Crown, demanding the payment of arrears of salary. The Duke received the importunate suitors in the most gracious manner, and gave them all good words, while the Cardinal had gibbets erected in the neighborhood of St. Germain, and caused it to be proclaimed three times by sound of trumpet, that all who came there to demand money should quit the place within twenty-four hours, on pain of being hanged forthwith,—one of the numerous instances in which the two brothers played with admirable effect into each other's hands.

But there were those for whom something worse than threatenings were prepared. King Henry died on 10th July 1559. On the 14th of the same month, an injunction was laid upon the Parliament of Paris to proceed instantly to the trial of Anne du Bourg, the Member of Parliament who had been arrested by the late King's order. The position, the youth, the eloquence, the piety of Du Bourg, fixed upon this trial a larger measure of public attention than on that of any other martyr of the Reformation. He asked to be tried by his peers; just and constitutional as it was, that plea was overruled by royal mandate. He drew up such a confession of his faith, as could not fail to send him to the stake. Few more touching scenes have ever been recorded than that of his last appearance before the Court when the sentence of death was passed upon him. He melted his stern judges to tears, and then turned those tears into fresh arguments against the course of persecution that was being followed in France. A rash attempt having been made to rescue him from prison, an old iron cage that had been used in the days of Louis XI. was sought out. Du Bourg was enclosed in it, clothed and fed in the meanest way. The 23d of December, the day before Christmas eve, was fixed for his execution. His deportment at the stake was so calm, so modest, yet so triumphant, and so sublime, that a Roman Catholic historian declared, that "his execution did more harm than a hundred ministers by all their preaching could have done."

Edict after edict was published, denouncing death on all who attended any private meeting for religious purposes; declaring that all who had knowledge of such assemblies, and failed to reveal them, should have the same penalty inflicted on them, offering large rewards to all who should inform against heretics, and ordering all houses in which it could be proved that secret assemblies had been held, to be razed to the ground. New courts were established, fitly called *Chambres Ardentes*, since they burned without mercy every one who was convicted of heresy. Popular fanaticism lent its aid to the execution of the law. In Paris, Bordeaux, Lyons, Grenoble, Dijon, and other cities where the Calvinists abounded, private houses were broken into upon the slightest suspicion, and whole families hurried to prison; espionage, pillage, confiscation, executions, multiplied day by day.

Men began at last to speak freely of taking up arms. A case was drawn up, and submitted to the most celebrated jurists and theologians of France, Switzerland, and Germany. They were asked,

"Whether with a safe conscience, provided no violence were offered to the King and the lawful magistrates, men might take up arms for the safety and liberty of the country, seize Francis of Guise, and the Cardinal his brother, and compel them to resign their usurped authority." True to the principle of almost unlimited submission to the civil power, which he had always taught, Calvin gave his judgment against the employment of force. The majority, however, decided in favor of the proceeding, provided it had the sanction of one of the Princes of the blood, and of the States of the kingdom, or the greater and sounder part of them. The Prince of Condé was consulted. He was not prepared, in the first instance, to appear as the leader of the movement; but should a successful commencement be made, he was ready then to acknowledge and to head it.

The perilous task was undertaken by Renaudie, a gentleman of Perigord. In executing it, he displayed an ability, activity, and devotedness worthy of a better fate. He crossed to England to see what hope of support he might count upon from the Government of Elizabeth, but got little encouragement. He traversed a large part of France, and conversed personally with the chief of the disaffected. He appointed a rendezvous to take place on the 1st February 1560 at Nantes. The Parliament of Brittany was to hold its sittings there. Some marriages among the nobility were at the same time to be celebrated. There would be a large concourse of people gathered, and Renaudie rightly calculated that he and his friends might assemble without exciting notice or suspicion. The day arrived. The engagements were all kept. By different routes, a goodly band, none indeed of the chief nobility, but one or two of the lesser barons, and many gentlemen of character and good position entered Nantes. Renaudie visited each of them separately in their hotels. In the evening they all met. Renaudie depicted in glowing terms the insolent tyranny of the Guises; the miserable condition into which the State had fallen; the danger to the King himself, if not rescued out of their hands. "Why, then," said he, "should we delay any longer? Let us deliver our King from peril, our country from its chains. Let all who agree with me stand up." They rose as it had been a single man. Not an objection was taken, nor shadow of hesitation seen. It was resolved that they should all return forthwith to their different provinces, to meet again, accompanied with a small but sufficient force, in the neighborhood of Blois, where the Court then was, on the 10th of the next month. A few of them unarmed were then to seek an audience of the King, to demand liberty of worship for the Protestants, and the dismissal of the Guises from power. On their demand being rejected, as they calculated it would, their armed followers were to seize upon the Guises, arrest them for trial, and call upon the Prince of Condé, who was not to be far off, to take the further guidance of affairs. The plan was admirably laid; the secret kept with astonishing fidelity, but the treachery of one man proved fatal.

Retiring from Nantes to Paris, Renaudie took up his quarters in the house of a Protestant advocate named Avenelles. Surprised at the number of persons coming at strange hours to see his guest, Avenelles expressed suspicion. To secure his silence, Renaudie took him into his confidence, and disclosed the project. Avenelles revealed the whole to the agent of the Cardinal of Lorraine in Paris. A courier with the intelligence set off at once to Blois. The frightened Cardinal was for instant seizures, imprisonments, and executions. The Duke took a different course. He removed the Court from Blois, where it was unprotected, higher up the Loire, to Amboise, whose strong castle, built upon a lofty rock, was of itself a bulwark of defence. He got himself appointed Lieutenant-General of the kingdom, an office conferring almost unlimited authority. He sent off letters to Condé, the Admiral, and D'Andelot, desiring their immediate attendance upon the King. If they came, it would keep them from rendering any help to the conspirators; if they came not, their absenting themselves would be presumptive evidence of their complicity in the plot. They all, however, without delay, presented themselves at Amboise.

The Admiral, who had no concern whatever with Renaudie's movements, strongly counselled that the best way to meet and counteract them was by the exercise of toleration towards the Protestants, a counsel that for the time was partially followed.

Renaudie was informed of the treachery of Avenelles. It did not change his purpose; but he had to alter his plan. The day of the meditated assault was shifted from the 10th to the 16th March, and fresh instructions were issued to his followers, their places of meeting on the morning of the 16th fixed, and the secret word of recognition given. Renaudie still fancied he should succeed, as the Duke had but a small body of troops at Amboise. One of his own number again betrayed him. All his preconcerted arrangements were communicated to the Duke. Met at every point by skilful dispositions of the royal forces, the attack utterly failed. Renaudie himself fell in one of the first encounters of the morning. His body was suspended for a day upon a gibbet on the bridge, then cut into four quarters, which were exposed in the most public places of the town; the head nailed to a plank, as keepers nail the birds of prey they shoot.

The Baron de Castelnau, one of Renaudie's associates, advancing at the head of his Gascons, found himself suddenly in front of a superior force. The Duke de Nemours, who led it, and who knew the Baron, warned him of the utter hopelessness of the enterprise, and entreated him to surrender. Castelnau did so, though not till he had got a written engagement (signed by Nemours on the spot) that his life, and that of his followers, should be spared. But few escaped. The great body of the insurgents fell into the hands of the victors.

And now commenced a series of butcheries that lasted for a whole month. During these four weeks, and within the small enclosure of that town of Amboise, 1200 men were beheaded, hanged, or drowned. The market-place was crowded with gibbets. Gallows enough could not be raised, and so they took them, and hung them up from the walls and battlements of the Castle. The Loire would soon have been choked up, and so they took the dead bodies, and sent them floating down the river on small rafts, whose ghastly freightage announced to the inhabitants of Tours and Nantes what was going on at Amboise. The Court had its daily festival of blood. At a set hour each day, the ladies of the Court, dressed in their gayest attire —our own Mary Stuart there among the rest— placed themselves at the windows of the château, before which, for their special behoof, a number of executions took place. The Cardinal was there, amusing them with his pleasantries, directing their attention to those minor incidents of the bloody drama that might otherwise have escaped their notice, turning occasionally to the young King, as the most intrepid heroism was displayed by his victims in meeting death, to say, "See, Sire, their shameless effrontery! The very fear of death can't quench their arrogance. What would they have done with you if they had had you in their hands?" The Duke had his own private entertainments of the same kind. A gentleman from the Duke of Longueville arrived to inquire after the Duke's health. He received him at table. "Tell your master," said he, "that I am well, and report to him (pointing his finger to the window) with what kind of viands I am regaling myself." As he spoke, a tall and handsome man, chosen for the occasion, was hung up upon the bars of the window.

One pities the poor sickly Francis, doomed to be the spectator of such scenes. It is a relief to notice that some bitter misgivings did at times come over him. "What have I done," said he once, bursting into tears, "what have I done to my people that they hate me so? I would like to hear their complaints and their reasons." Then, turning to the Lorraines, "I don't know how it is, but I hear that it is against you that they are so angry. I wish you would leave me for a while, that I might see whether it is of me or you that they complain." "If we left you," was the reply, "the Bourbons would quickly find the means of exterminating our house." The weak youth had nothing for it but to bury his misgivings in his heart.

Among the ladies of the Court one only shrank

from the frightful daily spectacle. She was not, as we could have wished her to be, the young King's beautiful bride. The Baron de Castelnau, with fifteen gentlemen who had surrendered along with him, were brought up for trial. Faith had been plighted to them, but it was ruled that with rebels as with heretics no faith should be kept. The Chancellor, Francis Olivier, whom Castelnau knew well, presided at the trial. Questioned as to his religious opinions, the Baron answered so well, that the Chancellor was tempted to ask him at what school of theology he had studied? "Have you forgotten," said the accused, "how, on my return from imprisonment in Flanders, you asked me once how I had spent my time, and when I told you it was in study of the Holy Scriptures, you praised my labors, advised me to attend the assemblies of the Reformed, and expressed your wish that all the nobility of France had chosen, like me, the better part?" Olivier hung his head in silence. The Cardinal took up the theological debate to be in turn confounded. Castelnau asked the Duke to notice how his brother had broken down. "I know nothing of arguments," said the Duke, "but I know very well how to cut off heads." "Would to God," replied the Baron, "that you did understand argument like your brother. I am certain you would not pervert your conscience. As to your threat about cutting off heads, it is unworthy of a Prince like you." Castelnau and his friends were subjected to torture, but no sufferings could extort from them any other declaration than that it was against the Guises alone, and not against the King, that they had taken up arms. They were condemned to death as guilty of high treason. "Treason!" said Castelnau, on hearing the sentence, "I ought then to have said that the Guises were kings of France. If it be treason to take up arms against those violators of our laws and liberties, let them be declared kings at once." The scaffold on which he and his companions were beheaded was erected in front of the castle. The Court ladies as usual, with the Chancellor and the Guises, were looking on. Castelnau, after praying aloud to God, and appealing to Him to attest his innocence, gave his head to the executioner. It came to the turn of Villemorgue, one of the fifteen. Stepping forward, he dipped his hands in the blood of his companions, and raising them to Heaven, exclaimed, "Lord, it is the blood of thy children unjustly slain. Thou wilt avenge it!" A cry came from the place where the ladies of the Court were sitting. The Duchess of Guise, who had uttered it, sprung from her seat, and rushed into the chamber of the Queen-mother. Catherine asked her why it was that she was in such deep distress. "Have I not seen," said the Duchess, "the blood of the innocent flowing? I fear, I fear, that cry for vengeance will fall heavy upon our house."

The Chancellor Olivier had been seen to weep at the execution. The last words of Castelnau kept ringing in his ears. He sought his chamber; he flung himself upon his bed. That room he never left; from that bed he never rose. Devoured by a terrible remorse that induced a consuming fever, he filled his chamber with the bitter cries of a self-accusing spirit. The Cardinal heard of his distress, and came to visit him. "Ha! Cardinal," said Olivier when he saw him enter, "you have damned yourself and all of us." "It is the Evil One who troubles you," said the Cardinal; "force yourself to stay firm in the faith." "Well spoken, well answered," said Olivier with a sardonic laugh; then turned his back upon him, and would not speak another word. The Cardinal retired. Two days afterwards Olivier died.[1]

It is from this conspiracy of Amboise that we date the giving of a new name to the Reformers of France. Up to this time, during the reign of Francis I. and Henry II., they had been called Sacrementaires, or those of "the religion," or heretics of Meaux, or more generally Lutherans. The impropriety of the last name was now generally felt. Both in doctrine and discipline the French Churches followed the guidance, not of Luther but of Calvin. A new term arose of local origin, at first a *soubriquet* of reproach invented and applied by their en-

[1] "Histoire de la Réformation Française," par F. Puaux, tome ii. p. 37. Paris 1859.

emics. In the superstitious belief of the times, each chief town had its own goblin of the night; its foul spirit doomed to make its purgatory there, haunting by day some dark subterranean dwelling, but sallying forth under cover of the darkness, to scour the streets and terrify the poor wayfarers it chanced to meet. At Tours it was Le Roi Huguet From this king, of whose historic character we know nothing, one of the gates of that city derived its name. Near this gate was an underground apartment in which the Reformers of the city held their nightly meetings. The time, the place, the object of these meetings connected themselves in the popular belief with the goblin King Hugo, and his terrible nightly forthcomings. They call the Reformers Huguenots. This term was taken up by others; it spread rapidly over France; time stripped it soon of its primitive and sinister signification. It was accepted at last by the Protestants themselves, who ever since for nearly three centuries have been familiarly spoken of as the Huguenots of France.[1]

But not only was a new name, a new character was now given to the Reformation. Up to this period it had been a purely religious movement. Now it became a political as well as a religious

[1] For a full discussion of the different etymologies of the word *Huguenot*, see "Les Huguenots et la Constitution de l'Eglise Reformée de France en 1559," par E. Castel, pp. 41–92. Paris, 1859.

one. There was as much, certainly, of political as of religious discontent at the bottom of Renaudie's enterprise. Its double aim was to overthrow the power of the Guises, and to protect the Huguenots from persecution. The victims of that enterprise died as heroically as any martyr at the stake; but those bloody hands of Villemorgue, the dying cry for vengeance, tell us that the purer age of religious martyrdom is over; that the strife of human passion and political faction has begun, with what gain and loss to the cause of Protestantism it remains for us to notice.

Condé's complicity in Renaudie's unfortunate attempt was more than suspected by the Court. Perhaps the Cardinal had in his hands sufficient proof of it. We know, at least, he urged that Condé should be arrested, and brought instantly to trial. The Prince cut the matter short by demanding an audience of the King; proclaiming in the royal presence that whoever charged him with being a conspirator against the King lied in his throat, and challenging him to single combat. The Duke of Guise stepped forward, not to take up the gauntlet, but to offer himself as the Prince's second. A few days afterwards, the Court, driven from Amboise by the stench of the putrefying bodies, removed to Tours, and Condé took advantage of the opportunity to effect his escape. He found the country everywhere in a ferment; the ranks of the Huguenots recruited by multitudes whom the cruelties of Amboise had excited against the Guises.

The demand for the calling of the States-General of the kingdom became so loud and so general, that the Guises yielded so far as to summon an assembly, consisting of Princes of the blood, the Ministers of the Crown, the chief Clergy and Nobility. This Assembly, called from the character of its constituency the Assembly of Notables, met at Fontainebleau on 21st August 1560. The King of Navarre and the Prince of Condé did not attend. The old Constable, however, appeared with his two sons, and his three Huguenot nephews, attended by eight hundred gentlemen. Coligni presented a petition from the Huguenot inhabitants of Normandy. The petitioners professed entire allegiance to the Crown; offered to pay double tribute, to prove how falsely they were accused of a seditious spirit; and humbly entreated that they might be allowed temples of their own in which they might assemble. It was remarked by some one that the petition was unsigned. "Prudence," Coligni said, "had dictated the omission, but he was instructed to say that in a few days 50,000 signatures could be obtained." "And I," said the Duke of Guise, "can as easily get a million of good Catholics to lead against them, and break their heads." In the debate which followed, two Roman Catholic Bishops—Montluc, Bishop of Valence, the Marillac, Archbishop of Vienne—distinguished themselves by the moderate and charitable sentiments they expressed. The Cardinal, seeing that the drift of the debate was running against his party, spoke in a conciliatory strain. "With regard to the States-General, he was decidedly of opinion that they should be called. A National Council to reform the Church he saw little need of, nevertheless he would not object to it. As to those seditious Huguenots, who cloaked their malice against the Crown under the guise of religion, he was for the severest punishment being inflicted on *them;* but as to those poor fanatics who, without arms, and for fear of being damned, went to their preachings and their psalm-singings, and other things of that sort, since punishment had as yet done nothing, he was of opinion that the King should no longer pursue them in that way; but as to allowing them places of worship of their own to practise their idolatry in, the King could not do it without being damned eternally."

One searches in vain through all the speeches on either side made on this occasion, of which large records have been preserved, for any expression in favor of religious liberty properly so called. It was not upon the ground that their faith and worship should be tolerated, though differing from that of the majority of their countrymen, that the Huguenots preferred their request, but alone upon the ground that theirs was the only true faith, theirs the only true worship. Nor was it with the idea that two different faiths and worships were to be allowed to dwell together, that those good and kindly Bishops pleaded for a National Council being held, but solely in the hope that the two might be brought together into one. One king, one law, one faith, was still the maxim universally accepted.

The Assembly of Notables broke up, after appointing a meeting of the States-General to be held at Meaux on the 10th December, and a National Council to be held at Paris on the 20th January 1561.

. Convinced by the results of this Assembly that a war *à outrance* was approaching, the Guises resolved to be beforehand with their enemies, and to cut them off at a stroke. The Cardinal was the contriver of the scheme, which he facetiously called his "rat-trap." A confession of Faith that no Huguenot could sign, was to be presented by the King to the States-General, and adopted as a fundamental law of the kindgom. This formula was to be presented afterwards to every individual in the kingdom arrived at years of discretion; whoever refused to sign it was to be executed next day without mercy shown. As a preliminary step, the Bourbon Princes, of whose treasonable practices sufficient evidence had now been got, were to be tried and executed.

A project so large and so perilous demanded that adequate preparations should be made for its execution. Nothing in this way was left undone.

The place of meeting of the States-General was changed from Meaux to the fortified town of Orleans; formidable forces were concentrated around the Court; camps were formed, and bodies of troops distributed over the provinces, and the King of Spain and the Duke of Savoy engaged to hold themselves in readiness to co-operate with the Lorraines when the time for action came. The Bourbons were now summoned to Court. Leaving Pau, the two brothers took their way to Orleans. All along their route they were met by those who entreated them to return, or at least allow themselves to be escorted by a sufficient force. At Limoges, they found between 700 and 800 gentlemen awaiting them, who engaged, that if they would but openly head the Huguenots, 16,000 well-armed men could be at once collected to open the campaign. Condé was ready for it, but Antony thought the enterprise too rash. Then they asked the King of Navarre to leave his brother with them in command, but Condé would not secure his own safety at his brother's risk. Blinded by a fatal infatuation, they pursued their ill-fated journey.

As they approached Orleans, a vague terror came over them. No one came out to meet them. They found the city crowded with military. Between two files of soldiers, drawn up as if to guard them as prisoners by the way, they reached the house in which the King was lodged. Its main entrance they found closed; they had to pass in by the wicket. As soon as they were in his presence, the King proceeded to accuse Condé of treasonable designs upon his person and crown. The dauntless Prince flung back the charge upon his accusers. "In that case," said the King, "we shall proceed according to the ordinary forms of justice." Rising to depart, he ordered the captain of the guard to arrest the Prince, and convey him instantly to prison. The iron-grated windows of the house to which he was conducted, the formidable guard placed over it, the triple row of cannon that faced each street by which it was approached, the order that none of his friends should be allowed to communicate with him, not even in the jailer's presence, all foretold to Condé his approaching doom. But nothing could daunt his spirit. They sent a priest to celebrate mass in his room. He dismissed him contemptuously. It was hinted to him that he should make some concession to the Guises. "My only way of settling with them," was the reply, "shall be at the point of the lance." His trial, irregularly conducted, was hurried through, and he was condemned to die, the 10th of December being named as the day of his execution.

Poor Antony had entered Orleans, idly talking of bearding these lions, the Guises, in their den. His brother's arrest shook all vain confidence out of him; he sank into despair. The meanest and most humiliating approaches were made by him to the Lorraines, which they haughtily repulsed. He, too, was to be removed, but in a different way. A plan for his assassination was concocted; it was to be managed so that the King should be personally implicated. The young King was to send for him, provoke a quarrel, draw and strike at him with his own dagger, and then fitter and stronger hands were to complete the deed. Navarre got notice of the plot. Sent for by the King he declined to go. The message was repeated. Navarre's blood rose, for he was brave, though weak. Accompanied by Renty, an officer who enjoyed his confidence, he proceeded to the royal residence. As he mounted the steps, he was entreated to turn back. "Mount not, sire," said a friendly voice; "you go to perish." "I go," said he, turning to Renty, "into a place where I know they have sworn my death, but never was life sold so dearly as mine shall be." With these bold words upon his lips, he passed into the royal presence. There was something in his bearing that quelled the King. Francis' courage failed him; no quarrel was raised, nor stroke of dagger attempted. The Duke of Guise, on seeing Navarre come out unhurt, was heard to say contemptuously, "The weak, cowardly child; his prey has escaped him." Some other mode of securing that prey was to be tried.

The scaffold for Condé's execution had been erected; the most expert executioners had been sent for, and were already in Orleans, when, on the morning of the 17th November, the young King was seized with a sudden illness. An abscess formed in the brain discharged itself through the ear. Symptoms of mortification manifested themselves. The Guises were in despair. The choleric Duke vented his abuse upon the physicians who could not cure the King. The Cardinal set the whole machinery of the Church in motion. Preachers in all the churches besought their hearers to pray for the prolongation of the King's life. The streets and squares were crowded with processions of the faithful. But the fatal malady pursued its course. Ambrose Paré, the celebrated physician, declared the case to be hopeless. In their extremity, the Guises offered their support to the Queen-mother, if she would consent to the immediate execution of the Bourbons. She was of too quick intelligence not to see that, in event of the young King's death, the destruction of the House of Bourbon would leave the Lorraines masters of the Crown. She closed her ear to the proposal, and calmly awaited the event that was to put so much power into her own hands.

Meanwhile, the poor young Prince was passing through his dying agonies. At first he had some hope, and then he made the vows that he had been taught to believe would be most acceptable to Heaven. He vowed, that if life were given him, he would extirpate every heretic out of his land. "May I die next moment," cried he, "if I spare mothers, infants, wives; any who have even the taint of the suspicion of heresy upon them." Vows and prayers were alike in vain. The sickly youth must die. His last hour, he himself felt, had come; and we are pleased to hear from those dying lips the words,—among the last he spake, " Oh Lord, pardon me my faults, and impute not to me those that my ministers have committed under my authority." The light of truth breaks in through the shades of death, and gentle nature triumphs over fanatical belief!

CHAPTER III.

CHARLES IX., 1560–1563.

Meeting of the States-General.—Catherine's letter to the Pope.—Colloquy of Poissy.—Conference at Saverne.—The massacre at Vassy.—Coligni at Chatillon.—Montluc and Des Adrets.—Battle of Dreux.—Death of the Duke of Guise.

The death of Francis II. terminated for a time the domination of the Guises. Relieved so suddenly from so heavy a pressure, France sprang to her feet and for a moment fancied she was free. The States-General met at Orleans on the 13th December 1560, only eight days after the young monarch's death. They sat daily for upwards of six weeks. Two of the Estates, the nobility and the Tiers-État, met some months afterwards at Pontoise to complete the work so auspiciously begun.

One of the first matters for consideration was the settlement of the Government. Charles IX. was only ten years old at his brother's death. The Estates conceived that it lay with them to nominate the Regent. Instead of waiting, however, even to consult with them, they found at their first sitting that the Regency had been filled up, and all the great officers of State appointed. They might have been less disposed to quarrel with this arrangement had the old custom of the State been followed, by the Regency being put into the hands of the nearest Prince of the blood. But Antony of Navarre had been set aside, and the Queen-mother installed in the place that should have been his. This had been done, however, with Navarre's own consent and concurrence; but it was more difficult to satisfy that party which had attached itself to the House of Bourbon, as furnishing it with its best heads and protectors. Coligni and D'Andelot were wisely chosen to conduct the negotiations between the Huguenots and the Court, and so thoroughly did Catherine convince them of her friendliness to their cause, that, mainly by their means, the controversy upon this point was closed by the Regency of the Queen-mother being ratified. One regrets to see that the Protestant ministers assembled in synod at Poitiers mixed themselves up with this affair, by drawing up a memorial demanding the exclusion of women from the government. It was stepping beyond their province, and that in the way most fitted to prejudice Catherine against them.

The state of the public finances came next under the notice of the Deputies. Matters here were in a quite ruinous condition. Not only had the surplus which Francis I. had left in the public treasury been exhausted, but a debt had been accumulated during the reigns of his two successors which amounted now to forty-three millions of livres.

What was worse, the excess of the annual expenditure over the annual income had been increasing till the one was now nearly the double of the other. To meet this deficit, the Nobles proposed that a new tax should be levied, two-thirds of which should be imposed upon the property of the Church, and one-third upon that of the general community. The Third Estate went further. It broadly laid down the position that the possessions of the Church, having no other origin than the liberality of kings and ancient barons, were in the hands of ecclesiastics only as administrators; that the right to dispose of them lay with the State. It proposed that, reserving to the Church its right to the ecclesiastical edifices, the entire remainder of its estates should be disposed of by public auction: one-third of the produce to be invested so as to furnish incomes to the clergy, one-third devoted to the liquidation of the public debt, and one-third to the general purposes of the State. It is curious to find a measure so sweeping and revolutionary in its character proposed in France at so early a period. Still more curious to remember that more than a century and a half before this time, in 1408, the Commons of England presented a petition to the King embodying a proposal identical in principle with that mooted by the Tiers-État of France. Alarmed at this threatened invasion of their property, the clergy of France voluntarily undertook the payment of nearly a half of the public debt, obtaining in return a secret pledge from the Queen-Regent that the Catholic religion should be exclusively maintained.

With respect to the Church and the state of religion generally, the Deputies of the two Estates demanded that all pluralities in the Church should be abolished; that ecclesiastical benefices should be conferred only by election; that free schools should be opened all over France, in which the children should be instructed in the truths of the Christian religion; that a national council should be held, in which all the existing controversies should be decided according to the Word of God; that in this council the Reformed ministers should be invited to take part; that meanwhile, churches should be allowed to the Reformed; and that all punishments on account of religious offences should cease. The States declared their belief that perseverance, even for one year, in such persecuting measures as had been pursued, would light a flame which no power under heaven could extinguish. Such were the proposals and demands of the first meeting of the Estates that had assembled in France since the leaven of the Reformation had begun to work. In the political and religious reforms which they suggest, they carry with them convincing proof of the extent to which their leaven had at this time permeated the middle and upper classes of society.

The assembly of the clergy, in which the differences between the Reformed and the Roman Catholic faiths were to be discussed, was summoned to meet at Poissy in September. Instead of calling it a council—a term obnoxious to Rome—the milder epithet of a Colloquy was bestowed on it. Called by whatever name, a conference upon equal terms between Huguenot ministers and the clergy of the Church was a scandal to all ultra Catholics. The Pope was alarmed and exasperated when he heard of it, nor were his fears apparently without foundation. A curious letter is preserved, written to him by Catherine de Medicis, in which she defends the calling of this assembly. "The numbers," she says, "of those who have separated from the Church of Rome are so great, the party has become so powerful through the multitudes of the nobility and magistracy that have adopted it, that it is formidable in all parts of the kingdom. But there are found among them neither libertines, anabaptists, nor holders of any opinions that are regarded as monstrous. All admit the twelve articles of the Apostles' Creed as they have been explained in the seven Œcumenical Councils. On this account, many zealous Catholics are of opinion, that they ought not to be cut off from the communion of the Church, which might prove a first step towards the reunion of the Greek and Latin Churches. Should your Highness not approve of the suggestion, they are of opinion, so urgent is the evil, that recourse must be had to extraordinary measures, in order to recall those who have separated, and to retain those who still adhere to the Church. To accomplish the first of these objects, they believe no better method will be found than frequent conferences between the Doctors on either side, and for the second, that all scandals should be removed." As instances of the scandals to be removed, Catherine goes on to specify the worship of images, communion only in one kind, the use of the Latin tongue in public worship, and the practice of private masses. The Pope, as he read this letter, must have felt as if France was on the eve of following the example of England. He immediately despatched the Cardinal of Ferrara to be present at the Colloquy, and Lainez, the general of the Jesuits, set out on the same errand. Catherine had written to Calvin inviting his presence. He did not come, but sent in his stead Theodore Beza, who, being an accomplished gentleman as well as a divine, was peculiarly fitted for the task assigned him. Beza was accompanied by Peter Martyr, a name familiar to us in the history of the Reformation in England.

The sittings of the Colloquy were opened on the 8th September in the refectory of one of the largest convents at Poissy. The young King, the Queen-mother, the members of the Court, all the great officers of state, six Cardinals, thirty-six Bishops and Archbishops, a whole host of inferior clergy and distinguished doctors of the Church, filled the Hall. The King opened the diet by announcing the object of the assembly. The Chancellor followed in a long address; then, at a given signal, the doors were thrown open, and, clad in their simple Geneva vestments, the twelve Calvinist ministers, escorted by two-and-twenty deputies from the churches, were seen to enter. They approached a balustrade that had been drawn across the hall to prevent their further ingress. Beza, addressing the King, entreated him not to be offended if in a matter of such great moment he had recourse to the Father of spirits for light and guidance. He and his colleagues then fell upon their knees, and, amid the breathless silence of the large assembly, Beza offered up a prayer still preserved in the liturgy of the French churches. Rising from his knees he entered upon a lengthened statement and defence of the doctrines of the Reformation. He was listened to with the utmost attention till he happened to let fall the words that he believed that in the Supper the real body and blood of Christ were as far from the bread and wine as the heavens were from the earth. A tumult of indignation was excited; some rose to depart, others exclaimed that he had blasphemed. The old Cardinal of Tournon entreated either that the speaker should be stopped, or that he and others should be permitted to retire. Order was at last restored. Beza resumed his address, which he closed by presenting to the King, on bended knee, the Confession of Faith of the Reformed Churches.

Beza's eloquent oration occupied the whole forenoon. The Cardinal of Lorraine undertook to reply to it. He demanded, however, some days for preparation. It was not till the 16th of the month that the sittings were resumed. The Cardinal's address came up to the highest expectation of his friends. Instead of going over the whole ground occupied by Beza, he confined himself to two points—the authority of the Church, and the real presence in the Communion. Opposing the unity of the one Holy Catholic Church to all the diversities of Protestantism, he drew a grand historic picture of that Church, surviving all the changes of the past, and destined to resist all the shocks of the future, ending by an appeal to the young monarch to attach himself more and more firmly to the ancient faith of his fathers. The assembly was electrified. The Bishops all rose from their seats, pronounced the reply unanswerable, demanded that the Reformed ministers should confess themselves conquered, and should either at once acknowledge the two articles the Cardinal had substantiated, or be driven from the presence of royalty. In the midst of the confusion Beza rose and requested to be heard immediately in reply. The Council, more reasonable than the Bishops, acknowledged the fairness of the request, but adjourned the hearing of the reply to a future diet.

Meanwhile, the Cardinal of Ferrara and Lainez

had arrived. Unable at once to stop the Colloquy, they persuaded the Regent that already by far too much publicity had been given to such discussions, and that if continued it would be much better to have a small number on both sides chosen, and to conduct the discussion in a smaller apartment of the convent. This suggestion was acted on, but the discussion in the Prior's chamber had no better issue than those in the refectory.

The Cardinal now tried a ruse, upon the success of which he confidently counted. Having selected those articles of the Confession of Augsburg to which he thought it most likely that the Calvinists would object, he presented it to Beza and his colleagues, and asked if they were ready to sign them as a basis of peace and reconciliation. Beza answered that these articles would be useless as such a basis, unless it were known in the first instance whether the Bishops agreed to them, and intimated that whenever their signature was attached to them, he and his friends would be prepared to take them into consideration. The wily Cardinal for once was foiled.

As a last effort, the Queen-mother required a few theologians on both sides to draw up a formula of belief as to the Lord's Supper which both could sign. They succeeded in doing so. The formula was shown to the Cardinal of Lorraine, who approved of it. For a moment it was imagined that a common ground or form of belief, on this one point at least, had been discovered. No sooner, however, had the formula been shown to the Bishops and the doctors of the Sorbonne than it was at once rejected. Another, drawn up according to the strictest tenets of Catholicism, was framed; and the Regent was required to extort a signature to it from the Reformed ministers, or, in case of their refusal, to drive them from the kingdom. Catherine was convinced that the attempt to reconcile the two religions was vain, and the Colloquy of Poissy was closed.

The adherents of the old faith, constituting the vast majority of the nation, regarded with an evil eye the favor shown to the Huguenots by the Government. All trials for heresy had ceased, the prison doors had been opened to those confined on account of their religion, the banished were invited to return, and though all public assemblies for worship were still legally prohibited, the law was not rigorously carried out. Under cover of the virtual toleration thus extended to them, the Huguenots made many open, in some instances offensive, exhibitions of their strength. They had not hesitated in a few cases to appropriate to their own use churches of the Catholics, cleansing them from all vestiges of idolatrous worship. Feeling the pulse of the nation beat strongly against the Government, the Guises saw that the opportunity for recovery of their power had come. By the help of that aged intriguer, the Duchess of Valentinois, they effected a reconciliation between the Constable and the Marshal St. André.

The Chancellor, De l'Hôpital, under whose wise and temperate guidance Catherine had hitherto been acting, felt that it was necessary to take a decided step. He resolved that it should be one in advance; nothing short, in fact, of the formal and legal recognition of the Reformed faith in France. In January 1562, he called together Deputies from all the seven Parliaments of the kingdom, the Council of State, the Princes of the blood, and the chief nobility. In his opening address, De l'Hôpital combated with the utmost strenuousness the advice of those who desired to see the King put himself at the head of one religious party in the State in order to crush the other. "It were a thing," he said, "unworthy not only of Christianity but of humanity. Whichever party gained, it would be a victory as sad for the conquerors as for the conquered. Deprecating all such remedies, let us seek one more analogous to the nature of the evil; an evil which being purely moral will never yield to mere physical applications. Waste not, then, your time in determining which of the two religions is the best. We are here not to establish a dogma of faith, but to regulate an affair of State. Ought the new religion to be tolerated according to the demand of the Nobles and Tiers-État assembled at Pontoise? Must one cease to be a good subject of the King when he ceases to worship God as the

King does? Is it not possible to be a good enough subject without being a Catholic or even a Christian? Citizens of different religious persuasions, can they not live together in all good harmony as members of the same society. These, gentlemen, are the questions you are called upon to decide."
New, strange words these; new even from De l'Hôpital's lips. Two years before, in opening the States-General, he had spoken in quite other terms, laying it down then as a maxim that it was folly to expect that persons of different religions could ever live together in peace and amity. But those two years' study of the state of France have opened the Chancellor's mind, and now he is the first public man in France to announce the true idea of toleration.

After twelve days' stormy debate he carried the measure—the Magna Charta of religious liberty in France—by which Protestantism was legally acknowledged and protected. This Edict, generally spoken of by historians as the Edict of January, suspended the execution of all pains and penalties on account of religion till the decision of a General Council, and granted liberty to the Huguenots to assemble for public worship, they binding themselves to teach no other doctrines than those contained in the books of the Old and New Testaments and in the Creed of the Council of Nice, and not to hold their Synods without permission from a magistrate. Moderate as it was in its concessions, this Edict was gratefully and joyfully accepted by the Huguenots. Their adversaries regarded it as so fatal a blow to the religious unity of the kingdom, so ruinous to the State, so dishonoring to God, that they resolved to disobey it, though at the cost of thereby generating a civil war.

Before plunging into the conflict, the Guises, knowing that it would be to the Protestant Princes of Germany that, in the event of hostilities breaking out, the Huguenots would apply for aid, invited Christopher, Duke of Würtemberg, whose position and character placed him among the first of these princes, to an interview at Saverne. The Duke, accompanied by his chief theologians, reached that city on the 13th February 1562, and found the Duke of Guise and his brother, the Cardinal, awaiting his arrival. Next morning the Cardinal preached a sermon, in which neither the Lutheran Duke nor any of his divines could find any thing objectionable. That evening Francis of Guise had a private interview with the Duke of Würtemberg. "I am but a man of arms," said Francis, "and know little about these matters. I have been brought up in the faith of my fathers, but if any one will convince me I am in error, I will readily acknowledge it. Those ministers at Poissy called us Catholics idolaters. What is idolatry?" "It is idolatry," said the Duke of Würtemberg, "when one adores any other God than the true one; when one seeks any other mediator than Jesus Christ; and when one puts his confidence for salvation in saints, the Virgin Mary, or his own merits." "I adore God only," said Guise; "I confide only in Jesus Christ. I know well that neither the saints nor the Virgin can aid me; that it is Christ alone and not my works must save me." Delighted at meeting one so open, so frank, already so far advanced, the Duke of Würtemberg discoursed at large to his attentive auditor. Apparently convinced by his arguments and eloquence, the Duke of Guise ended by saying, "Well, these things are quite new to me; but if it be as you say, then I am a Lutheran, but you must speak to my brother about all this."

Next morning at seven o'clock Francis entered the apartment of Christopher. "My mind," said he, "has been so full of the subject of our conversation that I have slept none last night. I have told something of it to my brother the Cardinal, who would like much to have a conversation with Brentius in your presence." The German Prince most readily assented. At eight o'clock the Cardinal preached a second sermon, more decidedly Lutheran than the first. A conference was held afterwards. Brentius, at the Cardinal's desire, stated the leading points of controversy between the two communions, the Lutheran and the Roman Catholic, dwelling particularly upon the mass. "No doubt," said the Cardinal, "Catholicism has gone too far in its exegesis of the Supper." They spoke then of the means of reconciling the two communions. "If the ministers at Poissy," said the Cardinal, "had accepted the Confession of Augsburg, I should have got the Prelates to range themselves on the same side." "Had Beza, then, and his friends," said the Duke of Würtemberg, "signed that Confession, would you have signed it?" "Certainly," said Charles of Lorraine, "I take God to witness that I think and believe as I now say, and that by the grace of God I shall live and die in these sentiments. I have read the Confession of Augsburg. I have read also those of Melanchthon and Brentius, and others. I entirely approve of their doctrines; I agree with them in all that relates to ecclesiastical discipline; but it is necessary that for a time I conceal these sentiments to gain those who are weaker in the faith." Brentius entreated him to labor for the advancement of the gospel and the attainment of religious concord in France. "I promise to do it," said the Cardinal; "but it is difficult to do any thing with those wrong-headed Calvinists," upon whose wrong-headedness he continued to descant. The strange conference broke up, the Guises having succeeded in injecting into the minds of the Germans an unmerited confidence in themselves, and a suspicion and dislike of the Huguenots.

Quitting Saverne, the Princes of Lorraine retired to Joinville, the residence of their mother Antoinette de Bourbon. Hearing strange rumors as to the progress of the Triumvirate, the Queen-mother despatched an order to the Duke that he should remain at Joinville. He got other instructions, however, from his friends in Paris, which he resolved rather to obey. Every thing was now ripe for open resistance to the Edict of January, and his presence was required to assist in carrying the preconcerted measures into execution. By the way, an event occurred which precipitated those measures, and plunged France at once into all the horrors of a wide-spread civil and religious war.

Three leagues from Joinville, on the way to Paris, lay the little town of Vassy. During the last few months a Huguenot congregation had sprung up in it, to which a large body of its inhabitants had attached themselves. His mother had complained bitterly to the Duke of Guise of a nuisance like this showing itself under the shadow of her château, and of the fruitlessness of all her attempts to suppress it. Early on Sunday morning the 1st day of March 1562, attended by a numerous and well-armed suite, the Duke was approaching Vassy on his way through it to Paris. Hearing the sound of bells, he asked what they were ringing for. It was for the service of the Huguenots, he was told. It threw him into a towering passion. Biting his lips and twisting his beard, as his custom was when in such a state, with his usual oath he exclaimed, "We will huguenot them presently in a different fashion; march, gentlemen, we must see them while they meet." Entering the town he dismounted before the convent, which stood about 200 paces from the building—a large barn—in which the Huguenots were assembled.

After a short interview with some of the town-authorities, he placed himself at the head of his followers and proceeded to the building, in which 1200 persons were engaged in worship. The Duke's company got wild with excitement by the way. The prayers were over, and the minister, Morel, had begun his discourse, when the hootings and shoutings of the approaching band was heard. Presently two shots were heard, fired by some of the Duke's people at the upper windows. Those within who were nearest the entrance-door rushed forward to close it. They were too late. Sword in hand the Duke's men broke in, stabbing and shooting right and left. Some stones were thrown; one struck the Duke. The fury of the assailants then knew no bounds. Unable to get out at the door, the Huguenots tore up part of the roof of the building, and some of them tried to escape along the tops of the neighboring houses. They were discovered and made shot-marks of, a servant of the Duke's boasting afterwards that with his own arquebuse he had brought down half a dozen of those pigeons. The Duke with drawn sword was himself within the building urging on the carnage. Sixty were killed upon the spot, more than two hundred severely wounded.

The minister kept his place and continued his discourse till a shot struck the pulpit. Throwing off his gown, he tried like others to escape. In doing so he fell over a dead body, and when down got a sabre-cut across the shoulders. He rose, but he had scarcely done so when several sabre-strokes fell upon his head. Again he fell, but some one recognized him and carried him to the Duke. "Are you the minister?" said the Duke; "what makes you seduce these people?" "I am no seducer," answered Morel, "but a preacher of the Gospel of Jesus Christ." "Does the Gospel, then," said the Duke, "preach sedition? You are the true cause of the death of all these people, and you shall be hanged this moment." He turned and gave an order to this effect to the Provost, but there was no one at hand to execute it.

The sackers of the chapel now brought the Bible that they had found in the deserted pulpit. Taking it into his hands the Duke went out, and calling to the Cardinal, who all the while had been lounging upon the walls of an adjoining cemetery, "There, brother," said he, "look at one of these cursed Huguenot books." The Cardinal, with the volume in his hands, cast a glance at its title-page, and said, "There's no great harm in it; it is the Bible, the Holy Scriptures." "How!" said the Duke, "the Holy Scriptures. It is fifteen hundred years since Jesus Christ suffered death and passion, and it is but a year since that book was made. Do you call that the Gospel? it is good for nothing." As he turned away in his blind passion, the Cardinal was heard quietly saying, "My brother is in the wrong." Walking up and down before the now blood-stained and desolated chapel, the Duke called for the Judge of the district, and demanded of him why he had tolerated this conventicle. The Edict of January was pleaded by the Judge in his defence. "Detestable edict!" said the Duke, grasping his sword: "this shall cut it asunder."

The massacre of Vassy,[1] committed in open day, in flagrant violation of the law that secured to them the free exercise of their religion, filled the hearts of the Huguenots with grief and indignation. The news of it spread speedily over the country. Rude engravings, horribly accurate in their details, were scattered over France, and copied and circulated in Germany. The whole Protestant world was filled with horror at the deed. The Duke of Guise, aware that the decisive step had at last been taken, hastened on to Paris. The tidings of the affair at Vassy had preceded him. His entry into

---

[1] Prior to the Revolution of 1789 there was a convent of Irish Capuchins at Vassy. At its suppression, Father Macnulty, known under the name of Père Casimir, left an old coffer of the convent in charge of a merchant of Vassy named Delauncy. The coffer was carefully preserved, and never opened till 1835, when its contents were inspected in the presence of a Justice of Peace. Among other papers which it contained was found a manuscript account of the Massacre of Vassy. M. Horace Gourjon published this account in 1844. It is almost verbatim the same with that given in the Martyrology of Crespin, that compilation whose accuracy every late historical investigation is serving to confirm.

the city was a triumphal ovation. On his right hand rode the Marshal St. André, on his left the Constable; more than 1200 noblemen and gentlemen followed in his train. The mayor of the city met him at the gate of St. Denis, and presented him with a congratulatory address. The assembled multitudes rent the skies with their acclamations, hailing him as the champion of the faith.

Catherine de Medicis had heard at Monceaux, where the Court then was, of what happened at Vassy, and of the Duke's approach to Paris. She wrote commanding him to lay down his arms, and to repair to Monceaux attended by twelve gentlemen. The order was disobeyed. The Duke preferred to receive the ovation that he knew awaited him at Paris. And now there came to Monceaux, couriers from Condé and deputies from the Reformed churches, entreating the interference of the Government. It was a critical moment in the history of the Queen-mother. She inquired eagerly as to the strength of the Huguenots. The Deputies showed her a list of 2150 churches, and assured her that they could bring into the field an army of 50,000 men. Still undecided, unwilling to throw herself into the hands of the Triumvirate by going to Paris, but as unwilling to throw herself into the hands of the Huguenots by going to Orleans, their stronghold at this time, she retired first to Melun, and afterwards to Fontainebleau. The arrogance of the Guises seems at last to have determined her.

From Fontainebleau she wrote in the most urgent terms to Condé, entreating him to come and take her and the young King under his protection.

Condé, forced to retire from Paris, was now at Meaux. Whether from distrust of the Queen-mother, or from thinking that the force he had was too feeble, he hesitated to take the step. The hesitation was fatal to the Huguenots; it lost them the opportunity of carrying the authority of the young King over to their side. Prompter and less scrupulous, the Triumvirs proceeded at once with a sufficient force to Fontainebleau, and informed the Queen-Regent that they came to conduct her and their young monarch to Paris. For the moment, Catherine resisted, and resented this attempt to coerce her movements. "She would not move," she said, "till moved by force." "She may remain here or quit the kingdom as she likes," was the haughty answer of the Duke of Guise; "the thing is indifferent to us; the King must go with us, whether she will or no." To part from her son was political death to Catherine. She gave way, and was conducted in triumph to Paris.

For months past, Coligni had been living quietly at his country-seat at Chatillon. A faithful picture of his daily life there has been handed down to us. It shows a household fashioned after the strictest Puritan model: the early hours, the fixed methodical routine, the frequent prayers, the fervent psalmody, the preachings almost every day.

But there was no tinge either of asceticism or fanaticism in the piety of Coligni. He was an unselfish patriot, and a far-seeing politician as well as a devoted Christian. Scarce a forenoon passed at Chatillon in which some deputy from one or other of the Reformed Churches was not received, coming to him for advice, and getting evidence, in the counsel that he gave, of his gentleness and moderation as well as his sagacity. But now the quiet of that country life is broken. He hears of the massacre at Vassy. Couriers from the impetuous Condé come to the château, telling him of the occupation of Paris by the Triumvirate, of the resolution openly avowed to trample under foot the Edict of January. Fresh messengers arrive to tell him that all Protestant France is up in arms, ready to take the field, and summoning him to join the Prince of Condé and share in the command. His wife and brothers press him to depart. He hesitates. Calvin's repugnance to the use of arms is also in a large measure his. No eye in France sees half so far as his into the miseries and crimes into which a religious war must plunge his country. Would they but let that edict stand; would they but let the true faith live and breathe, though it were within narrow limits, and in a hampered straitened way, he should be content. Strifes of rival houses struggling for political power, what were they to him? Besides, if war were entered on, failure would doom Protestantism to extinction:

and was there any thing like a fair promise of success? Coligni could not see his way at first to draw the sword.

But now came tidings, day by day, of the atrocities of Vassy repeated here and there all over France; of the Catholics rising upon the Calvinists at Chalons, Sens, Auxerre, and Tours; of 3000 men, women, and children murdered. Coligni's heart was rent by the recital. One night, with sobs and tears, his wife, the truly noble Charlotte de Laval, besought him to depart. "Are you prepared," he said to her, "to receive the intelligence of defeat, to see your husband branded as a rebel, and dragged to a scaffold; your children disgraced and ruined, begging their bread at the hands of their enemies? I will give you three weeks to reflect." "The three weeks are already past," was her chivalrous reply. "Go, in God's name, and He will not suffer you to be vanquished." Next day Coligni was on his way to join Condé at Meaux.

If slower than others to draw it, Coligni was for decisive measures when once the sword was drawn. His advice was to march instantly on Paris, and meet the enemy in the open field. The Huguenot troops might be inferior in number, but Coligni's own companies were men upon whom he could fully count. He had inspired his own spirit into them. They were under the strictest discipline; no license of any kind was given. A Calvinist minister was placed over each regiment. They were drilled daily, not only in martial movements, but to know and feel that they were soldiers of the Cross, called to do battle for the true faith. Had the Admiral been at the head of the movement, with none but his Huguenot soldiers under him, there might have been seen in France, a hundred years before Cromwell's time, a little army of Ironsides, that had proved invincible in the field. But the Barons brought other kinds of men, and other kinds of ideas into the field. The Prince, to whom the chief command belonged, shrunk from following the Admiral's advice. The Queen-mother, whose boast was that her tongue and pen were more powerful than the swords of the greatest captains, got him entangled in negotiations. The summer months of 1562 were wasted thus.

But while the chiefs on either side hesitated, the country took the matter into its own hands. The note of open war was no sooner sounded, than in the south-western provinces, in which the Huguenots prevailed, they rose against the Catholics; in the north-western, in which the Catholics prevailed, they rose against the Huguenots. For weeks and months, the blindest, wildest, bloodiest, fanaticism ran riot over France. Where the Huguenots had power, the Catholic worship was abolished. The priests were driven away or killed; the churches were sacked, their altars overturned, their images broken, their relics scattered and defiled, their baptismal fonts turned to the vilest uses.

The shrines of saints, the tombs of kings, whatever monument was venerable by age or otherwise, was marked for ruin. The ashes of Irenæus were flung into the Rhone, those of St. Martin of Tours into the Loire, the sepulchres of Louis XI. at Cleri, of Richard Cœur de Lion at Rouen, of William the Conqueror at Caen, were rifled and desecrated. The Catholics had no churches of their opponents to pillage, no images of theirs to break. Their wrath directed itself not against dead monuments, but against living men. In that region, spurred on by the priests, and encouraged by a terrible Edict of the Parliament of Paris, which doomed every Huguenot to death and called upon the faithful everywhere to arise, and without form of law, to execute that doom, it was a frightful havoc that they wrought. We read of a stream of Huguenot blood running in one place nearly a foot deep. We would shut our eyes upon such horrors, were it not that it is so useful, by thorough inspection of them, to be taught into what fearful excesses religious wars have run.

Blaise de Montluc was commissioned by the Government to reduce the Huguenot district of Guienne. Let us listen to Montluc himself, as in his commentaries, written many years after, and in cold blood, he describes to us the beginning of his operations. "I privately," he says, " got two hangmen (whom they have since called my lacquais, because they were often at my heels), determining to execute all the cruelty I could, for I saw very well that gentle means would never reclaim those cankered and inveterate rascals. So soon as I came to St. Mezard, Monsieur de Fontenelles presented three prisoners, all bound in the churchyard, in which there was yet remaining the foot of a stone cross that they had broken. I had my two hangmen behind me, well equipped with their tackle, and especially with a very sharp axe, when, flying in great fury upon one of the three, I took him by the collar, saying, 'O thou confounded rogue, dost thou defile thy wicked tongue against the majesty of thy King and Sovereign?' To which he replied, 'Ah, Sir, have mercy upon a poor sinner!' At which, more enraged than before, I said to him, 'Thou ungracious rascal, wouldst thou have me to have mercy upon thee who hadst no reverence nor respect for thy King?' and with that I pushed him rudely to the ground, so that his neck fell exactly upon the piece of the cross, crying to the hangman, 'Strike villain,' which he did, and so nimbly, that my word and the blow were the one as soon as the other, which fetched off his head, and, moreover, above another half-foot of the cross. The other two I caused to be hanged upon an elm that was close by. This was the first execution I did at my arriving from my own house."

The thousands that followed were done by Montluc in the same style, so that, as he seems pleased to tell us, "one might mark the road I took by the trees on which my ensigns hung."

Montluc's terrible doings in Guienne were rivalled by a Huguenot captain, the Baron des Adrets in Dauphiny. So swift in motion, so fiery in assault, was Des Adrets, and his name at last carried with it such a spell of terror, that the best fortified cities flung open at once their gates at his approach. But few escaped who fell into his hands. The garrison of the lofty stronghold of Maugiron were all put to the sword, with the exception of a few whom he reserved till after dinner, to enjoy the savage glee of making them, one after another, leap down from the highest tower. One of them alone escaped. Three times he had taken the preparatory run, but each time had halted at the brink. Des Adrets reproached him with cowardice in having three times failed. "Baron," said the man, turning quickly round to him, "brave as you are, I will give you ten trials to do it in." The Baron spared him for his reply. Equal in cruelty, on opposite sides, as were Montluc and Des Adrets, there was this difference between them: the one gloried afterwards in the blood he had shed; the other endeavored to excuse it. The one received for his services a letter of thanks from the Pope, the acknowledgment of his own government, and the rank of Marshal in the French army; the other was openly censured by Condé and Coligni, took offence at the manner in which he was treated by the Protestants, and finally forsook their ranks.

The leaders on both sides, at Orleans and at

Paris, fearing to act upon the offensive with so small a body of native troops as they had been able to muster, had, during the summer months, been seeking foreign aid,—the Huguenots at first unwillingly, the Admiral strenuously opposing it. When it was known, however, that Spanish and Swiss troops had been engaged to act against them, Coligni withdrew his opposition. On the 20th September, a treaty was signed at Hampton Court, by which the English Government agreed to furnish 140,000 crowns and 6000 men, on condition, however, that the town of Havre should be put into their hands,—a condition, the granting of which did no small injury to the Huguenot cause in France. D'Andelot was despatched to Germany, where, after overcoming many difficulties, he gathered round him some thousands of those *Reiter*, heavy cavalry, armed with pistols, whose attacks, in close, deep columns, had proved so formidable in so many fields. Instantly on their arrival, Condé took the field and marched on Paris. The wily Catherine once more entangled him in her snares, and kept him inactive till such a large body of Spaniards and Swiss had entered the city, as to cut off all hope of successfully assaulting it. Condé retired into Normandy. The army of the Triumvirs hastened after him to cut off his retreat.

On the 18th December, near the village of Dreux, on the plain that stretches between the Blaise and the Eure, two tributaries of the Seine, the two armies found themselves in front of one another, and the first great battle of those wars was fought. The Catholic army was composed of 16,000 infantry and 3000 cavalry, in all 19,000 men; the Huguenot army of 5000 infantry and 8000 cavalry, in all 13,000 men. The great numerical inferiority of the Protestants was in part made up for by the ground being so favorable for the movements of the cavalry, that branch in which they were the strongest. Condé, with Coligni and D'Andelot under him, led the one army; the old Constable, with the Duke of Guise and the Marshal St. André under him, led the other. For two hours the armies stood gazing at each other in perfect stillness, many in each thinking of the friends and relations that were in the opposing ranks. But when the close-handed fight began, which lasted for full seven hours, it was carried on with extreme ferocity. At first all seemed to go in favor of the Huguenots. Condé, with his natural impetuosity, flung himself with his gallant French lances on the Swiss, who sustained the shock with a steadiness worthy the reputation gained upon so many fields. At last, however, their ranks were broken, and they were forced into retreat. The Admiral, leading 1200 German *Reiter*, was no less successful against the division of the French army led by the Constable in person. That gallant old general, his horse shot under him, his jaw broken by a pistol-bullet, his throat choked with blood—unable any longer to let his word of command be heard—was forced to yield himself prisoner. The confusion of the Catholic army became general, apparently irretrievable. The Huguenots looked on the day as already theirs. Scattered over the field, they had already begun the work of pillage.

The eyes, however, of the two best captains in the field were still studying the bloody fray. The Admiral felt insecure. He had noticed a dense company of the enemy, which had remained motionless on the left. While the shout of victory was ringing in his own ranks, he fixed an uneasy look upon that company, and said,—" We deceive ourselves. We shall soon see that great cloud discharge itself upon us." He was not mistaken. The Duke of Guise, with a chosen troop of men-at-arms, had stationed himself at the beginning of the action on a rising ground somewhat in the rear. He watched there the progress of the fight. The retreat of the Swiss, the confusion and flight of a large body of the Catholic army, did not seem to move him. The Constable's son, Damville, galloped up to him, and entreated him to fly to his father's rescue. "Not yet, my son; not yet," was the Duke's reply. All he did was to command his ranks to open. He rode out to the front, rose upon his stirrups, and looked round upon the field. At last the time for action came. Turning to his men, and putting spurs to his horse, he cried, " Come on, my friends, the day is ours." Dashing forward, he took up by the way the yet unbroken division of St. André, and threw himself upon the surprised, exhausted Huguenots. The charge was decisive. The Protestants were utterly routed. Condé was taken prisoner. Coligni and D'Andelot, after the most determined struggles to retrive the fortunes of the day, were forced to retire. It was a proud day for the Duke of Guise: for the victory was wholly of his gaining. The Constable was in the hands of the enemy. The Marshal St. André had fallen in the fray. The undivided command of the royal army was in his hands, nor was there any one to dispute his general influence over the Government. He closed a day that raised him to such a pinnacle of power, by an act of chivalrous courtesy to his distinguished prisoner. The Prince of Condé was received by him into his own tent. They slept that night in the same bed, Condé relating afterwards that he never closed his eyes, but that the Duke slept as soundly as if nothing had occurred.

The Duke was too good a general not to follow up his success at Dreux. Taking a few weeks to recruit his army, he led it, flushed with victory, forward to Orleans. That city was the stronghold of the Huguenots. Their ablest ministers, the wife and eldest son of Condé, the wives and families and movable estates of many of their nobles and gentry, their important prisoner the Constable, were all shut up within its walls. Trusting mainly to the bridge and towers which guarded it—the Tourelles which had witnessed one of the greatest exploits of the Maid of Orleans—D'Andelot, who commanded the garrison, had engaged to keep Guise before the city till the Admiral returned from Normandy to raise the siege. An accidental and unexpected success put the southern suburb, that part of the city which lay on the south side of the Loire, into the Duke's hands. The bridge and towers were captured in a night attack. The other fortifications of the city were too weak and the garrison too feeble to resist an assault. The Duke looked upon the city as already his, and proceeded to lay before his officers his plan for terminating the war. Orleans taken, he was to call out the Arrière-ban—all the nobility of France from eighteen to sixty years of age, with their retainers—to gather all the regular forces scattered throughout the kingdom, pursue the Admiral into Normandy, cut his troops to pieces, drive the English into the sea, and so quench the Huguenot spirit in France,—a bright and not improbable perspective.

The first step, at least, seemed sure. The 19th February was fixed on as the day for the assault at Orleans. The Duke wrote to the Queen-mother that the city must inevitably be taken, and that he hoped she would not blame him if he slew every living thing within the walls, razed it to the ground, and sowed its foundations with salt. On the 18th, he visited the trenches, and saw that all was ready for next day's bloody work. In the dusk of the evening, he was returning to the château in which he slept. He had just passed two walnut trees which stood where two roads met, when the click of a trigger was heard immediately behind his back; a shot was fired; three balls entered his right shoulder and passed out through his breast. At first he bent to his horse's neck, then raising himself, he said, "They owed me this, but it will be nothing." He tried to grasp his sword, but his arm hung useless by his side; another impression came over him, he felt that the wound was mortal. They bore him to his chamber. All that the surgical skill of those days could do was done, but without effect. The skill of the regular practitioner failing, there was presented to the Duke's notice some early discoverer of the water-cure—one reputed to have done wonders in the cure of wounds, by use of linens and of water. The Duke refused to be treated in that way. "He would have," he said, "no other remedies than those proceeding from the Divine goodness; he would rather die than give himself to enchantments forbidden of God."

His end approaching, he met his fate, that came upon him at the very time when all that ambition sought for seemed within his grasp, with the utmost fortitude and resignation. In the most urgent terms he asked that his death should not be avenged. Most tenderly he warned his son against ambition, bidding him beware how for worldly distinction he stained his soul with violence or crime.

Some of his own excesses he admitted, but tried partially to excuse. The Massacre of Vassy he frequently alluded to, solemnly declaring that on his part it was unpremeditated. He advised the Queen-Regent, who had hastened to Orleans to see him, to make peace as speedily as possible. Long speeches and prayers have been preserved, not likely to have been spoken as they are given. But there is reason to believe that the last hours of the Duke of Guise were those of an affectionate, devout, and generous spirit; nor do we remember another to whom the familiar words of Shakspeare might more fitly be applied—

"Nothing in his life
Became him like the leaving it."

CHAPTER IV.

JEANNE D'ALBRET, QUEEN OF NAVARRE,
1528–1572.

Kingdom of Navarre.—Birth, education, and marriage of Jeanne D'Albret.—Birth of Henry IV.—The Queen becomes a Protestant.—Letter to the Cardinal d'Armagnac.—Bull of the Pope.—Plot of Phillip II.—Code of laws.—Conferences at Bayonne.—Glimpses of Prince Henry.—Breaking out of the war.—Battle of St. Denis.—The Queen, Prince Henry, and Condé at Rochelle.—Battle of Jarnac.—The Queen's address to the soldiers.—Battle of Moncontour.—Invasion of Navarre.—Arnay-le-Duc.— Proposed marriage of Prince Henry with Marguerite of Valois, sister of Charles IX.—Illness and death of Jeanne d'Albret.—Her character.

For seven centuries the Pyrenees saw both their northern and southern slopes occupied by a small but separate sovereignty, which owed the independence it had so long preserved not so much to the strength of its natural defences as to the distracted condition of the neighboring countries of France and Spain. It boded ill for this little kingdom of Navarre when Aragon and Castile were united, the Moorish kingdom of Granada overturned, and Ferdinand the Catholic planted on his brows the crown of a broad and powerful monarchy. He had scarcely done so when, casting a covetous eye upon the province that obtruded itself between Castile and Aragon, he sought and found a pretext for invasion, and in the year 1515 united it to the other provinces of Spain. Besides the Spanish province thus appropriated, which gave its name to the kingdom of Navarre, that kingdom embraced a large tract of country lying on the French side of the Pyrenees, including the principality of Béarn and the counties of Foix, Armagnac, Albret, Bigorre, and Comminges. Catherine de Foix, the heiress of this kingdom, had in 1491 carried it by marriage into the house of D'Albret. Henry, the second King of Navarre belonging to this house, was in 1528 united to Marguerite d'Angoulême, the favorite and devoted sister of Francis I. of France. Pampeluna, the ancient capital of their kingdom, being in the hands of the King of Spain, Henry and Marguerite held their Court at Nérac, the chief town of the duchy belonging to the family of D'Albret. It was at Nérac that Marguerite, herself more than half a Huguenot, opened an asylum to her persecuted fellow-countrymen. Farel, Calvin, Beza sought temporary refuge and found glad welcome there, while to Lefèvre, Clément Marot, and Gérard Roussel it became a second home. Marguerite died in 1549, leaving only one child, a daughter, who, in the event of her father having no issue by any second marriage, became heiress to the crown of Navarre. Born in 1528, Jeanne d'Albret had early and bitter experience of what heirship to such a crown involved. The Emperor Charles V. was believed to have early fixed his eye on her as a fit consort for Philip, his son and successor. Such an alliance would not only have prevented the question of the recovery of the lost province of Navarre from being raised, but would have given to Spain a footing on French soil, of which large advantage might have been taken. Suspecting and determined to thwart the project of his great adversary, Francis I. took his little niece into his own especial custody, would not let her pass out of France, nor go to receive her education at Nérac. Assigning the royal castle of Plessis-les-Tours to her, he insisted that she should live there, apart from her parents; and to remove any objections on that score, he undertook himself to defray the expenses of her household. It was in that gloomy abode (familiar to us from the pages of *Quentin Durward*), every legend of whose past history she greedily devoured, that so many as fifteen years of her childhood and youth were spent, years that threw a sombre shade over her character—for often, we are told, "her chamber echoed with her lamentations, and the air was laden with her sighs,"—but years, at the same time, in which, under the ablest instructors, she received an education more solid, as well as more extensive, than she might have got had she been living in the neighborhood of the Court. Her uncle had in the first instance destined her to be the bride of his second son, who was afterwards his successor upon the throne. Changing his purpose, however, to suit his political designs, Henry was affianced to Catherine de Medicis. How different that dark and troubled reign of Henry II. of France might have been had Francis's first purpose been carried out! One day, when Jeanne was about twelve years old, the dreariness of her abode at Plessis was disturbed by the sudden appearance of her royal uncle. She received him with transports of delight. The joy, however, was but short-lived. He came to tell her that it was his royal will and pleasure that she should wed a German prince—the young Duke of Cleves. The abrupt proposal was resisted and resented by the young Princess with a vehemence which she was at no pains to conceal. But Francis was inexorable. She must come to Court at once, to be betrothed to her intended husband. Jeanne appealed to her parents. They told her she must submit. By her as by them the will of Francis must be done. Not by her, however, without token of vigorous resistance. All outward opposition vain, she drew up with her own hand the following protest, which she got three of the officers of her household to witness:—" I, Jeanne de Navarre, do hereby again affirm and protest that the marriage which it is desired to contract between the Duke of Cleves and myself is against my will;

that I never have consented to it, nor will consent; and that whatever I may say or do hereafter, by which it may be attempted to prove that I have given my consent, will be forcibly extorted against my wish, from dread of the King my father, and the Queen my mother, who has threatened to have me whipped by my Governess. By command of the Queen, my mother, the said governess has also several times declared that if I do not all in regard to this marriage which the King wishes, I shall be punished so severely as to occasion my death, and that by refusing I might be the cause of the total ruin of my father, my mother, and of their house, the which has impressed me with such fear that I know not to whom to have recourse excepting to God, seeing that my father and my mother abandon me, who both know well what I have said to them, that never can I love the Duke of Cleves, and that I will not have him. Therefore I protest beforehand, that if it happen I am affianced or married to the said Duke in any way or manner, it will be against my heart and in defiance of my will; and that he shall never become my husband, nor will I hold and regard him as such." The girl but twelve years old who thought of making such a protest, and who put it into such pithy words, gave early proof of that independence and strength of will, which, brought afterwards under the control of the highest principles of action, contributed to the formation of one of the noblest female characters that has ever filled a throne. Despite of her protests, again and again repeated, Jeanne was betrothed to the Duke of Cleves, and the marriage ceremony was performed. The marriage, however, was not to be consummated till three years afterwards. Within that interval the Duke acted so that Francis became as eager to prevent as ever he had been to promote the marriage. The bond already formed was broken, and the union never took place.

The next hand offered to Jeanne, and which she accepted, was that of Antoine, elder brother of the Prince of Condé, and head of the Bourbon family. They were married in 1548, a year after the death of Francis I., and a year before that of his sister Marguerite, Jeanne's mother. The marriage was an unfortunate one. Ambitious, yet weak and vain; frivolous and vacillating yet headstrong and impetuous, faithless to his wife, faithless to his principles, faithless to his party, Antoine became the butt and victim of the policy of the Court. But though unfortunate in so many respects, this marriage gave to France, if not the greatest, the most fortunate, the most popular, the most beloved of all her monarchs. At first, indeed, Jeanne's hope of giving an heir even to the small kingdom of Navarre seemed doomed to disappointment. Her eldest child, a son, was confided to the care of an infirm and crotchety old lady, whose fancy was that of all hurtful things air and exercise were the most hurtful, who immured her infant charge night and day in an apartment close hung with arras, which not a breath of fresh air was permitted to enter, and which was heated to an oppressive degree. Under this treatment the infant wasted away, and in its second year expired. The second child, also a son, treated differently, was healthy and strong. One day, however, in his parents' absence, the nurse who carried the infant coming to an open window of the palace engaged in a somewhat too lively talk with one of the gentlemen ushers of the Court. The talkers amused themselves by passing the infant to and fro between them. Unhappily he fell between their hands upon the pavement beneath, and a few days afterwards expired. Jeanne's father, Henry, who was still living, grew irritated at the second disappointment of his hopes. He charged his daughter roundly with neglect of her maternal duties, and threatened to marry again himself, a threat which he was by no means unlikely to execute. He soothed himself, however, by exacting from his daughter a solemn promise, that if she had another child, she should repair to his city, Pau, and from its birth put the management of the child entirely into his hands—a promise that she was all the readier to make, as she had got alarmed at the ascendancy which a certain lady of noble birth had got over the old King, and at the rumor that he meant to marry her, and so legitimate a son whom he had by her since Marguerite's death. It was the heart of winter, and Jeanne was in Picardy, when the time came for her to fulfil the promise she had made. So great was the excitement in Béarn, that a deputation from the States of the Principality was deputed to Picardy to remind Jeanne of her engagement, and entreat her to keep it. Travelling back in company with these envoys, she reached Pau on the 4th December 1553, nine days before her son was born. She had heard that her father had made his will, and aware how deeply her own and her children's interests might be affected by it, she longed to penetrate the secret of its contents. Henry teased her by stimulating her curiosity. One day, when alone with her in his cabinet, the topic of the will once more was broached. Henry rose, and bringing out a little gold box, with chain and key attached, and holding it up before her, "My daughter," he said, "you see this box; well, it contains the will; and it shall be yours, and its contents, provided that during the birth you sing me a Gascon or Béarnois song, for I don't want you either to give me a peevish boy or a whimpering, whining girl." The hour came, and with it a summons to the King, who rose in haste to visit his daughter. As soon as Jeanne heard his approaching footsteps, in a firm clear voice she raised the Béarnois chant—"Notre Dame du bout du pont, Adjuda mi in questa houre." And bravely she sang on—not one of the many verses of the chant omitted; and so was sung into this world of ours the conqueror of Cintras, of D'Arques, of Ivry—Henry IV. of France. The old King took the babe and wrapped it carefully in his robe. Approaching his daughter, he put the gold box into her hand. "That is thine, my daughter," said he, pointing to the box, "and this is mine," pointing to the child. Jeanne got the box, but it is told that the mischievous old King forgot to let her have the key. The King carried the infant into his own apartment, where, upon committing him to his nurse, an ancient Béarnois ceremony was gone through. First the lips of the infant were gently rubbed with a clove of garlic, then a wine-cup of the best Jurançon wine was brought, and a few drops were put into its mouth. It is said that at the smell of the wine, as it approached, the infant raised its head—the drops at least it swallowed eagerly. "Ha," said the fond old grandfather, as in rapture he looked on, "Ha, thou shalt be a true Béarnois!" On the twelfth day the child was christened; and in a room of the ancient castle of Pau a curious relic is still preserved, called the cradle of Henry IV.,—a large tortoise-shell, upon which, inverted, and hung upon cords like the scale of a balance, the infant was carried to the baptismal font. From the castle of Pau the child was removed to that of Coarasse, lying at the mouth of one of those Alpine valleys by which the southern slopes of the Pyrenees are diversified. Here he was brought up after the true rough Béarnois fashion—nursed by a peasant woman—playing with peasant children—dressed like them—fed like them—bare-headed, bare-footed—climbing with them the hill side—wading with them the burns—scrambling with them over the rocks—braving all the heats and colds, and winds and rains, to which those children of the mountain were exposed—laying thus the foundation of that extraordinary physical energy by which the toils of so many a long and arduous campaign were borne, not only without fatigue, but with unflagging and unshadowed light-heartedness.

Happy we doubt not in the thought of leaving such a child behind him to fill his throne, the old King Henry of Navarre died in 1555, when Jeanne and Antoine succeeded. Antoine was summoned immediately to the Court of St. Germain. Henry II. thought the opportunity a favorable one of attaching the Principality of Béarn and its dependencies to the French crown by offering in exchange territories of equal extent lying in the heart of France. The facile Antoine would have yielded. He was King of Navarre, however, only by courtesy, and nothing could be done without his wife's consent. Her indignation on coming to the French Court and at first hearing of a design, the obvious effect of which was not only to strip her and her children of their ancient patrimony, but to bring them into complete subjection to the French monarchy, was unbounded. Knowing, however, the extent to which she was already in Henry's power, holding, as she did, more than one of her dependencies as fiefs under the French crown, she assured the King that if the States of Béarn sanctioned the proposal she would not resist. Meanwhile she summoned to her presence the wisest and firmest of her Béarnese councillors and friends, spread by their means through the Principality a knowledge of the sinister proposal, and roused the old spirit that so many centuries of independence had nurtured. There were popular outbreaks against all supposed to be friendly to the scheme. The house of the Chancellor, who had lent himself to aid the French intrigue, was burnt to the ground. The States met and issued the most energetic protests; and as if to show how seriously they took it, and were already preparing for the worst, reinforcements were voted to the garrisons of Navarreins, Oléron, and Pau. In consequence of the Queen's prompt action things were in this condition when she entered the Principality accompanied by the French Commissioners, who came prepared to absolve the States from their oath of allegiance to their existing sovereign, and to receive their abdication of the kingdom. Jeanne found herself in a position to write to Henry "that her subjects, far from yielding to persuasion upon the projected transfer of Béarn to the Crown of France, had been transported with fury at the simple report of such a project; that it was quite out of her power to control their repugnance; that they had risen tumultuously in defence of their ancient privileges, as his Majesty's Commissioners could testify; and that she must therefore pray the King to forego his purpose, and hold her absolved from pressing a subject so distasteful to her subjects of every rank." Henry unwillingly had to yield.

It was not long, however, ere he again sought and found the opportunity of interfering with the government of Navarre. Jeanne venerated the memory of her mother. She was aware of Marguerite's strong leanings in favor of the Evangelical doctrines. The instructors under whom she had been educated did much to instil these doctrines into her mind; but slower in all her movements than her mother, Jeanne did not readily imbibe the principles of the Reformation. When she ascended the throne she was still in faith and by open profession a Roman Catholic. She showed much less favor to the Reformers than her husband did, who was then on the eve of openly joining their ranks. She did not, however, revoke or abridge that toleration which for so long a time had been granted them in Navarre. It was of this toleration that Henry now complained, demanding the instant expulsion of the Calvinist ministers, and threatening an armed intervention should the demand not at once be complied with. To ward off this second peril, Jeanne and her husband repaired again to the French Court, taking with them upon this occasion the young Prince Henry, then about five years old. A somewhat bitter altercation was going on between the royal relatives, when the young Prince, tired of waiting in the anteroom, burst in upon them. The sprightliness and beauty of the boy quite disarmed King Henry, who, calling him to his side, took him up upon his knee. "Well," said he, "will you be my little son?" "That's my father," said the bold little Prince in his native Béarnese dialect, pointing to Antoine. "Well then," said Henry, "if you won't be my son, will you be my son-in-law?" Oh, with all my heart!" said the child, and from that day, it is said, the ill fated marriage was projected.

Jeanne returned to the comparative seclusion of her own Court, less than ever reconciled to Rome. She now gave herself to the serious study of the differences between the two faiths. The gravity of the inquiry deepened the constitutional sadness of her disposition. Often she was so absorbed as to be totally unconscious of all that was going on around; then, suddenly awaking to a sense of her position, her large and lustrous eyes would beam with intelligent kindness as she hastened to repair the rudeness she confessed. The result was a firm, intelligent, and devoted adherence to the Protestant faith. Nor was it long till she made an open avowal of her attachment to it. She chose as her time for doing so the accession of Charles IX. to the French throne. Her husband's weak submission to the Guises and the almost fatal peril in which he had involved his brother Condé and himself during the short reign of Francis II., had already taught her to act without him, and prepared her even to act against him. She did not consult him when she openly joined the communion of the Reformed, but she acted with the consent and on the advice of her own Council. Seduced by the wiles of Catherine de Medicis and the Triumvirate to desert the Huguenots, Antoine first desired her, and then commanded her, to cease attending the services of the Calvinist ministers, telling her of the false but flattering hopes that had been held out to them should they conform to the Roman Catholic worship. Jeanne resolutely refused, telling her husband that it was not her purpose to barter her immortal soul for territorial aggrandizement, and that she would not be present at the Mass or any ceremony whatever of the Romish Church. Exasperated by her pertinacity, Antoine at last intimated to her that it was his intention to sue for a divorce. She knew already of his infidelity, but she was not prepared for a proposal so coarsely made. For a moment she was silent—tears filled her eyes—but indignation soon dried up those tears, and now Antoine had to listen while with terrible distinctness she pictured to him all the humiliations to which he had been doomed, and all the treachery he had been drawn into, and all the arts that he had been the dupe of, and all the meanness he had committed, and all the vileness of that pit of political degradation into which he was doomed to fall. "And as to that divorce with which I have been threatened, Monseigneur, though *my* fate does not move you, at least have mercy on your children. Know you not that to repudiate in this way the mother is to brand the children as bastards?" The poor craven husband had no answer to all this to make, but to shrink away and go and report to those who sent him the failure of the attempt. Antoine was not likely to succeed where Catherine de Medicis herself failed. Once in her most honeyed accents she tried to win Jeanne over to the same temporizing policy that she was at the time herself pursuing. The Queen of Navarre, after listening to the discourse, inquired what step in her conscience her Majesty would advise her to take. Catherine suggested that to preserve her kingdom for her son she should reconcile herself with Rome. "Madame," exclaimed Jeanne, with a passionate earnestness, "if I at this very moment held my son and all the kingdoms of the world together, I would hurl them to the bottom of the sea rather than peril the salvation of my soul;"—a reply that sounded about as unmeaning and extravagant in Catherine's ear as her proposal had sounded dishonorable and soul-endangering to that of Jeanne. No two women could be more unlike, and when we think how often all the one's fair speech and wily policy was dissected and exposed by the clear-cutting, deep-cutting weapon of the other's sharp and honest indignation, can we wonder that Catherine hated Jeanne with a hatred that followed her, if indeed it did not send her, to the grave!

Antoine of Navarre died at the siege of Rouen in 1562. The first use that the Queen made of the increased measure of freedom she thus acquired was to publish an edict establishing the Protestant and interdicting the exercise of the Roman Catholic worship in Béarn. So bold an act by so weak a sovereign—by one whose political position was so perilous and insecure—drew down upon her the instant and severe displeasure of the Pope. The Cardinal d'Armagnac was despatched from Trent to resume his Legatine functions in the south of France; one of his first acts in that capacity being to address a monitory letter, couched in no ambiguous terms, to the Queen of Navarre. Her answer is one of the boldest that ever came from royal pen. Among other not less tart and pungent things, she says, "I clearly perceive, my cousin, that you have been deceived as to the condition of my subjects generally. They all, without a single exception, have tendered me obedience in religious matters, and continue daily to pay me the same deference, which you will own differs materially from your assertion of their menaced rebellion. I do nothing by compulsion. I condemn no one to death or to imprisonment, which penalties are the nerves and sinews of a system of terror. . . . I blush for you, and feel ashamed when you falsely state that so many atrocities have been perpetrated by those of our religion. Purge the earth first from the blood of so many just men shed by you and yours. Pull that mote from your own eye, and then you shall see to cast the beam out of thy neighbor's. . . . As to what you remark respecting the books of the ancient Fathers, I hear them constantly quoted by our ministers, and approve them. Nevertheless, I own that I am not so learned as I ought to be in this matter, but neither do I believe that you are more competent than myself, having observed that you have applied yourself more to the study of politics than to that of divinity. . . . You request me not to think it strange, nor to take in bad part what you have written. Strange I do not deem your words, considering of what order you are; but as to taking them in bad part, that I do as much as is possible in this world. You excuse yourself, and allege your authority over these countries as the Pope's Legate. I receive here no Legate at the price which it has cost France. I acknowledge over me in Béarn God only, to whom I shall render account of the people He has committed to my care. As in no point I have deviated from the faith of God's Holy Catholic Church, nor quitted her fold, I bid you keep your tears to deplore your own errors, to the which act of charity I will add my own, putting up at the same time the most earnest prayer that ever left my lips, that you may be restored to the true fold, and become a faithful shepherd instead of a hireling. I must entreat that you will use other language when next you would have me believe that you address me, impelled, as you affirm, by motives of respect; and likewise I desire that your useless letter may be the last of its kind." Hundreds of copies of the Cardinal's letter and of the Queen's reply were printed and circulated through the country. The Pope himself arose to avenge the insult put upon his representative. In October 1563 a Bull was issued by him, in which the Queen of Navarre was cited to appear before the Holy Tribunal of the Inquisition at Rome, to clear herself from the stain of heresy, failing which she was declared excommunicate and accursed, her kingdom given to the first despoiler, or "to them on whom his Holiness or his successors might please to bestow it." The mark was in this instance overshot. Such revival of the intolerant pretensions of Pope Gregory VII. was what no monarch of the sixteenth century was ready to allow. Jeanne appealed against the Pope to the French Court. The Queen Regent warmly espoused her side, and despatched a special ambassador to Rome. "We have given," she said in her letter of instructions to him, "the said Sieur d'Oysel charge to make his Holiness understand that we don't acknowledge his authority and jurisdiction over those who bear the title of King or Queen, and that it is not for him to give their kingdoms and territories to any conqueror whatever." The Pope had to give way, and the Bull was expunged from the ecclesiastical ordinances of the Pontificate.

And now that arch-enemy of Protestantism and of liberty, Philip II. of Spain, who a few months after Antoine's death had offered his son's hand to the widowed Queen, and had seen his offer set aside, employed his own peculiar weapons. A conspiracy was organized, the object of which was to seize Jeanne and her children, carry them off to Spain, have *her* tried and condemned before the Holy Inquisition, and them disposed of afterwards according to Philip's own royal pleasure. Lower Navarre was to be seized and occupied by Spanish troops; while, to conciliate the King of France, he was to be invited to annex Béarn to the French monarchy. With consummate skill every contingency was provided for. The scheme was on the very eve of execution, when Dimanche, one of the agents engaged to execute—during a serious illness at Madrid revealed the plot in confidence to a valet of the Spanish Queen, Elisabeth of France. Elisabeth, struck with consternation at the impending fate of her relative, took instant but secret means of apprising her of her peril. The information came just in time. The Queen fled to her strong castle of Navarreins, and the designs of the conspirators were defeated.

It was during her abode in this fortress-palace of Navarreins that Jeanne resumed those severe studies to which, in the course of a former residence there, she had devoted herself. With a view to the reformation and codification of all the existing laws of Béarn, she now set herself to the examination of the general principles of jurisprudence, and of the best existing specimens of ancient and modern legislation. After seven years' labor bestowed on it, and as the fruit mainly of the Queen's own work, a code of laws was sanctioned and published by the States of Béarn in 1571, which, without modification, was in force throughout the domains of the house of D'Albret till after the great Revolution. This code remains as the abiding monument of the Queen of Navarre's capacity as a legislator and governor.

By its ordinances all ecclesiastical property alienated from the Church of Rome was attached to the revenues of the Crown. No part of it, however, was appropriated to the ordinary purposes of government. One-third was devoted to educational purposes, one-third to the support of the poor, one-third to the support of the Protestant Church. The monasteries were, for the most part, changed into schools. The college for higher instruction established originally at Lescar was transferred to Orthez, and by liberal allowances distinguished professors were attracted to it. Fifty theological students were maintained here out of the public funds for the term of ten years. Under Jeanne's own personal direction the Bible was translated into the Béarnois and the Gascon dialects, and the greatest efforts were made by her to provide a ministry that could preach to the inhabitants of each of the provinces in their vernacular tongue.

Many of the fiscal ordinances of Jeanne's code—especially some of its sumptuary regulations—exhibit that unwise interference with the personal liberty of the subject which characterized all the legislation of the period. But when we discover that by this code the equality of all subjects in the eye of the law was affirmed and enforced; that the venality of all public offices was abolished; that a system of instruction offering the benefits of education to all, and providing especially for the education of the poor, was organized; that mendicity was proscribed and all poor widows and orphans provided for; that the punishment of death was restricted to the single crime of murder; that all burial of the dead within churches or near inhabited places was forbidden,—when these and other regulations of a like kind meet our eye, we rise from our review of this code with the conviction that Jeanne d'Albret was the wisest and most enlightened sovereign of her age, and that she needed only to have had a wider and more conspicuous theatre to act in to have had her name as broadly and as deeply engraved on the page of history as either of her two great contemporaries—Elizabeth of England and Catherine de Medicis of France.[1]

[1] "La France Protestante," par M.M. Haag, vol. i. pp 31–59. This important work is a mine of information on the subject of French Protestantism.

In reviewing her legislative and administrative measures, perhaps the most interesting thing is to notice the exact stage to which the idea of religious toleration was carried out in them. The liberty of individual belief was freely and fully granted. No trial on the charge of heterodoxy, no execution for heresy, was permitted. And here is the great and striking contrast between this little Protestant kingdom of Béarn and all the great Roman Catholic kingdoms by which it was surrounded. This assertion and protection of the liberty of the individual conscience was one of the chief services that the Reformation rendered to modern Europe. The public exercise, however, of the Roman Catholic religion was interdicted in Béarn. At first Jeanne showed herself willing to tolerate it. In some parts of her dominions where division of opinion existed she directed that the churches should be used both by Catholics and Protestants. On the ground, however, of the rebellion raised by the priesthood, Catholicism was at last interdicted (1569). Not only was all exercise of the Roman Catholic worship suppressed, but all were bound under certain penalties to attend the Calvinistic services, any one absenting himself more than once from the Communion without good and reasonable excuse being liable to banishment. At that period the almost universal conception was that the King or the State was responsible, not indeed for what was thought or believed, but for all that outwardly was done in the way of religious worship. In Protestant eyes the Mass was an act of idolatrous worship; and to permit its celebration was to countenance idolatry,— a countenance, it was thought, that no true Christian, no true Protestant prince could give. It is to an after age, and not to that of the Reformers, that we owe our emancipation from such a conception of the duty and the prerogative of the State, that we owe the establishment of the great principle that neither with the mode of worship nor with the religious faith of its subjects has the State any right authoritatively or dictatorially or punitively to interfere.

In 1565 Catherine and her son Charles IX. made a progress through France, and had their memorable interview with Queen Elisabeth and some of the most distinguished Spanish courtiers at Bayonne. The young Prince of Béarn, then in his twelfth year, accompanied the French Court. His singular sprightliness made him a great favorite with the Queen-mother. Imagining that he was wholly given up to boyish sports, Catherine admitted him to many of those private conferences which she held with the Duke of Alva, and other members of the Spanish Cabinet. In one of these Henry overheard the Duke recommend that the leading Huguenots should be cut off as a first step towards the entire extirpation of heresy,—" For, Madame," said the Duke, " the head of one salmon is worth that of a hundred frogs." The saying stuck fast in the memory of the Prince, who repeated it soon after to Calignon, one of his mother's privy councillors, who was in attendance on him. Calignon despatched a messenger to Pau, conveying it in cipher to his Queen, who from that time, it is said, had a dark presentiment of the Massacre of St. Bartholomew.

After a few years' residence at the French Court, the young Prince of Béarn was, at the age of thirteen, restored to the guardianship of his mother. She found him a proficient in all manly exercises. He rode well, fenced well, wrestled well; had all the gallant bearing of the young cavalier. His taste for poetry had been cultivated, and the chivalrous lays of France and Spain were his especial delight. His mother set him now to the harder task of mastering the Greek and Latin tongues; and instead of books of fiction gave him volumes of history, politics, and religion to study. She acted frequently herself as his preceptor. With her son's quick intelligence and power of rapid acquisition she must have been more than pleased, but many a strange misgiving must have shadowed her hopes as she noticed how averse he was to any exercise requiring steady, continuous, serious thought, and how fond he was of pleasure—of all kinds and at all costs; the mercurial Gascon spirit that was in him already effervescing in more ways than one. We get glimpses of him about this time in two letters written by one of the magistrates of Bordeaux.

"We have here," says the writer, "the young Prince of Béarn. One can't help acknowledging that he is a beautiful creature. At the age of thirteen he displays all the qualities of a person of eighteen or nineteen. He is agreeable, he is civil, he is obliging. He insinuates himself into all hearts with inconceivable skill. I shall hate the new religion all my life for having carried him off from us." A year or two later the writer says, "We have the pleasantest carnival in the world. The Prince of Béarn has besought our ladies to mask and give balls by turns. He loves play and good living. When money fails him, he has skill enough to find more, and that in a manner quite new and obliging towards others. He sends to those whom he believes to be his friends a promise, written and signed by himself, begging them to return to him either the note or the sum which the promise bears. You may judge whether there is any house where he is refused. People regard it as a great honor to have one of these billets from the Prince, and every one does it with joy, for there are two astrologers here who declare that either their art is false, or that the Prince will some day be one of the greatest kings of Europe."

More serious matters were soon to occupy this gay young Prince. The Duke of Guise died on the 24th February 1563, six days after he received his wound. So prompt was the Queen-Regent in carrying out the advice which he had given her, that on the 12th of the following month the basis of a peace was fixed upon in a conference between the Prince of Condé and the Constable. Before formally concluding it, Condé consulted his co-religionists. He had no difficulty with the Huguenot officers and gentlemen, who were willing that some sacrifice should be made for peace. It was otherwise with the ministers. The question whether it would be right or lawful to lay down arms on any terms less favorable than those of the Edict of January, was submitted to an assembly of seventy-two ministers assembled at Orleans. They declared energetically that peace purchased on less favorable terms would be treason against God, and they insisted that it should form one of the terms of the settlement that all atheists, libertines, anabaptists, and disciples of Servetus, should be burnt alive.

Turning a deaf ear to such advisers, without waiting even to consult with Coligni, Condé signed a pacification on the 18th March, known under the title of the Edict of Amboise. By this edict the exercise of the Reformed religion was prohibited in Paris, somewhat limited in the provinces, but it secured individual liberty. "Every one," said the Treaty, "shall be permitted to live at liberty in his own house, without search or molestation, and without being forced or constrained for conscience' sake."

The peace established thus lasted for four years.

Not that the Huguenots enjoyed during these years any thing like security or repose. The repeated abridgment even of those narrow liberties conferred by the Edict of Amboise, and the frequent outbreaks of popular hatred in which numbers of them perished, kept them in perpetual alarm. Still more alarming was the meeting at Bayonne in the summer of 1565. The Pope had long sought to bring about a personal interview between Catherine de Medicis and Philip of Spain, with a view to concert measures for the suppression of Protestantism. Taking advantage of a royal progress that Catherine was then making with her son the King through France, it was arranged that the two Courts should meet in the border town of Bayonne. Philip himself did not come, but sent as his representative his Queen and the Duke of Alva. Amid the Court festivities which took place, it was known that there had been many secret meetings between Alva, Catherine, and Charles. The darkest suspicions as to their objects and results spread over France. It was generally believed—falsely, as from Alva's letters it now appears—that a simultaneous extermination of all heretics in the French and Spanish dominions had been agreed upon.

To anticipate this stroke, Coligni proposed that the person of the King should be seized upon. The Court, but slenderly guarded, was then at Monceax. The project had almost succeeded. Some time, however, was lost. The Court got warning and fled to Meaux. Six thousand Swiss arrived, and by a rapid march carried the King to Paris. After such a failure, nothing was left to the Huguenots but the chances of a second civil war. Condé entered boldly on the campaign. Though he had with him but 1500 horse and 1200 infantry, he marched to Paris, and offered battle to the royal troops beneath its walls. The Constable, who had 18,000 men at his command, accepted the challenge, and on the 10th of November 1567, the battle of St. Denis was fought. The Huguenots displayed unexampled bravery. "Ah!" said the Ambassador of the Sultan, who was looking on, "had my master but 6000 men like these, all Asia would be at his feet." Neither party could well claim the victory, as both retired from the field. The royal army had to mourn the loss that day of its aged and gallant commander the Constable. Condé renewed next day the challenge, which was not accepted.

The winter months were spent by the Huguenots in effecting a junction with some German auxiliaries, and in the spring they appeared in such force upon the field that, on the 23d March 1568, the Peace of Longjumeau was ratified, which re-established, free from all modifications and restrictions, the Edict of Amboise. It was evident from the first that this treaty was not intended to be kept; that it had been entered into by the Government solely to gain time, and to scatter the ranks of the

Huguenots. Coligni sought Condé at his château of Noyers in Burgundy. He had scarcely arrived when secret intelligence was given them of a plot upon their lives. They had barely time to fly, making many a singular escape by the way, and reaching Rochelle, which from this time became the head-quarters of the Huguenots, on the 15th September 1568.

During the first two religious wars, marked respectively by the battles of Dreux and of St. Denis, the seat of war was so remote from her dominions that the Queen of Navarre had satisfied herself with opening her country as an asylum for those Huguenots driven thither out of the southern counties of France. But when she heard that Condé and Coligni, only barely escaping the attempt to seize them at Noyers, were on their way to Rochelle, to raise there once more the Protestant banner, convinced that the French Court meditated nothing short of the extermination of the Huguenots, she determined openly to cast in her lot with her co-religionists, and to give them all the help she could. Dexterously deceiving Montluc, who had received instructions to watch her movements, and seize upon her person if she showed any intention of leaving her own dominions, after a flight as precipitous and almost as perilous as that of Condé and Coligni, she reached Rochelle on the 29th September, ten days after their arrival. This town, for nearly a century the citadel of Protestantism in France, having by its own unaided power freed itself from the English dominion, had had extraordinary municipal privileges bestowed on it in return—among others, that of an entirely independent jurisdiction, both civil and military. Like so many of the great commercial marts of Europe, in which the spirit of freedom was cherished, it had early welcomed the teaching of the Reformers, and at the time now before us nearly the whole of its inhabitants were Huguenots. Knowing how zealous the Rochellese were for their independence, Condé, in the first instance, took his wife and family into a neighboring town, and entering the city alone, and in the disguise of a sailor, suddenly presented himself in the midst of the Council, and cast himself and the cause he represented on their sympathy and aid. The frankness and confidence shown by one who came thus without a single follower won at once all hearts. The citizens vowed to assist him by every means in their power, and he in his turn vowed never to sheathe the sword till liberty of conscience should be achieved. When, a few days later, the approach of the Queen of Navarre and her son was announced, all were ready to give them an enthusiastic greeting. At the Hotel de Ville the Mayor and other city authorities welcomed the Queen in an elaborate address. Her answer, for she was eminently eloquent, made the hall of audience re-echo with applause. Then the Mayor turned to the young Prince, addressing him in a like style. "Gentlemen of the city," said young Henry in reply, "I have not studied enough to be able to speak as you do, but I assure you that if I don't speak so well I will act better, for I know better how to act than to speak." Next day an important assemblage was summoned to deliberate as to the future conduct of the war. The Prince of Condé rose and tendered his resignation as commander-in-chief, offering to serve under the Prince of Béarn, to whom, as the first prince of the blood, the command by right of birth belonged. "No, Messeigneurs," said the Queen of Navarre, promptly rising to decline the offer, "I and my son are here to promote the success of this great enterprise, or to share in its disaster. We will joyfully unite beneath the standard of Condé. The cause of God is dearer to me than my son. My son and I would rather return and abandon our share in this great design than permit a resignation so pernicious." In vain the leading councillors remonstrated—in vain Condé assured the Queen that he would be all to Henry that Tavannes and Biron were to his young cousin Henry of Anjou, who was to lead the forces of the Royalists. Condé was proclaimed general-in-chief. "My son," said Jeanne then to Henry before the assembly, "policy, gratitude, necessity combined to render it expedient that you should resign the command to your uncle. That privilege in truth belonged to you in virtue of your birth, but it is a privilege you could not safely claim without exposing your party to ruin—a ruin that would entail your own. You have ceased to be a child—you have become a man. Europe is at this moment watching your actions. Go then, and under Condé learn to obey, that it may be yours some day in your turn to command."

The Court had thrown off all disguise. About the very time that the Queen of Navarre entered Rochelle a royal edict appeared, prohibiting, under pain of death, the exercise of any other than the Roman Catholic religion in France, imposing upon all the observance of its rites and ceremonies; and banishing from the realm all preachers of the doctrine of Calvin, fifteen days only being allowed them to quit the kingdom. It was by the sword that this stern edict was to be enforced or rescinded. Two powerful armies of nearly equal strength mustered speedily. One was nominally under the command of the Duke of Anjou, but really led by Tavannes, Biron, Brissac, and the young Duke of Guise, the last burning to emulate the military glory of his father; the other under the command of Condé and Coligni. The two armies were close upon one another; their generals desired to bring them into action; they were more than once actually in each other's presence, but the unprecedented inclemency of the weather prevented an engagement, and at last, without coming into collision, both had to retire to winter quarters. The delay was fatal to the Huguenots. They were still in winter quarters,—a large part of their force, many of them being volunteers, still in their own homes, scattered over the country,—when the intelligence arrived that, largely reinforced and fully organized, the Royal army was on its march. Not in a condition to fight upon any thing like equal terms, Condé and Coligni resolved to retire behind the Charente, breaking down the bridges behind them. But their object was frustrated, partly by the negligence and insubordination of their own troops, and partly by the superior skill of the Royalist generals. On the 13th March 1569, with an army inferior in numbers, and so scattered that it could not all be brought at once into action, Condé was forced to halt near Jarnac, and face the Royal troops. For some days before a cloud had been seen to rest upon the fine spirits of the Prince. His arm was in a scarf as he entered the battle-field, and just as he took his helmet to lead his own division to the charge, his leg was broken by the kick of a horse in so frightful a way that the bone obtruded through the boot. But his gallant soldier-spirit nothing could subdue. "Gentlemen of France," he cried, "the hour so long desired has come. Forward then! sweet is the combat for Christ and for one's country." With these words, at the head of his little troop he charged the enemy. Overpowered by numbers, thrown from his horse, resting on one knee, he fought on with desperate resolution. "Around him," says Agrippa d'Aubigné, "was the bitterest and most obstinate contest that ever was seen, it was thought, during the civil wars. One old man, La Vergne, fell with fifteen of his descendants in a heap around him; but what could 250 gentlemen do, opposed to 2000 in front, with 2500 *Reiter* on the right and 800 lances on the left, but die?—as they did, two-thirds of them upon the spot." Seeing at last how needless it was to prolong such slaughter, Condé raised his visor, and calling to a Roman Catholic gentleman (D'Argence), gave his name, presented his sword, and surrendered himself as prisoner. D'Argence treated him with all due respect and tenderness, had him borne to a neighboring thicket, and laid on the grass with his back against a tree. A number of Royalist officers surrounded him, with whom Condé was speaking with his usual courtesy, when Montesquiou, captain of the Swiss Guard of the Duke of Anjou, galloped up to the spot, and hearing who the prisoner was, deliberately levelled his pistol at him and shot him through the head. The Duke passed no censure on his officer, and expressed no regret at his deed. The grossest indignities were afterwards, by his orders, heaped upon the dead body of the slain.

The defeat of Jarnac, and still more the death of Condé, threw the Huguenot army into despair. It had suffered comparatively little loss, for a large part of the infantry had not been in action, and had retired in almost unbroken order from the field. At Cognac, on the day after the battle, Coligni, D'Andelot, La Rochefoucauld, Teligni, Montgomery, and the other Huguenot chiefs, found themselves still at the head of no inconsiderable force; but all heart and hope had gone out of the soldiery, and with the spirit of despair had come the spirit of suspicion, detraction, insubordination. The Admiral especially was blamed—blamed falsely for neglect in leaving a bridge undefended—accused even of cowardice in retreating so early from the fight. The utter dissolution of the Army seemed at hand. The Admiral sent a messenger to the Queen of Navarre at Rochelle, entreating her to come to the camp. She was already on her way. On arrival, and after a short consultation with the Admiral, the army was drawn up to receive her. She rode along the ranks—her son Henry on one side, the son of the deceased Condé on the other. Cheers rose from the ranks as they passed along. They formed around her as she prepared to address them. "Children of God and of France," she said, "Condé is no more; that heroic prince, whom even his enemies were constrained to honor, has sacrificed his life for the noblest of causes. He is dead. A sacrilegious hand has severed the thread of life. His enemies have deprived him of being by a deed of cowardly perfidy. What say I? have they not even added foul insult to his cold remains? Oh, how by this base outrage have they not augmented his renown, and defiled forever the laurels gathered from the fatal field of Jarnac! Soldiers, you weep—but does the memory of Condé demand nothing more than tears? Will you be satisfied with fruitless regrets? No! let us unite and summon back our courage to defend a cause which can never perish. Does despair overpower you?—despair, that shameful failing of weak natures, can it be known to you, noble warriors and Christian men? When *I* still hope, is it for you to fear? Because Condé is dead, is all therefore lost? No! the God who placed the arms in his hands for our defence has raised up others worthy to succeed him. To these brave warriors I add my son. Make proof of his valor. Soldiers, I offer to you every thing I have to give,—my dominions, my treasures, my life, and, what is dearer to me than all, my children. I make here solemn oath before you all—I swear to defend to my last sigh the holy cause which now unites us, which is that of honor and of truth!" Heroic words, that carried with them a quickening power. The soldiers crowded round the Queen, and unanimously, as if by sudden impulse, hailed young Henry of Navarre as their future general. The Admiral and La Rochefoucauld were the first to swear fidelity to the Prince; then came the inferior officers and the whole assembled soldiery, and it was thus that, in his fifteenth year, the Prince of Béarn was inaugurated as general-in-chief of the army of the Huguenots.

7

All eyes were now directed to the celebrated march of the Duc de Deux-Ponts with a division of German auxiliaries from the banks of the Rhine. Through a part of France whose inhabitants were hostile, all whose towns and the bridges of whose rivers were held by his enemies, surrounded all along by superior forces that hung upon his flank and rear, the Duke made good his way to the banks of the Loire, attacked La Charité, made himself master of the bridge there, across which and without loss he conveyed his troops. No sooner did the Admiral hear of his passage of the river than he set out to meet him. A junction of the two armies took place at St. Yrieix on the 23d June. Once more the Queen of Navarre hastened to the united camp to renew and re-ratify the articles of confederation between the Protestant Princes of Germany and the Huguenots of France. Before leaving Rochelle she got a gold medal struck with the heads of herself and her son upon the one side, and on the reverse the inscription—*Pax certa, victoria integra, mors honesta*—" a sure peace, an entire victory, an honorable death." Hung upon a chain of gold, the Queen threw one of these medals round the neck of each distinguished chief at St. Yrieix, as he stooped to kiss her hand at the close of one of her receptions. Among the chiefs who thus presented himself was William of Orange, who, with his brother Louis of Nassau, on this occasion accompanied the German army; and never surely by worthier hands was medal hung upon a nobler breast.

The Duke of Anjou, who had approached St. Yricix in the hope of preventing a junction of the two armies, retired to La Roche-Abeille. Here the Huguenots attacked and gained a slight advantage, the first occasion in which young Henry of Navarre shared in the actual perils of the battle-field, giving proof, while he charged at the head of the line, of that brilliant courage which shone out so conspicuously in many an after field. Coligni was preparing to follow up this partial success when the Royal army melted away before him. Its sagacious leaders calculated that a few months' want of pay, provisions, and of any well-defined object, would disorganize the Germans and exhaust the Huguenots, and that then the royal forces, refreshed and re-invigorated, would be prepared, under favorable auspices, to take the field. Acting on this counsel the Duke of Anjou disbanded his army, but appointed a general rendezvous for the 18th of August. The scheme was but too successful. The Huguenots, contrary to the advice of Coligni,—one of whose favorite maxims was that great towns were the sepulchres of great armies,—resolved to lay siege to Poitiers, tempted by the hope of capturing the young Duke of Guise and his brother, to whom the defence of that place had been intrusted. The Duke however conducted the defence with such great skill and bravery that when, after many weeks' preparations, the general assault was given, the assailants were beaten back. The Duke of Anjou at last appeared with a relieving force, and the siege was raised. Conscious of his weakness, Coligni would have retired before the advancing enemy, but his counsel was rejected, and the fatal battle of Moncontour—the most disastrous of all to the Huguenots—was fought. His jawbone broken by a pistol-shot, his throat half-choked with blood, unable any longer to articulate the word of command, Coligni was forced to retire. The rout of his army was complete; 5000 dead and wounded Huguenots were left upon the plain. The Prince of Béarn took no part personally in this engagement. Anxious about his safety, as being so doubtful of the result, the Admiral had placed him in the rear, and given strict orders that he should not mingle in the fray. Henry shed tears of vexation and impatience as he obeyed. He watched the battle eagerly from a rising ground, and it is said that he marked a crisis in it when, had the quick suggestion he made been acted on, it might have had a different result.

At Niort, after this great defeat, the wreck of the broken forces was gathered. Regret for the past, terror for the future, seized every heart; nothing was spoken of but submission upon any terms. The Admiral found himself surrounded by the discontented and the despairing; his power weakened, his merits forgotten, the defeat wholly attributed to his imprudence. Again Jeanne d'Albret hastened to his side. "He was abandoned," says D'Aubigné, "by his officers, his nobles, and all, save by one woman who heroically advanced to hold out her hand to the afflicted, and to assist in retrieving the affairs of the confederates." Tears filled the old man's eyes as he grasped the hand so opportunely held out to him. It was her own familiarity with suffering which made the Queen of Navarre so good a soother and supporter of others. The bygone summer months had been months to her of the most painful anxiety.

Returning from Cognac to Rochelle, she kept the promise she had made to the assembled army. To furnish the needful funds for carrying on the war she had literally given all she had. She pawned at last the jewels of the Crown, depositing, among the rest, in the hands of our own Queen Elizabeth one of the most precious heirlooms of the house of D'Albret—a necklace "set," it is described, "with eleven large table diamonds, one diamond being set clear as a pendant, the whole being valued at the sum of 160,000 crowns." While straining thus every nerve, and making every sacrifice to sustain the cause, her own kingdom, in her absence, excited by French emissaries, broke out into revolt. A French army, under the command of Terride, entered and took possession of it. One fortress, that of Navarreins, alone held out, and Terride's victorious army was already besieging it. A bitter grief rent the Queen's heart as she heard of towns and villages sacked and pillaged; her country suffering all the horrors of a foreign invasion and occupation; her capital itself in the hands of the enemy. Idle grief however gave way to vigorous effort. A little Béarnese army, called the Army of the Viscounts, from its being led by those Barons of her States who still stood faithful, lay encamped at Quercy, inefficient through discord among its leaders. Jeanne instantly despatched the Count de Montgomery to take command; bestowing on him unlimited authority, civil as well as military. The task imposed was so difficult, and the means at his disposal for accomplishing it so apparently inadequate, that one can well imagine that when he took his oath of allegiance to the Queen, and swore either to win back her dominions or perish in the service, the latter seemed to Montgomery by much his likelier fate. But fortune smiled on the skilful soldier who threw himself into so hazardous an enterprise with all the dash of a chivalrous devotion. He left Rochelle in the end of June, escorted by 200 horse. In less than six weeks he traversed 150 leagues of country, gathering troops together in the face of no fewer than five hostile armies, all on the watch to intercept him. With the troops collected thus he joined the Army of the Viscounts, entered Béarn, and within fourteen days the siege of Navarreins was raised—the royal army beaten in a pitched battle, Terride, its general, and all the rebel lords taken prisoners, the whole Principality reconquered, and the standard of Navarre once more planted on the castle of Pau.

This brilliant success set Montgomery free to join the Admiral afterwards in the boldest and most successful of all his military exploits. After the disheartening defeat at Moncontour, the Huguenot chiefs generally were in favor of acting for a time solely on the defensive, confining themselves to those provinces in which they had the greatest strength. Coligni, on the other hand, determined to force a peace by demanding it before the walls of Paris. Keeping what troops he could collect around him, he marched into the remotest southern counties, up into the valleys of the Pyrenees, where he and they were as far out of sight as they well could be, little thought of and less feared by the pleasure-loving Court of St. Germain. But soon as spring came he turned his steps northward, passed rapidly through Montpellier, Nismes, the Vivarrais, along the banks of the Rhone, over the mountain defiles of the Cevennes, by roads impassable for artillery, covered with the snows of winter; descending at last into Burgundy, after a march of 400 leagues. About 6000 men perished in the course of the march: of 100 Englishmen under Chapman, who had joined Coligni at Rochelle, only twelve survived. But, amid all the exposure and fatigues, there was one youth whose strength never failed, and whose spirits never flagged; whose gay and ever buoyant activity was of infinite service in keeping up the spirits of the troops—the young Prince Henry of Navarre. The Court was thunderstruck when it heard that a Huguenot army was in the heart of the country, approaching the Loire. The Marshal de Cossé, at the head of 12,500 men, was despatched to arrest its progress. Coligni had less than 7000 men under him, but, taking up his position on the slope of a declivity at Arnay-le-Duc, he resolved to await the attack of the enemy. Counting on an easy victory, Cossé led his soldiers to the assault. Again and again his charges were impetuously and successfully repelled. A recent illness kept Coligni from engaging personally in the fight, but the Huguenots had a fresh and brilliant leader in the Prince of Béarn. "My first exploit in arms," said Henry many years afterwards to the historian Matthieu, "was at Arnay-le-Duc, where the question was whether to fight or to retire. I had no retreat within forty miles, and if I fought I ran the risk of being taken or slain, for I had no cannon, and the King's forces had. A gentleman was killed by one of their balls not ten paces from me. I decided to fight, and, commending the success to God, it pleased Him to make the day favorable and fortunate." Though it was but a partial victory, it accomplished the design of the Admiral. This happened in the end of June, and on the 8th of August the Peace of St. Germain-en-Laye was signed, and France had two full years of quiet.

These years were divided by Jeanne d'Albret between the cares of her domestic government and the agitations of that negotiation which embittered her latter days. The proposal for the marriage of her son Henry with Marguerite of Valois, the sister of Charles IX., was one to which, from the beginning, she had the strongest aversion. She could not at first believe in the sincerity of the French Court in making such a proposal. When all ground for disbelieving in that sincerity was removed, she cherished the darkest surmises as to the real and final ends and objects of the proposers. When these suspicions were overruled, and she was forced, by the advice of her own Council and almost the entire body of the Huguenot leaders, to entertain the project, it was with the utmost difficulty that she was dragged from her own capital to go and adjust the marriage articles with Queen Catherine at Blois. It was arranged that the two Queen-mothers should settle all between themselves. The very first conference, however, revealed the irreconcilable difference of their ideas. The Queen of Navarre felt hurt and aggrieved at its being laid down at once, as a necessary preliminary to all minor stipulations, that after the marriage her son and his wife should reside at the French Court; that Marguerite, whereever she was, should have the free exercise of her religion, but that Henry, while in France, should be debarred the public exercise of his. On her part, Jeanne as peremptorily insisted that after the

7*

marriage the Prince and his consort should reside at Pau, and that the Mass should not be celebrated there. Her letters to her son tell us how bitterly Jeanne felt the annoyance to which she was exposed. "I assure you, my son," she says (Blois, 21st February), "that I am in great trouble; for they taunt me without mercy, and I have need of all the patience in the world. I must inform you that Madame Marguerite has given me every honor and welcome in her power to bestow. She has frankly owned to me the agreeable idea she has formed of you. With her beauty and wit she exercises great influence with the Queen-mother, the King, and his younger brothers. Should she embrace our faith, I may say it will be the most fortunate event in the world; not only for our house, but for the entire realm of France. If she, however, remain obstinate, it is to be feared that this marriage will prove the ruin of our souls and of our country, and the destruction of all the Reformed Churches of France. Therefore, my son, if ever you had need to supplicate the Almighty, it is now in this our extremity." On the 8th March she writes—"I am in travail and in such extremity of suffering that had I not forseen all that has happened I must have succumbed beneath the torrent. I am compelled to negotiate quite contrary to my expectations and to their past promises. I have no longer liberty to speak even to Madame, but only to the Queen-mother. I have remonstrated with the

Queen upon three separate occasions, but she ridicules me, and afterwards repeats to every one just the very contrary to what I said. Therefore, when many of my friends blame me, I know not well how to contradict the Queen's words, for when I venture to say to her Majesty, 'Madame, it is reported that I have said such and such a thing to you,' although it was she herself who spread the statement she denies the thing flatly, laughing in my face, and treating me in such shameful fashion that you may believe my patience surpasses that of Griselda herself. As for Madame, she is beautiful and graceful, but she has been educated in the midst of the most vicious and corrupt Court that can be imagined. I see no one here exempt from its evil influences. Even cousin (Marie de Cleves) is so greatly altered that she exhibits no signs of religion. My sister the Princess sets even a worse example. The bearer of this letter will tell you what license the King already indulges in. I would not for the world that you should abide here. For these reasons I desire to see you married, that you and your wife may be withdrawn from this corrupt society; for though I believed the license great, it surpasses my anticipations."

The two Queen-mothers could make nothing of the matter. It was referred next to four Commissioners on either side. These also failed. Indignant at the delay, the King broke in, declaring, in one of his impulsive moods, that it was his royal will and pleasure that the marriage should take place without any conditions whatever. But now a new difficulty arose. The pope refused to grant a dispensation for the marriage. Jeanne hailed the refusal as an obstacle thrown by Providence in the way, and expressed her intention of retiring from Blois. "No, no, my aunt," said the choleric King, "I honor you more than the Pope, and I love my sister more than I fear his Holiness. I am not a Huguenot, but neither am I a fool. If M. le Pape demeans himself too absurdly in this affair, I promise you I will take Margot by the hand, and lead her to be married in full prêche." A Papal dispensation was at last procured; the general belief being that it was forged for the occasion. All impediments at last removed, the Queen of Navarre left Blois for Paris, to make the many needful purchases in preparation for the approaching ceremonial. It was in the midst of these occupations that the fatal malady seized her which in five days carried her to the grave. She early intimated her conviction she should not survive. But death was to her neither unexpected nor unwelcome. "Ought you to weep for me," she said to her weeping attendants, "when at length God takes pity on me, and calls me to the enjoyment of that blessed existence for the which I have unceasingly prayed?" One regret alone in quitting life was expressed by her,—that felt in leaving her children at such an age, exposed to so many dangers. Her sufferings were intense; her patience and confidence in God unbroken. "My pains," she said, "are indeed most grievous, but I know that He doeth nothing but what is right and good." The Queen-mother came to visit her. Not a word about the approaching nuptials was spoken; indeed, throughout her illness Jeanne never once alluded to the event. Sunday the 8th June was her last day in life. She summoned two notaries to her bed-side, and declared to them her last instructions. "Tell my son," she said, "that I desire him, as the last expression of my heart, to persevere in the faith in which he has been brought up, and to remember that those who honor God He will honor. Tell my daughter that her dying mother besought her to depart into Béarn, far from the corruption of the Court." Her last instructions given, she desired that the 14th, 15th, and 16th chapters of the Gospel by John should be read to her; they had been, she said, her support and consolation through all the troubles of her troubled career. Her ministers Merlin and Espina, at her desire, engaged frequently in prayer. "O my Saviour," she was heard herself to say, "hasten to deliver my spirit from the miseries of this life, and from the prison of this suffering body, that I may offend Thee no more, and enter joyfully into that rest which Thou hast promised and that my soul so longs for." A few hours' more suffering, and the prayer was heard —the prison-door was opened and the eternal rest was reached.

Two short months after her decease the marriage that Jeanne d'Albret so shrank from was consummated, and within a week thereafter the Massacre of St. Bartholomew took place. One of the darkest features of that dark deed was the shameless treatment by Catherine de Medicis, and the ladies of her Court, of the bodies of the slain—treatment whose very shamelessness forbids its recital. A previous scene, however, described by one of themselves, prepares us for their conduct upon that occasion. Marguerite of Valois—so soon to be the daughter-in-law of the deceased—tells us in her Memoirs that she and other ladies of the Court went to see the dead body of the Queen of Navarre as it lay in state. It shocked them to notice that it lay exposed upon an ordinary bed, the curtains drawn back: no darkening of the room, no dim-burning wax-lights, no crosses, no priests, no vases of holy water. But it did not shock them when one of their number, the Duchess of Nevers—the one who disliked the late Queen most—slipped from their side and to use now Marguerite's own words, " with several fine, low courtesies approached the bed, and taking the Queen's hand in her own, kissed it, and then, with another profound obeisance, retired to their side." One's blood curdles at the recital of such polished, courtly, heartless, inhuman mockery of the dead.

Very different the sentiments with which, could we have entered that chamber, we should have lifted that hand, and looked down upon the face of the dead. Her life, her death, do they not kindle in our hearts profound admiration and esteem? Her intellectual gifts, her great capacity for legislation, her sagacity in council, her promptness and energy in action, would rank Jeanne d'Albret among the most gifted of our European Queens. But she gets a peculiar hold of our sympathies, and takes a peculiar place in our regard and reverence, as we think of the difficulties, trials, temptations, seductions, that lined her chequered and sorrowful path; of the heroic spirit that she displayed, the pure and noble principles by which she was ever animated. Born and brought up in connexion with a Court in which, as Sully, who knew it so thoroughly, says, next to gallantry nothing was so cultivated as falsehood, she kept her integrity entire,— nothing false or deceitful, nothing mean or ignoble, nothing shifting or tortuous, appearing in any action of her life, or any course of public policy she pursued.[1] There hung a shade of sadness, sometimes of sternness, over her: yet she was not ungentle or unfeminine. She had a passionate fondness for

[1] The only moral charge brought against her is that contained in a letter of the Duchess of Ferrara, in which the Queen of Navarre is said to have maintained in the Duchess's presence the position that one might lawfully deceive and falsify to promote religion. The letter is authentic, but the Duchess may have been mistaken. This at least is true, that no deceit nor falsehood can be detected in the long course of Jeanne d'Albret's reign.

flowers, and in tapestry-work, to which she gave much of her time, she had few rivals. The sadness and the sternness let us in part attribute to natural temperament, in part to early education, in part to the crowded difficulties and sorrows of her life, and in part also to the serious aspects in which truth and duty were always regarded by her. This was her crowning excellence,—that she was so sincere and devout a believer in the truths of our holy religion. It was a light that shone from Heaven she loved to follow, and following it she closed a public career unstained with crime, in a death of patience and Christian hope.

CHAPTER V.

CHARLES IX., 1570–1574.

Pope Pius V.—Philip II. of Spain.—How the peace of St. Germain-en-Laye was brought about.—Proposal of breach with Spain.—The anti-Spanish policy advocated by the Admiral.—Conduct of Catherine de Medicis and the Duke of Anjou.—Marriage of Henry of Navarre.—Coligni wounded.—Massacre of St. Bartholomew.—Sieges of Rochelle and Sancerre.—Party of the *Politiques.*—Francis Othman.—Death of Charles IX.

POPE PIUS V. was a chief instigator and promoter of the third religious war in France. He had furnished both troops and funds for its prosecution. The spirit in which he desired to see it conducted appears from the instructions issued to his soldiers, that no quarter should be given to the enemy. After the battle of Jarnac, he wrote thus to the French King:—"If your Majesty continue to pursue openly and ardently the enemies of the Catholic religion, even to their extermination, be assured the Divine succor will not be wanting. It is only by the entire destruction of the heretics that you can restore its ancient worship to your noble realm." Hearing that negotiations for peace were opened, his Holiness wrote to Charles, warning him against all advisers of a peace as deceivers of his Majesty; as men who, under the false pretext of the general good, forgot at once their faith and their loyalty. When, notwithstanding his remonstrances, the peace of St. Germain-en-Laye[1] was concluded, he complained of it as pernicious, infamous, abominable; reproaching Charles in such strong terms, that he was obliged at last to say that he was King in France, and would do there what he thought best.

Ever since the inglorious treaty of Cateau-Cambresis, Philip of Spain had insisted, without ceasing, that the course which he was taking in the Low Countries should be followed also by France. He had fomented every rising against the Huguenots; had opposed every concession made to them; had lent his aid in the last war expressly on the condition that no treaty should be made with them; did his utmost to prevent the peace; and, when he could no more, Alva expressed his monarch's sentiments when he declared that it was a peace most dangerous to Christianity. How then was a peace, so offensive to Spain and the Holy See, brought about? Chiefly through the influence of a party inaugurated by De l'Hôpital, which rose at this time into power, by obtaining a dominant influence over the mind of the young King.

[1] The treaty of peace was signed on the 8th August 1570. For an abstract of its contents see Drion's *Histoire Chronologique*, p. 121.

At the head of this party were Montmorency, the eldest son of the old Constable, his brother Damville, and the Marshals Cossé and Biron, all zealous Roman Catholics, but men tired of civil war, impatient of Spanish bondage, who wished to see their country resume the position of power and independence which it had held in the days of Francis I. "Montmorency," says Walsingham, the English ambassador at Paris, writing on the 29th August 1570, "who has had the chief part in bringing about the peace, insinuates himself more and more into power." A few days afterwards, Walsingham writes again—"Montmorency is at present all-powerful at the Court; the Government of Paris has been put into his hands." The young King, who had opened his ear to these wise advisers, came to regard himself as the author of the peace; took pride in calling it *his* treaty, *his* peace; watched strictly over its execution; and punished severely those who violated its provisions. He repeatedly declared that he had been mistaken in the Huguenots; that he now counted them good and loyal subjects; and he gave orders that the nomination to all public offices should be made without distinction as to religion. There was every external indication that he had adopted the moderate policy of De l'Hôpital and Montmorency.

It was from the same party who brought about the peace, that the proposal emanated, of the marriage of Henry of Navarre with the King's sister,

Margaret of Valois. The marriage, like the peace, met with open and violent opposition from the Pope, who in the first instance sent his relative the Cardinal Alessandrino to dissuade Charles from entertaining the proposal; and when that intervention failed, refused the dispensation necessary for the completion of the marriage. It was as strenuously opposed by Philip, by the Guises, the Duke of Anjou, and the whole Spanish party in France, who looked upon it as a step towards the amicable adjustment of the religious strife which had rent the kingdom. There were difficulties with the Huguenots themselves. Jeanne d'Albret, Henry's mother, shrunk from the idea of such an alliance for her son: Coligni and the Huguenot chiefs were equally indisposed to it. They could not indeed be insensible to the great benefit to their cause that would arise from Henry's becoming the brother-in-law of the reigning monarch; but they were naturally mistrustful of all propositions emanating from the Court. Montmorency, however, wrote to Coligni, informing him of the origin of the proposal; Biron and Cossé visited him and the Queen of Navarre at Rochelle. Long conferences were held, such explanations made, and such assurances given, that at last all obstacles in that quarter were removed.

What mainly indicated, however, the entrance upon a new line of policy was the manner in which the proposal of a breach with Spain, by supporting the Netherlanders in their noble struggle, was entertained by the Court of France. Montmorency and his friends saw in such a course the salvation of their country from intestine discord, and its advance upon a new career of conquest and glory. Many of their best affected Roman Catholic fellow-subjects felt bitterly the degradation of that subjection to Spanish influence under which France had so long been groaning. A war with Spain then would be popular. It offered besides to French ambition the easy acquisition of provinces that lay contiguous to its own territory. The fact of their inhabitants being Calvinists could create no difficulty, as Charles had only to extend to them the same toleration which he had already given to his own subjects of the same faith. The Netherlanders themselves had their eyes quite open to the advantage of coming under French rather than Spanish rule, and in despair of achieving their independence unaided, made tempting offers to Charles to espouse their cause.

The project was opened to Coligni, with a view to secure the co-operation of the Huguenots. He embraced it with the entire devotion of his heart. To assist in its execution became the ruling passion of his being. To William of Orange—the soldier, the patriot, the Christian—kinship of spirit linked him. They were in fact the two first and greatest men of their age. To Coligni nothing could be more attractive than to fight side by side with William and his gallant brother Louis, and to assist them to throw off the yoke of Spain and its terrible Inquisition. The more he thought of it, the more persuaded was the Admiral that this was the best course for France upon purely national grounds to take. When he heard therefore that the King welcomed the proposal, wished to consult with him, and thought of putting him at the head of the enterprise, Coligni hesitated no longer, but repaired to Court. The King gave him the most gracious reception, and restored him to all his honors.

Charles was a weak, impulsive, passionate, capricious youth; but he was not insensible to generous emotions, nor incapable of perceiving and estimating true worth. He saw through and despised the men who were his mother's favorite advisers and friends. The simple, earnest, grave, truthful unflattering man—Admiral Coligni—gained day by day a growing ascendancy over him. He delighted to hear the brave old soldier and statesman descant upon the future prosperity of France, her domestic wounds all healed, taking a first place once more among the great military powers of Europe.

For a time all went favorably. An envoy was sent from France to cement a union with the Protestant Princes of Germany. Though marriage projects failed, there still might be effected a close political alliance between France and England, directed against Spain, their common enemy. So eagerly and successfully was this matter pressed, that a treaty offensive and defensive between these two powers was signed at Blois on the 29th April 1572. Montmorency, who had been its chief promoter, passed over to London to have it ratified, and had the most distinguished reception given him at the British Court. All seemed pointing to a speedy open rupture between France and Spain.

A counter-movement, however, had commenced. The Spanish party, at the head of which were Guise, Tavannes, Nevers, De Retz, Birague, wrought now upon the fears and now upon the pride of the Queen-mother. The life of this singular woman, whose character it is so difficult to decipher, had been one of extraordinary vicissitude. Of a nervously diseased constitution form her birth, she had been a prey from infancy to terrors of all kinds. Raised to share the throne of France, she had for twenty years to endure the infidelity of her husband, the dominion of a rival, and the perpetual threatening of divorce. The death of her husband, Henry, only brought with it to her a change of masters. During the brief reign of Francis II., the Guises, through their young niece, Mary Stuart, had exercised a sway scarce less despotic than that of Diana of Poitiers. With her son Charles's advent to the throne, she had risen to a larger, a dominant share in the management of public affairs. Fond of intrigue, and perfect mistress of it, she was keen of insight into all the motives by which men are moved; and passionate herself (if we except that one passion, the love of power), cunning and mean in her methods of playing upon the passions of others. Superstitious, as the towers she built for her astrologers still tell, she had no strong faith in the truths of Christianity. Bound by hereditary attachment to the Papacy, she could yet sportingly say, when told by the first messenger from the field of Jarnac that the Protestants had gained the battle, "Well, then, we shall have to say our prayers in French." Seeking supremely the secure possession of the throne, and the aggrandizement in it of her family, she cared for little else than the indulgence of a gay and cultivated but unrestrained frivolity.

Disposed at first to follow the moderate course marked out by the counsels of her wise and tolerant Chancellor, De l'Hôpital, by degrees she had got estranged from the Huguenots. Heartily disliking from the first their strict morality, she had given up the hope, perhaps relinquished the desire, of ruling by their help. The results of the first two religious wars had taught that they were not easily to be subdued by open force; but they had convinced her, at the same time, that the scheme was vain of bringing the two religions to dwell together in harmony. Regulating her movements by no fixed principles, nor by any broad political ideas, she had gone in for the moment with the measures that Montmorency and Coligni had proposed, their accomplishment offering such strong temptations to personal and family ambition.

But it was with a quick and jealous eye she watched the estrangement of Charles, for whom she had little of a mother's affection, from his brother Henry, the Duke of Anjou, the only one of all her family that it was thought she loved. Still quicker, and still more jealous was the eye with which she watched the growing influence of the Admiral over the passionate but generous spirit of the King. Coligni, on his part, was not slow to perceive, what soon openly revealed itself, that Catherine would be on the side of Spain, against the aiding of the Netherlands; and that if Charles was to be kept firm in his purpose, it could only be by emancipating him from that maternal thraldom in which he had hitherto been held. All depended upon whether he or she should gain the supremacy over Charles. The simplicity, the earnestness, the noble candor the unselfish patriotism o the Admiral, for a time prevailed. Charles dared to assert and express his independence of his mother. One day that Catherine entered his closet after a long conference he had had with the Admiral, in a piqued and taunting tone she asked him what it was that he was learning in all those endless conversations? "I have learned, madam," said the King, "that I have no greater enemy than my mother."

8

Her part now chosen, Catherine resolved to break a spell that she foresaw would be used against herself. The King had gone to his hunting-seat at Montpipeau, where she knew he would be alone. Thither she followed him. Shutting herself up with him in a cabinet, she burst into a flood of tears. "You hide yourself," she said, "from me, your mother, to take counsel with my enemies. You forsake the arms that have preserved you, to take refuge in those of an assassin. You would plunge your kingdom into a war with Spain, that would make you and all of us a prey to the Huguenots. Rather than that I should witness such a catastrophe, give me my dismissal, and send me back to the place of my birth."

All that Charles had been secretly planning with Coligni, every step that had been taken to bring on the war, she showed him that she knew, representing all as a device of the Huguenots, by which they hoped to climb to power. Every instrument that a strong-minded, strong-willed mother can exercise over a weak child that had long been subject to her Catherine wields. Astonished, affrighted, overcome, Charles yields, confesses error, pitifully asks pardon, and promises obedience.

Released, however, from the pressure of these threats and tears, once more under the sway of Coligni's calm but resolute council, he returns to the anti-Spanish policy. More decisive steps than ever are now taken. A large body of French troops under Genlis march to the help of William of Orange, carrying with them an autograph letter from Charles, which fell afterwards into Alva's hands, betraying the King's complicity in the movement. Accurate information of all that had been going on had been forwarded to Alva, who, falling unawares upon Genlis in his march, cuts to pieces the 3000 men that he commanded. Catherine gets more impatient, Charles more irritable than ever. Violent altercations take place in the Council of State. Coligni is for an immediate and open rupture with Spain. "He is no true Frenchman who opposes it:" these are his bold words. The King holds fast by Coligni. Catherine and Anjou notice with alarm that he is becoming more and more suspicious of them.

One day the Duke of Anjou entered unexpectedly the cabinet of the King, who had just had an interview with the Admiral. "Without speaking a word to me," said Anjou, afterwards describing the scene, "the King began in the most furious manner to stride back and forward across the apartment, casting at me savage looks, and put his hand so often in such a threatening way upon his dagger, that I thought every moment he was about to collar and to stab me. Perceiving myself in such danger I lost no time in retreating as hastily as I could, while his back was turned to me, to the door by which I had entered, and with a much curter salute that I had given on entrance disappeared, counting myself happy at having effected my escape." Henry went instantly to his mother with the news. Something prompt and decisive must be done. They agreed at last (we have Anjou's own word for it) that the Admiral must be assassinated.

All the difficulties about young Henry of Navarre's marriage had by this time been got over, and the 18th August 1572 fixed as the day of the nuptials. Henry came to Paris escorted by the flower of the Huguenot nobility and gentry. There were not wanting many among their number whose hearts misgave them as they entered the capital, and thought how entirely they were in the hands of their enemies. Their reception by all parties went far to remove their misgivings, especially their reception by the King. The regard and confidence so openly manifested by him towards the Admiral relieved their fears; his personal kindness to many of their number confirmed the confidence. With Rochefoucauld and Teligni, young men about his own age, the latter a son-in-law of Coligni, he was so frank, so familiar, so confiding, as to dispel the shadow of suspicion. None of those who had the best opportunities of knowing intimately his sentiments, up to this time, doubted his friendliness to the Huguenots. Still there were those who would not be persuaded, who carried their alarms to the Admiral, and entreated him to leave Paris. Firmly always, sometimes indignantly, he repelled their suggestions and alarms. Was he, on the very eve of seeing a great scheme executed that would unite all true Frenchmen, heal all internal strifes, and give back to his country her old place and renown among the nations, to do what would not only defeat that scheme, but plunge France once more into a religious war? He would rather die than do it, rather die than distrust a monarch who had given him every assurance of protection and support.

On the morning of Friday the 22d August, four days after the marriage, Coligni was sent for to the Louvre. Returning on foot to his hotel, some one put a paper into his hand which he opened and was reading, walking slowly as he passed the cloister of St. Germain l'Auxerrois, when a shot was fired. Coligni owed his life to a sudden movement that he made. But he had not wholly escaped the shot of the assassin. Two balls took effect; the one shattering the forefinger of the right hand, the other lodging in the left arm. Pointing to the house from which the shot had come, Coligni fell into the arms of one of his attendants, asking another to go and tell the King. Several of his suite now rushed to the house that had been indicated, forced an entrance, sought eagerly for the perpetrator of the deed, but he was gone.

The King was playing at tennis with the Duke of Guise and Teligni. When told of what had happened, he flung his racket upon the ground, exclaiming, "What! am I never to have peace?" and retired to the Louvre. Grief and fury in his looks, he paced his chamber to and fro. His mother and the Duke of Anjou ventured into his presence and tried to soothe him; he turned on them disdainful looks, but would not say a word.

Henry of Navarre and the young Prince of Condé came straight from the bedside of the Admiral. Full of sorrow and indignation, they told the King that neither they nor their friends could deem themselves any longer safe in Paris, and solicited permission to depart. The King burst out now into a tempest of rage against the attempt on Coligni's life, swearing with the most terrible oaths that he would have justice done to the uttermost on all concerned in it. Relieved of their own fears, the two Princes returned to tell their friends the King's feelings and his purposes.

The wounded man was now lying upon his bed. It was found necessary to amputate the finger, and to make deep incisions in the arm to extract the ball; the operations were painful, the result uncertain. But the composure of the sufferer was unruffled. Many were weeping around him.

"My friends," said he, "why do you weep? I am, indeed, sorely wounded, but it is the will of God, and I thank Him that He favors me by permitting me to suffer for His name."

"I wonder," said Marshal Damville, who came to visit him, "whence this can have come."

"I suspect," said Coligni, "no one but the Duke of Guise, but I do not feel sure even as to him. By the grace of God, I do not fear my enemies; the worst they can do to me is to bring me a little sooner to my eternal rest. I grieve, however, to be deprived of the opportunity of showing my King how greatly I desire to serve him. I wish his Majesty might be pleased to listen to me for a few moments. There are things which it concerns him to know, and which, perhaps, no one but myself will tell him."

The desire was communicated to Charles, who hastened to gratify it. Catherine and the Duke of Anjou, alarmed about the interview, accompanied the King. On coming to the bedside, the King manifested the strongest and tenderest emotion.

"Ah, my father," he said, "the wound is yours, but the anguish, the injury is mine; and by God's death, I will take such vengeance as shall never be effaced from the memory of man!"

"May God never be my help," said the wounded patriot, "if I desire vengeance. Justice, I feel certain, I shall obtain."

Coligni asked to be permitted to speak with the King alone. Charles motioned Catherine and Anjou away. The Admiral, believing himself to be dying, then unburdened his mind. The conversation was deepening in its earnestness. In her impatience the Queen mother at last interfered, and under the plea that it would be cruel to Coligni to tax his strength any longer, forced Charles from his side.

On their way back to the Louvre, Catherine asked her son what the Admiral had been saying to him. He would not tell. Again and again, with increasing importunity, she urged him to let her know. Provoked at last, Charles turned to her, and said, "If you will have it, then, he told me that the power and management of affairs was too much in your hands, and that this superintendence and authority of yours was certain one day to be deeply injurious to myself and to my country. That is what, as one of the best and most faithful servants of the Crown, he wished to guard me against before he died; and *Eh, bien! mon Dieu!* what he said was true."

The King's conduct was in keeping with his words. He gave instant orders that the gates of the city should be closed, and every corner of it searched for the assassin. It soon appeared that the house from which the shot was fired belonged to one of the household of the Duke of Guise; that the piece which, so soon as it had been discharged, had been flung upon the floor, belonged to one of the Duke's body-guard; that the horse in attendance behind the house, on which the assassin had escaped, came from the Duke's stud. No sooner, in fact, had Catherine and Anjou resolved upon the deed, than they took into their counsels the widow and son of the late Duke of

Guise, who, believing the Admiral to be implicated in his death, cherished the bitterest hatred towards Coligni.

The suspicion that directed itself against the young Duke of Guise was well founded. He had taken a chief part in the management of the affair. But as no evidence had been got to implicate him, he was bold enough to go next day into the royal presence, complain haughtily of the injustice that was done him, and request permission to retire from Court. His reception by Charles was gloomily ominous. He was told he might go when and where he liked; but if proved to be guilty, Charles would know well enough where to find him. But if the royal vengeance fell on him, what were Catherine and Anjou to do? They could not disown and forsake one who had acted only as their instrument. Even if they tried it, Guise and his mother could easily establish their connexion with the crime. Out of the meshes of those difficulties, in which this failure of the attempt on the Admiral's life had involved her, what way was there for Catherine to escape?—the one that for years she had been keeping as an *arrière-pensée* in her mind; the one that, thirteen years before, Henry II. had whispered into the ear of William of Orange in the woods of Vincennes; that Alva had boldly proposed to her in those midnight interviews at Bayonne; that her son-in-law, Philip of Spain, had never ceased to urge upon her adoption; that her son himself, the

King, in some of his fits of antipathy to the Huguenots, had entertained; that Pope after Pope had recommended, and which from so many pulpits had been proclaimed to the populace as the only fit cure for the plague of heresy in France—the cutting off, not of Coligni alone, but of all the chief Huguenots at a stroke. Here now, in Paris, as if brought together for the very purpose, were the head and flower of that party, that a vigorous hand might lop off by a single blow. It could be done, however, only under royal warrant, and how, in his present mood and temper, could Charles be brought to give the order?

Catherine knew her son too well—his weakness, his fitfulness, his suspiciousness, his proneness to sudden turns and frightful gusts of passion—to despair. Late in the evening of Saturday the 23d, in a summer-house in the gardens of the Tuileries, there met in secret conclave Catherine, Anjou, Tavannes, De Retz, Birague, and Nevers; three out of the four chosen advisers of the Queen being foreigners. Their plans concerted, they sought and found the King in his cabinet in the Louvre. The fatal colloquy which followed was managed mainly by Catherine herself. "The Huguenots are arming everywhere," she told the King; "not to serve, but to crush you. Their envoys are already off with instructions to raise 6000 *Reiter* in Germany, and 10,000 infantry in Switzerland. The Catholics on the other hand, are determined to be done with this. If you won't do as they desire, they have resolved to choose a General of their own. The citizens are already under arms."

"But I have forbidden it," cried the King.

"It is done notwithstanding; and now, between the two, what are you to do?"

The King asked her, what?

"One man," she said, "is the chief author of all this mischief. The Admiral has been playing the king, using you as the tool of his ambition and his party; let him be killed. Remember the conspiracy of Amboise against your brother; that of Meaux against yourself, when you had to fly before your own subjects." Then, by every argument that could move his pride, his fear, his jealousy, his thirst of vengeance, she pictured to him all the wrongs done to the throne by Coligni and his friends.

Tavannes, Birague, Nevers, Anjou seconded the Queen, insisting that not Coligni alone, but that all the Huguenots should instantly be cut off.[1]

"And now," added the Queen. "These Huguenots are coming to-morrow to demand vengeance on the Guises. But you cannot sacrifice the Guises. They will defend themselves by throwing the blame on your mother and brother, and justly too. Yes; it was we who did it. We struck at the Admiral

[1] The Duke of Anjou mentions in his narrative of this interview that De Retz at first objected to this proposal, but afterwards gave in to it.

to save the King; and you must finish the work, or you and all of us are lost."

"But my honor," exclaimed the King; "and my friends, the Admiral, Rochefoucauld, Teligni. Can no other way be thought of?"

"Sire, you refuse," said the Queen; "then give to me and your brother permission to retire and take our own steps to save ourselves and the monarchy."

Charles trembled at the thought of being deserted.

"Sire," she said, as she made a movement to depart, "is it for fear of the Huguenots that you refuse?"

This taunting him with cowardice was the last touch of that cruel and cunning hand. Charles sprung up, mad with rage, and with a fearful oath exclaimed—

"Then since you think it right the Admiral should be killed, let every Huguenot in France perish with him, that there be not one left of them to reproach me with the act. Let it be done," he said, and the meeting hastily broke up.[1] It was

[1] The details of what took place at this eventful meeting are derived from the narrative of the Duke of Anjou, who was present. The authenticity and truthfulness of this remarkable narrative are now generally admitted, Ranke being the only modern historian who expresses any doubt regarding it. The main fact in it, that Charles was difficult to be persuaded, and only gave way at last after extreme pressure, is supported by the Memoirs of Tavannes, another eye-wit-

already past eleven o'clock when the royal sanction was got. It was settled that the massacre should begin at daybreak.

The Queen and Anjou took the arrangements into their own hands. Marcel, the ex-Provost of the city, was summoned to the Louvre, and told to close the city gates and summon the Catholic citizens to arms in all their quarters. This was scarcely needed; emissaries had been among them all forenoon stimulating their passions against the Huguenots. To the young Duke of Guise was assigned the task of slaughtering all in and round the Louvre, beginning his bloody work by killing the Admiral. He called together the captains of the French and Swiss guards. "Gentlemen," he said, "the hour is come when, under sanction of the King, we may at length avenge ourselves upon the accursed race, the enemies of God. The game is in the snare, you must not suffer it to escape." He then posted the troops on each side of the Louvre, with command to suffer no servant of the house of Bourbon to pass.

At midnight the city authorities assembled in the Place de Grève. The Duke addressed them thus: "It is the King's good pleasure that we should take up arms to kill Coligni, and extirpate all the other Huguenots and rebels. The same is

ness, and by the Memoirs of Marguerite de Valois, which Michelet regards as the chief document bearing on the massacre.

to be done in all the provinces. When the clock of the Palais de Justice sounds its bell at daybreak, let each good Catholic bind a strip of white linen round his left arm, and put a white cross on his cap, and begin the work."

They had not to wait so long. It wanted yet an hour and a half of daybreak, when the Queen-mother, impatient of the delay, or fearing some change in the purpose of the King, gave orders that the bell of the church of St. Germain de l'Auxerrois should be sounded as the signal to commence. Then she and Charles and Anjou passed into a small apartment above the gate of the Louvre, and, opening the window, looked out to see the tragedy begin. All was still and dark: a pistol-shot was fired; the solitary report struck terror into their hearts. Seized with a spasm of remorse, they sent a gentleman to the Duke of Guise, bidding him proceed no further. It was too late.

No sooner had the signal been given than Guise galloped to the dwelling of the Admiral. Cosseins, the captain of the King's Guard, knocked at the outer gate and demanded entrance. Suspecting nothing, the servant in charge opened, and fell under the stroke of Cossein's dagger. His followers rushed in and filled the inner court of the hôtel. The noise had awakened the Admiral, who lay upstairs with one or two faithful attendants in his room. Fearing some popular outbreak, but relying on the King's Guard stationed there for the purpose of protecting him, Coligni rose, put on his dressing-gown, and asked Merlin, his favorite minister, to engage in prayer. A servant rushed into the room.

"My Lord," he said, "it is God who calls you. The hall is carried, and we have no means of resistance left."

"I have long been prepared to die," said the Admiral; "but save yourselves, all of you, if you can."

Behme, a German, and other retainers of the Guises, now broke into the apartment.

"Are you the Admiral?" said Behme.

"Yes," was Coligni's calm reply; "but, young man, you should have some respect to my gray hairs and my infirmities."

With a savage oath, the German plunged his boar-spear into his breast. Rapid sword-strokes from others followed. Covered with wounds, Coligni sank mangled among their feet.

"Behme, have you done it?" shouted the Bastard of Angoulême, from the court below.

"It is done, my Lord," was the reply.

"But Guise will not believe it unless he see him with his own eyes. Throw him out of the window."

The brutal command was instantly obeyed. The body was flung down upon the pavement. The two Lords alighted and bent over it; the face was besmeared with blood, and disfigured; they took their handkerchiefs, and wiped the blood away. "'Tis he," they said, as each kicked the corpse. Then in haste they mounted, and dashed out through the gate, shouting in triumph as they galloped forth, "Courage, soldiers, courage! we have made a good beginning—now for the others."

At this moment, responding to the first signal sound, the bells of all the churches rung out their summons to that shameless slaughter. In a few hours, within a short space round the Louvre, 500 noblemen and gentlemen were sabred or shot. Rochefoucauld had parted from the King but an hour or two before, the last to leave the palace. He was awakened by men entering his chamber in masks. Fancying it some frolic of the Prince, he rose to meet them, and fell pierced by their rapiers at the door. The young Teligni was seen creeping along a house-top; but he was such a favorite that more than one, who as they pointed their pieces recognized him, held back their fingers from the trigger. At last the fatal shot was fired, and he fell dead upon the street.

Margaret, the young Queen of Navarre, gives us a glimpse into the interior of the palace. "I saw every one in agitation," she says, "but no one told me any thing till the evening, when being with the Queen my mother, sitting near my sister of Lorraine, who I saw was very sorrowful, the Queen noticed me, and told me to retire. As I made my courtesy, my sister seized me by the arm, and stopping me began to weep, saying, 'My sister do not go.' This frightened me excessively, which the Queen perceived, and calling very angrily to my sister forbade her to tell me any thing. My sister said it was shocking to send me to be sacrificed in that way. The Queen answered, Be it as it might, I must go, lest they should suspect something. They continued to dispute, but I could not hear their words. At length the Queen told me very roughly to go to bed, and my sister bursting into tears bade me good-night. I went away shivering and trembling. . . . At daybreak the King rose and quitted the room. I begged my nurse to shut the door, and fell asleep. . . . I had only slept an hour when I was startled by the cries of some one striking with hands and feet against the door, and calling loudly 'Navarre! Navarre!' My nurse rose and opened it, when a gentleman called Tejan rushed in, having a sword-wound in his elbow, and one from a halberd in his arm, pursued by four of the Guard. He threw himself upon the bed, from which I sprang, and he after me, catching me in his bloody arms, both of us screaming with terror. At last, by God's help, Monsieur de Nançay came in, who finding me in that situation could not help laughing. He scolded the archers for their indiscretion, and having ordered them out of the room, granted me the life of the poor gentleman, whom I hid in my cabinet till he was cured.

"While I was changing my dress, which was

covered with blood, M. de Nançay told me what was going on, assuring me that the King, my husband, was in the King's own apartment, and was safe. Throwing a cloak over me, he led me to the chamber of my sister of Lorraine, where I arrived more dead than alive. As I entered the antechamber, the doors of which were all open, a gentleman named Bourse, flying from the archers who were pursuing him, received a blow from a halberd and fell dead at my feet. I swooned in the arms of M. de Nançay—who thought the same blow had struck both at once, and was carried into my sister's room."

But the archers' work in the chambers and passages of the Palace, daring and desperate as it was, was a restrained and orderly execution, as compared with that perpetrated throughout the city by sixty thousand men—princes, nobles, soldiers, citizens—with all kinds of murderous weapons in their hands, under no command, throwing off all restraint, all pity, every vestige of human feeling, turned for the time into incarnate demons; Guise, Tavannes, Nevers, and others, hounding them on with shoutings of " Down with the Huguenots! Kill! kill! blood-letting is as good in August as in May! Kill! kill! 'tis the command of the King!" And king never had command more thoroughly obeyed. Two thousand unsuspecting, helpless, half-naked men were slaughtered that morning, their bodies flung out at windows, dragged through the mire, pitched into the river, amid whistlings and howlings, and yells of delight, and oaths of a horrible blasphemy.[1]

At mid-day of that Sunday, the King thought good to hold his hand, and sent an order to the authorities of the city to check the massacre. And his mother and he employed the leisure of that Sunday evening in writing despatches to foreign Powers, attributing the massacre wholly to the Guises, going so far even as to say that they had had enough to do to protect themselves in the Louvre.

But Charles had raised a demon he could not lay. Next forenoon, in the Cemetery of the Innocents, a miracle was announced; a hawthorn

---

[1] *Geschichte des Französischen Calvinismus.* Von Gottlob von Polenz. Gotha, 1859. Vol. ii. pp. 432–563, and 718–720.

Geschichte des Protestantismus in Frankreich bis zum Tode Karls IX. Von Dr. Wilhelm Gottlieb Soldan. Leipzig, 1855. Vol. ii. pp. 399–472.

It is from this historian that the general view of the origin of the Massacre of St. Bartholomew given in this volume has been derived. A French translation of the part of Soldan's History relating to this event appeared under the title, *La France et la Saint Barthélemy.* Par M. G. G. Soldan, traduit de l'Allemand, par Charles Schmidt. Paris, 1855.

Henri Martin in his *Histoire de France* takes the same view, referring to Soldan as the "learned and judicious Professor of Giessen." Michelet's narrative in *Guerres de Religion,* chapters 21–26, is of the same tenor.

See also *Essai sur l'Avenir de la Tolérance.* Par Ad. Schæffer. Paris, 1859, pp. 203–282.

La Saint Barthélemy. Par Ath. Coquerel, Fils. Paris, 1859.

had flowered in the night—emblem of the Church flourishing once again. The fanatic city mob got more excited than ever. The bells all rang out again. The massacre began with greater barbarity than ever, and went on more or less throughout the week. The business now was to search out every Huguenot that was left, to let not even the youngest child escape. Infants packed in baskets, amid jeering laughter were flung over the bridge into the Seine. Little boys not ten years old were seen dragging with cords in triumph along the streets, a Huguenot infant torn from its slaughtered mother's breast.

Upon the streets, there lay together, weltering in their blood, a father and his two sons, apparently all dead. Many as they passed stopped for a moment to gaze upon the group. "'Tis all the better so, they said; it is nothing to kill the wolves, if you do not kill their little ones along with them." The bodies lay all still. At last there came a solitary man who, as he stopped and looked, gently raised his hands to heaven, and said in pitiful indignation, "God will avenge that deed!" And then the youngest of the children raised its little head from out its bath of blood, and said, "*I am not dead.* Take me to the arsenal, and M. de Biron will pay you well." The child that had the singular self-possession to feign itself dead so long, and was thus preserved, was Caumont de la Force, the head of a distinguished family, who lived to do good service afterwards to the Huguenot cause in France.

As little respect was paid to character as to age. Pierre de la Place, a distinguished jurist and historian, had a message sent to him that he was wanted at the Louvre. Suspecting the object, he fled out of his own house, tried the houses of three friends, was repulsed from each, returned to his own dwelling, gathered his family round him and engaged in prayer. The message came a second time, with an urgency that he could not resist. He bade adieu to his household, but had not gone far upon his way when he fell under the daggers of the assassins.

Peter Ramus—still a name of renown in the world of scholarship and philosophy, the highest name, in fact, that France had then to boast of—retired into his library in the fifth story of the house, and was kneeling there in prayer when they broke in upon his retirement. They stopped a moment. They heard him say, "O my God, have mercy on me, and pardon those who know not what they do!" A sword was passed through his body, a shot fired at his head. He still breathed. His murderers seized him and flung him out of the window. Still he breathed, but no one would give him the *coup de grace*. They tied cords, instead, about his feet, and dragged him through the streets. At last, by the river's side, they cut the head off, and flung the trunk into the stream.

Coligni's body was exposed to still more barbarous treatment. His head was carried to Catherine, as the Baptist's was to Herodias, and sent by her as a trophy to the Cardinal of Lorraine at Rome. The headless trunk, subjected to indescribable indignities, after having been dragged to and fro through the streets, was hung up by the feet, half burnt upon a gibbet at Montfaucon. Two days afterwards, the King and Catherine, and the Court ladies, made a holiday excursion to the spot, shamelessly to gaze on and to jeer at the marred and mutilated remains of the greatest man that France had in that age produced.

With marvellous speed the news of the Parisian massacre spread over France, and so ripe and ready for it was the Catholic population, that each city, as it got the tidings, had its own St. Bartholomew. They heard of it at Meaux on the Sunday evening; that night the streets of Meaux were drenched in blood. They heard of it at Orleans on Tuesday the 26th; for a week onward from that date Catholic Orleans gave itself up to the pillage and murder of its Huguenot inhabitants. They heard of it in Lyons on Thursday the 28th, and scenes of horror, outrivalling those of Paris, were day by day enacted, the Rhone literally so red with blood, that the inhabitants of Arles, and other towns below Lyons, for days abstained from drinking its waters. Orleans, Rouen, Bordeaux, Toulouse, Angers, Saumur, Bourges, and other towns, followed the lead. Premeditated as to the general design, but not preconcerted as to the time and mode of its execution, the massacre of St. Batholomew was not the gusty act of a single night. It was the prolonged and wide-spread massacre of six weeks and more, all over France, in the course of which 30,000 Huguenots were cut off.[1]

The King at first, as we have seen, would have thrown the odium upon the Guises. A day's reflection satisfied him, or rather convinced Catherine and her advisers, that it must be openly avowed. On Tuesday the 26th, Charles, accompanied by his Court, appeared before the Parliament of Paris, acknowledged that the order had been given by himself, vindicating it by asserting that Coligni and his friends had embarked in treasonable designs, and had meditated an assault upon the throne The obsequious Parliament heard and applauded, appointing an annual festival in Paris to commemorate the day.

Philip of Spain got speedy information of the event, and sent off immediately six thousand crowns to the murderer of Coligni. "The news,"

[1] *Histoire de France*, par Henri Martin, tom. ix. pp. 327 and 339. *La France et le Saint Barthélemey*, par M. G. G. Soldan, p. 93.

Pérefix gives the number slain all over France as 100,000; Le Reveille-Matin, 100,000; Sully, 70,000; De Thou, 30,000; Popilinière, 20,000; Papyre Masson, one of the panegyrists of the massacre, 10,000.

says the French Envoy at Madrid, "arrived here on the 7th September. The King, on receiving the intelligence, showed, contrary to his natural custom, so much gayety, that he seemed more delighted than with all the good fortune or happy incidents which had ever before occurred to him. I went to see him next morning, and as soon as I came into his presence, he began to laugh, and with demonstrations of extreme contentment to praise your Majesty as deserving your title of Most Christian, telling me there was no king worthy to be your Majesty's companion, either for valor or prudence. I thanked him; and I said that I thanked God for enabling your Majesty to prove to his master that his apprentice had learned his trade."

At Rome the joy was greater than at Madrid. Gregory XIII., who had just ascended the pontifical throne, went at the head of his Cardinals, and all the ambassadors of the Catholic Princes, in solemn procession to the different churches of the city, to have masses and *Te Deums* chanted over the deed. In the evening the guns of St. Angelo were fired as for a great victory, and for three nights the city was illuminated, the Pope exclaiming that the massacre was more agreeable to him than fifty victories of Lepanto. Vasari was instructed to execute a large picture, still to be traced on the walls of the Sixtine Chapel, representing the massacre, beneath which were the words, "*Pon-*

tifex Coligni necem probat."¹ A medal was struck; on one side the crest of the reigning Pope, on the other, that of a destroying angel smiting the Huguenots. Mark Antony Muret, preaching before the Pope, exclaimed: "O memorable night, worthy of a distinction all its own among our festivals! I love to think that the stars that night shone with a more silvery brilliance, that the Seine rolled its waters more impetuously, as if in haste to fling into the sea the corpses of the impure it carried. O day full of joy and gladness, when you, thrice holy Father, received the tidings, and went to render solemn thanks to God! What happier commencement for your pontificate could you have desired?"

Very different was the reception given to the news in England. Elizabeth was at Woodstock with her Court. She had heard all from her own ministers before La Motte Fénélon, the French Ambassador, came down from London personally to announce it. It was a dull and rainy day. The ambassador was ushered into a room hung with

---

[1] See a learned and elaborate article on the Massacre of St. Bartholomew in the *North British Review*, vol. li. p. 30–70. The writer succeeds in proving that many persons anticipated such a slaughter of the Protestants, and that members of the French Government had given reason to some of the foreign ambassadors to expect it; but he does not succeed in disproving the view that Soldan, Martin, and Michelet have presented of the general current of events, and especially of the conduct of the King.

black. The Queen and Court were all in mourning. Every eye was bent upon the ground. "Sir," said Elizabeth to him in reply to his communication, "Heaven weeps for the miseries of France. Your King must be a very cruel master to have so many traitors among his subjects. It seems that men were wishing to put that commandment out of the Decalogue, Thou shalt not kill." A touch of Elizabethan stiff formality, and Elizabethan masculine boldness in that reception, but such a touch of nature, too, as has made all the world akin; for, that sentiment of the English Court, is it not now the sentiment of broad humanity, which in every land weeps over and abhors that massacre of St. Bartholomew as one of the foulest crimes that ever stained our globe?

The massacre was at its height, the streets of Paris were running with blood, the courts of the Louvre were ringing with the shouts of the murderers, the paroxysm of fury into which Charles had been lashed was still on him, when Henry and Condé were summoned into the King's presence. Pouring blasphemous rebukes on them, he demanded an instant recantation of their faith. Henry bent before the storm, and in ambiguous phrase declared that, provided his conscience was left at peace, he was willing to do whatever the King required. With greater boldness, Condé said that he would die rather than deny the truth.

The King gave him three days to deliberate. The three days made no change in Condé's purpose, nor had they done much to mitigate the choler of the King. "The Mass," he fiercely exclaimed to the young Prince, when brought again into his presence,—"the Mass, or death, or the Bastile." Condé told him that he might choose for him between the two latter, as with the Mass he was resolved to have nothing to do. The King would have taken his life with his own hand upon the spot had he not been restrained. Time, however, the hopelessness of their condition, and the persuasion and the example of others, effected what Charles's threatenings failed to bring about, and both Princes for a time conformed to the Roman Catholic worship.

Those fearful gusts of passion into which Charles IX. was so easily hurried had terrible interludes of despondency and remorse. "Ambrose," said he one day soon after the massacre, to his cherished physician Paré, "I don't know what ails me; my whole frame seems in a fever. I see nothing round me but hideous faces covered with blood. I wish the weak and innocent had been spared." Years afterwards the King of Navarre was in the habit of telling his intimate friends, never however but with horror painted on his countenance, that eight days after the massacre a multitude of ravens, croaking dismally, settled on the great pavilion of the Louvre. The noise they made brought out every one to look at them, and the superstitious ladies of the Court infected the King with the terror they felt at the sight. The same night the King, two hours after he had gone to rest, sprang up, called to those who were in his chamber, and sent for the King of Navarre and others to listen to a loud noise in the air; a concert of screams, groanings, howlings, and furious voices, menacing and blaspheming, just as they were heard on the night of the massacre. The sounds seemed so distinct and articulate, that, fearing a new disaster, Charles despatched in all haste his guards into the city to stop the carnage, but they brought back word that all was quiet there. The King continued greatly agitated, and for seven successive nights the sounds returned, being heard precisely at the same hour.

Other things than sounds in the air soon came to trouble the Court. In that bloody grave of St. Bartholomew's Day it had imagined that the power of the Huguenots lay buried. But now, before the summer was over, the startling news reached Paris that the whole south of France was once more in arms, and that Montauban, Nismes, Sancerre and Rochelle were in the hands of the Huguenots. A powerful army was despatched to reduce Rochelle, as their strongest and most important hold. The army was composed of nearly the whole available force of the kingdom. It was led by the young Duke of Anjou, the conqueror of

Jarnac and Moncontour. He was accompanied by the Dukes d'Aumale, Guise, Mayenne, Nevers, Bouillon, the Marshals Biron, De Cossé, Montluc, and a large body of the nobility. Against all this array of war the Rochellese had but about 1000 regular troops and 2000 volunteers of their own citizens trained to arms. Animated not so much by a political as by a religious spirit, this spirit fired and stimulated by the fifty ministers who had found refuge within their walls, the brave inhabitants resolved to defend their city to the last. They marched to the ramparts, not at the sound of the trumpet, but singing one or other of their favorite Psalms. In the thick of the conflict women of all ranks, the wives and daughters of the combatants, were to be seen carrying off the dead and wounded, supplying refreshments to the weary, not unfrequently mingling personally in the strife. The enthusiasm rose as the danger rose, and happily, though the town was strictly blockaded both by land and by sea, the extreme pressure of famine was unfelt. The siege lasted for four months; twenty-nine assaults were given; seventy mines dug and attempted to be sprung; 35,000 cannon-shot were hurled against the walls; 12,000 of the besiegers were slain in the fight, and a still greater number perished from disease on the march and in the camp. Yet Rochelle remained untaken.

Even this defence, heroic as it was, fails in comparison with that made by the little town of Sancerre. A few hundred men, many of them without fire-arms, furnished only with their slings, in the use of which they were proverbially expert, placed behind ill-built walls, that crumbled under every cannon-shot of the enemy, defended themselves there for ten months against 5000 troops supplied with all the munitions of war. Again and again the attempt to take the town was made, but made in vain. The siege was then turned into a blockade, and the horrors of famine fell upon the besieged. The details have been preserved in the Journal of one of the ministers, De Leri. The supply of food failing, orders were at last issued that the allowance for each man, whether soldier or citizen, should be half a pound of bread per day; a few days later this was reduced to a quarter pound per day; still later, to one pound per week. Horses, asses, dogs, and cats were all devoured in turn. Half-famished children were to be seen eager in the chase of rats, moles, and mice, roasting them and ravenously devouring them when caught. De Leri, who had suffered all the horrors of famine on a five months' voyage from the Brazils, remembered that life had been sustained among the crew and passengers by leather soaked and cut in strips and then dressed like tripe. The suggestion was eagerly caught at. Every article of skin or leather was sought for, and various ways of preparing this unnatural food invented. This resource too failed, and then parchments, letters, title-deeds, manuscripts, and books hundreds of years old, were turned into food. "I myself," says De Leri, "have seen them eagerly eaten when the writing was still visible on the fragments served up in the dish, and could be read distinctly." The mortality from sheer want of food grew to be so great that from twenty-five to thirty funerals occurred daily. Pale countenances, with tearless eyes, gazed into the open graves, as if envying the rest that was to be found there. Of the children under twelve years old, scarcely one survived. Only 84 men fell under the shot of the enemy, while 500 perished from hunger. A spectacle more horrible than all beside met the eye when in the public square of the town a scaffold was erected, and the death-knell tolled for an execution. Parents, vicious in their habits and brutalized by want, had been found feeding on the dead body of their child. The horrors of Samaria, of Numantia, of Jerusalem, were equalled if not exceeded at Sancerre. But though wandering about like phantoms, sinking to the ground from weariness and want, the inhabitants resolved to die to the last man, rather than put themselves in the hands of those by whom the Massacre of St. Bartholomew had been perpetrated.

The same political event brought relief both to Sancerre and to Rochelle. The Estates of Poland had elected Henry of Anjou to be their king. Polish ambassadors, many of whom were Protestants, came to lay their crown at the young Duke's feet, charged at the same time to do their uttermost to mitigate the sufferings to which their coreligionists, the Calvinists of France, were exposed. It became for the time the policy of the French Court to deal tenderly with the Huguenots. A treaty was concluded, by which the free exercise of the Reformed faith, as well as their ancient municipal privileges, were granted to the three cities of Rochelle, Nismes, and Montauban. Sancerre was cruelly disappointed on learning that it was left out. It still, notwithstanding the disappointment, stood out in its defence, and won the due reward of its bravery in the same terms being formally conceded to it. The Protestants generally were disappointed with an arrangement which, though it allowed liberty of conscience to all, confined within so narrow limits the public profession and exercise of their faith. On the 26th August 1573, the anniversary of St Bartholomew, deputies from all the Protestant Churches of France met at Montauban and drew up a petition to the Crown, in which they not only craved a free and universal liberty of worship, but demanded that the authors of the late massacre should be punished, the sentence against Coligni reversed, the charges against him pronounced to be calumnious, and a full pardon granted to all who, since the massacre, had taken up arms in their own defence. As the bold, outspoken document was publicly read to him, the King stood stupefied; but the Queen-mother, who was by his side, could not restrain her surprise and indignation. "Why!" she exclaimed, "if Condé were still alive, with 50,000 foot and 30,000 horse at his command, he could not have asked the half of what is here demanded." Bland speeches, however, had to be made to quiet in the mean time the presenters of this petition. But it effectually taught the Court how signally, as a means of crushing Protestantism, the great crime of the massacre had failed. The spirit that had risen up so fresh and strong in the Huguenots was still further reinvigorated by the approach now made to them by that party which had dictated the Peace of St. Germain. This party, the *Politiques*, at the head of which were the Montmorencys, Biron, Cossé, Brissac, and others, were Roman Catholics, but they had imbibed the tolerant spirit and principles of the great Chancellor De l'Hôpital. They were lovers of peace, tired of the religious strife by which France had been so torn and weakened. They longed to see her—once more united—regain that position and that strength from which she had fallen. There was nothing that they dreaded more than Spanish intervention in French affairs,—a sure step, as they took it to be, to Spanish domination and control. They were jealous of the influence that so many foreigners had already attained at Court, and they were satisfied that by their means it was the design of the politic Queen-mother to raise and establish the royal power on the ruins of the ancient nobility of the realm. They formed the project, therefore, by union with the Huguenots, to deliver their country from the rule of Catherine and her courtiers, and to establish a pure and strong, a broad and tolerant government, in France. The more religious section of the Huguenots shrank from a coalition that had in it so much more of the political than the religious. But they were overruled by the majority, and at the first of their purely political meetings, whose separate history has been given to the public by Anquez,[1] the terms of the union between the Huguenots and the *tiers parti* were adjusted.

Learning and genius hastened to lend their aid to the great cause of union and of liberty. The tyranny of the government was based on the assumption of the Divine right of the sovereign to dictate in all things absolutely to all his subjects. Thoughtful men began to question an assumption that covered and justified so much cruelty and oppression. In numerous pamphlets the bases of the social contract were discussed with a freedom that indicated the rise of a wholly new set of political ideas. A posthumous work on Voluntary Servitude, by Étienne de la Boëtie, the friend of Montaigne, made an impression on the public mind of France inferior only to that made about this time by a

---

[1] *Histoire des Assemblées Politiques des Réformés de France.* Par Léonce Anquez, Professeur de l'Histoire au Lycée Saint Louis. Paris, 1859.

treatise coming from the pen of the celebrated jurisconsult Francis Othman. Touched by the sight of the martyrdom of Anne du Bourg, Othman had in early life become a Protestant. His prospects in life were blasted; his father disinherited him; he was driven as an exile from France. Lausanne opened to him the Chair of Belles-Lettres in its college; and in that quiet retreat he devoted himself for years to a profound study of the civil law, especially of the Roman jurisprudence. The learning, the originality, the genius displayed in his writings, won for him a European celebrity. Tempting offers came in upon him from all quarters. German Universities strove to appropriate him; our own Elizabeth invited him to Oxford. But he refused all their invitations, resolved to devote himself to the interests of his native land. Othman was at Bourges when the news of the massacre of St. Bartholomew spread over France. He saved himself by flying to Sancerre, mourning the loss of his valuable library. From Sancerre he escaped to Geneva, from which city of freedom he now launched the famous volume *La Gaule Franque*. The author boldly put the question, Have the people ever the right to resist and revolt against the royal authority? and as boldly he answers that at times they have. The contract is a mutual one between the King and his subjects, and whichever of the two parties flagrantly violates one of the primary natural and indefeasible conditions upon which all such contracts rest, forfeits all the rights that it bestows. The notion of a Divine right examined and repelled, Othman places the sovereignty ultimately in the people. The King, he says, is for the people, not the people for the King. It was but a reduction of this theory into practice when so many of the Reformed communities in France adopted, as they did at this time, a federate democratic constitution, providing not only for the conduct of a war in defence of their liberties, but for all the ordinary purposes of government—an early and premature shadow of the French Republic of modern times, with this great difference, that the prime principle and motive in the projected Huguenot republic of 1574 was a strong religious faith. That central element of power which, if preserved, had guided and restrained the others, was trampled out in the course of the eighteenth century, under the iron hoof of civil and ecclesiastical oppression. The purely political element was left to act alone against the oppressors, and France reaped the fruits in the impieties and fearful inhumanities of the Republic of 1798.

For the new confederacy between the Huguenots and the *tiers parti*, a temporary chief was found in the King's youngest brother, the Duke of Alençon. The Duke had gained the favor of the Protestants by having protested against the attempt on the life of Coligni, and his having taken no part in the massacre of St. Bartholomew.

His intense jealousy of his elder brother, Henry of Anjou, who was the acknowledged leader of the extreme Catholic party, threw him naturally into association with the Montmorencys and the Tiers-État which they headed. When his brother went to Poland, he cherished the design of excluding him from the succession, and taking the French throne on the death of Charles; and it was alone by the help of the Confederates that any such design could be carried out.

It was arranged that D'Alençon, Navarre, and Condé, escaping from the semi-bondage in which they were held at Court, should place themselves openly at the head of the malcontents. The 10th March 1574 was the day fixed on for their flight. The Huguenots were to rise in the south under the gallant La Noue, whilst a chosen band under Guitre was to approach St. Germains, and cover the escape of the Princes. When the day came, D'Alençon's courage failed. To cover himself from the consequences, he went and revealed the whole plot to the Queen-mother. Catherine felt or simulated an extremity of terror. There was a midnight flight of the whole Court to Paris. La Mole and Coconas, two friends and agents of D'Alençon, were tried and beheaded. The Marshals Montmorency and Cossé were thrown into the Bastile, and the young Princes of Navarre and Condé confined under strict watch in the castle of Vincennes. Undaunted by these events, La Noue advanced to meet the storm gathering to overwhelm him, when the death of Charles IX., on 30th May 1574, once more changed the current of affairs.

Charles never recovered the shock of the fatal night at Paris. We cannot lay on him, indeed, the chief burden of that crime. He was the dupe of deeper designs. Neglected in his education, worse taught—he often complained—than many of his valets, he had not only been suffered, he had been encouraged and excited, to gratify some of the worst and strongest propensities of his nature; and when the hour for using him as their tool arrived, those who had so encouraged and excited knew well how to play upon his passions. At his death it was suspected that poison had been administered. But it seemed needless to imagine this in order to account for his death. He had never been robust. To invigorate a frame diseased from the beginning, he had recourse to the most violent exercises. A smith's forge was erected for him, at which he would toil for hours forging great iron bars or beating out suits of armor. Often he would rise at midnight, mount one of his fleetest steeds, and gallop off to the chase, blowing furiously on the horn, or hallooing at the top of his voice to the hounds. Again, for hours together, he would play at tennis till he had utterly exhausted himself. These were the pastimes to which, when his strength began to fail, he would insist on betaking himself, aggravating the malady under which he sank. The evil demon of his life—that grew in its tyranny over him as he grew less able to resist it—was his liability to those tornadoes of passion by which all the better principles and feelings of his nature were for the time scattered to the winds. Such better principles and feelings undoubtedly were there. The fine taste for poetry and music that broke out in him so spontaneously revealed sensibilities that, rightly cultivated, might have made him a very different man. Let us give him, besides, the benefit of the belief that he carried by inheritance the seeds of a semi-insanity in his constitution—seeds fostered rather than repressed; under better treatment in his youth and with better influences around him on the throne, he might have escaped the ignominy with which his name and reign are now so deeply covered.

CHAPTER VI.

HENRY III., 1574–1589.

Origin of the League.—Henry and his *Mignons*.—Projects of Philip II. of Spain.—Alliance contracted at Joinville.—Treaty of Nemours.—Effect upon Henry of Navarre.—Papal Bull against Henry, and his reply.—Exploit at St. Foy.—Interview with Catherine.—Battle of Coutras.—The day of the Barricades.—The Spanish Armada.—Meeting of the Estates at Blois.—Assassination of the Duke of Guise.—State of Paris.—Interview between the two Henrys at Plessis-les Tours.—Arrival before Paris.—Death of Henry III.

The first ten years of Henry III.'s reign were years of comparative repose for the Huguenots. At first, indeed, he seemed disposed to prosecute the war against them, fired with all his early hatred of heresy. The strength however that their union with the politicians gave them, the presence of D'Alençon, Navarre, and Condé, each of whom had in turn escaped—the two latter throwing off their profession of Roman Catholicism instantly on their liberty being regained,—and the imposing military preparations which were in progress, induced the King to pause. The Queen-mother had recourse to her ordinary expedient of negotiation and, on the 5th of May 1576, a treaty was concluded, in which very favorable terms¹ were granted to the Huguenots. So little intention however had Henry to abide by the terms of that treaty, that when the Estates of the realm assembled in December of the same year, he actually proposed a measure for the utter extirpation of the Calvinists. A verbal resolution to that effect the Estates were quite willing to pass, but when the question as to the raising of the supplies necessary to the carrying on of the exterminating campaign came up for discussion, not only were all the projects of taxation that Henry and his council submitted rejected, but measures, some of them trenching deeply on the royal prerogative, and all of them in the highest degree offensive to the King, were openly proposed and generally supported. Henry took his revenge by returning to the policy of toleration, and in the years 1577, 1579, 1580 the successive edicts of Poitiers, Nérac, and Périgord gave even larger privileges to the Huguenots than those they had previously enjoyed.

Slowly however throughout all these ten years a power had been gathering that was about to plunge France into the broadest and bloodiest of all her civil wars. At the very commencement of Henry's reign the extreme Catholic party had been scandalized at the ease with which toleration

---

[1] Drion's *Histoire Chronologique*, etc., p. 145.

had been extended to the heretics, and its disaffection grew as that toleration was continued and enlarged. Many of the chief offices of State, as well as many of the leading provincial governments, had ordinarily been in the hands of some of the old nobility, members of this party in the State. But it now saw these gradually withdrawn from them to be put into the hands of those young favorites—his *Mignons* as they were called—by whom the King delighted to be surrounded. To make these gay and giddy youths the daily and nightly companions of his pleasures might have been tolerated; but to elevate them to places of dignity and power, and that to the exclusion of old and able servants of the Crown, was more difficult to endure. The effeminate frivolities and puerile superstitions in which the King indulged added contempt to scorn, and deprived Henry of that respect which a belief in his sincere attachment to Catholicism might still have preserved for him. It was truly one of the strangest pictures that royalty ever presented which Henry III. offered to the eyes of his subjects. Let us take a glance or two at life in the Louvre as it then went on. Henry sleeps in an apartment whose floor is strewn with roses and other flowers, on a bed hung with cloth of silver, his head reposing on crimson satin pillows, his body wrapped in a white satin night dress, his hands covered with richly embroidered gloves, and his face protected by a half mask saturated with odoriferous oil. The chief valet enters, and the laborious toilet begins. What this was in the royal chamber may be imagined from what meanwhile goes on in another room in the palace, in which one of his Mignons is passing through the process. The patient seats himself upon a chair, one valet holds a mirror before his face, another comes and with powder from a box of cypress wood powders his head. Another approaches, and with a delicate instrument removes all superfluous hair from his master's eyebrows; another comes, and after washing them with perfumed waters, first lays strongly one deep chosen color upon the beard, and then gently tinges with all appropriate corresponding hues the cheeks, lips, neck, and forehead. Then the various articles of dress are put on and adjusted—the doublet drawn so tight that two or three of these valets have to assist in buttoning it. Let the rings now be put upon the fingers and the chains of gold hung over the neck, and his embroidered handkerchief, and his portable mirror, and his comfit-box, and his hat and plumes be handed to him, and he is in fit attire to go and spend the forenoon with his royal master. Some idle hours of the forenoon are lounged away in a divan; the King and his favorites resting on velvet cushions, drinking sherbet, and serving out to one another the last and richest morsels of the current Court gossip, generally some tale of scandal that one blushes now to hear or read.

All the while the King is fondling the lap-dogs that lie in dozens around him, or making one of his best-taught parrots repeat the ribald refrain that he has been taught, or exciting one of his tame apes to grin and show its teeth. These little lap-dogs are especial favorites with their master. At one time he had about 2000 of them in his different palaces. Each half-dozen had a keeper with a yearly salary of 200 crowns. They slept generally in a room adjoining to the royal bed-chamber, fitted up with baskets and cushions of green velvet. But now the divan breaks up. A notion has seized the King to have an hour or two's amusement in the streets. The Chamberlain, the Chancellor, all the chief officers of State, are summoned to attend the King, and told the object of the summons. Once more the services of the numerous valets are in requisition, and, all richly and fantastically dressed, the cortége issues from the gates of the Louvre. And now the eyes of the Parisians are greeted by the King and his chief councillors, each with cup and ball in hand, trying, as they marched along the streets, to rival one another in the management of the new and wonderful toy. His favorite buffoon is by Henry's side; but it needs no jester to make the scene ridiculous. Bursts of laughter break from the ranks of the performers, echoed by like laughter from the spectators, in which one's ear catches undernotes of pity, contempt, or scorn. But let them wait till to-morrow, and these Parisians shall see their King and his attendants marching through the streets in a very different guise and on a very different errand. Overnight the King is seized with one of his superstitious fits. On first entering France as King, Henry had headed at Avignon a procession of the sacred society of Flagellants, whose habit it was to perambulate the streets dressed in sackcloth, each member holding a torch or olive-branch in the one hand, and a scourge in the other, with which he flogged his neighbor as they marched. For three hours, in the depth of winter, under inclement skies, did Henry, bareheaded and clad like the rest of them, lead such a company through the streets of Avignon—a procession that cost the great Cardinal of Lorraine his life. Not content with repeating the same in the streets of Paris, Henry instituted a new order of Penitents. And now at the head of this new order of his own, the King and the cup-and-ball players of yesterday are seen issuing on foot from the Monastery of the Augustinians to hold a Chapter of the Order in the cathedral of Notre Dame. Over the head of each penitent is drawn a sack of coarse canvas, with holes cut out for the eyes to look through, and long loose sleeves attached, the waist bound round with a hempen cord, from which a string of wooden beads, the rudest of rosaries, depends. Dressed thus, counting his beads, muttering his Paternosters and Ave Marias, scourged by his one neighbor, and scourging the other in his turn, the King of France is to be beheld on his way to prostrate himself before the high altar at Notre Dame, to lie prostrate there for hours. No wonder that all respect for royalty was well-nigh weeded out of the hearts of the Parisians. But with the folly of the Court there was vice—vice that one chooses not to describe; and with the vice there was cruelty—that heartless kind of cruelty with which licentiousness seems so naturally associated;—for these Mignons of the King were bullies too, as expert at the use of the sword as of the cup and ball: their bravery in part redeeming their effeminacy, and the strong attachment that they kindled in the breast of the King in part atoning for the follies and vices of their intercourse. Two of them fell once in a duel in which half-a-dozen of them were engaged, and the long and bitter agony of grief into which their death threw the King, tells us that a warm heart lay beneath that frivolous exterior.

It could only have been over very calm waters and under very quiet skies that such a royal bark as Henry guided could have gone on in safety. Unfortunately for him there came a terrible tempest, a storm that swept over Europe, and the frail vessel was wrecked. The demon that stirred this storm was Philip II. of Spain. Guided by the greatest and best man of his age, the Netherlanders had risen to throw off the Spanish yoke. Philip resolved to quell the insurrection by not leaving a heretic alive in the Low Countries. Alva labored hard to realize his monarch's project. The heads of Horn and Egmont, and the lives of 18,000 lesser victims, were the offering that he laid at his master's feet. But still the Netherlanders held out. England helped them, feebly yet openly, and they were helped, though clandestinely, by France. For the help so given Philip was resolved that both countries should feel the weight of his anger. With England it should be open war. The one great object of Philip's ambition—the idol of that dark den in which he lived—was to see a purely Romish and purely despotic policy dominant in Europe— the Spanish monarchy its centre and chief support. To the furtherance of that scheme England and Elizabeth stood out as the greatest obstacle in the way—England and Elizabeth must be crushed. To that first, and above all things, the efforts of the Spanish monarchy must be directed. So the scheme of the great Armada, of the invasion and conquest of this country, was devised. If France could not be got to help, she must be kept from hindering, by giving her enough to do in her own territories,— by Spain employing there the same weapons that France had used against her in Holland. The spirit of intestine discord was to be secretly fostered, and at the proper stage effective help was to be given. That stage arrived when, on the 15th June 1584, the Duke of Alençon, Henry's younger brother, expired. Neither Francis II. nor Charles

IX. had left any issue. Henry, the reigning monarch, was childless; with him the race of Valois became extinct. The next heir to the French throne was the young King of Navarre. But he was a heretic, and a heretic on the throne of France what true Catholic could tolerate? Serious but secret negotiations had already been going on between Philip and the house of Guise, the acknowledged head of the ultra-Catholic movement in France—a movement that had lately taken more and more the form of direct opposition to the reigning monarch. So early as in 1576 a Holy League had been formed in Picardy, its members bound by signature and solemn oath, under penalty of forfeiture of goods and life, to strive to the uttermost for the entire suppression of heresy. This League, though originally confined to a single province, had taken deep root and spread widely over the country. It now took a new, a more definite, a more formidable shape. In the Castle of Joinville, one of the châteaus of the Guises, there is still shown the chamber in which there assembled, in January 1585, two commissioned delegates from Spain, the Dukes of Guise, Mayenne, Aumale, Elbœuf, and others. Secret articles were drawn up, and a solemn oath was taken, by which the Leaguers bound themselves to resist unto death all toleration of heresy by whomsoever sanctioned; to labor in every way for its entire extirpation, and to oppose the accession of Henry of Navarre to the throne of France. The blow was aimed as well at the reigning monarch as at the heir-presumptive to the throne. As the direct if not the only effective way of gaining their ends, the Leaguers, on promise of help from Spain, resolved at the point of the sword either to compel Henry of Anjou to yield to their demands, or drive him from the throne, leaving the way to that throne temptingly open to the Duke of Guise himself. The standard of revolt was raised. A manifesto, setting forth the principles and objects of the League, appeared. All true Catholics were summoned to join it. To its deepest depths the spirit of religious fanaticism was stirred—the pulpit, the confessional, every instrument that the priesthood possessed, was employed to inflame the public mind. Large bodies of troops hastily assembled, and never did persecuted Huguenots rise to defend their lives and liberties with greater enthusiasm than did these heated adherents of Rome rise now to follow the young Duke of Guise as he embarked in this new crusade against heresy. The means were not wanting for Henry to have met and braved the rising storm, but the spirit was. Instead of throwing himself upon the support of the Montmorencys and the Huguenots, he bent ingloriously before the Guises, and on the 7th July 1585 he signed the celebrated Treaty of Nemours, by which all profession as well as all exercise of the Reformed faith in France was forbidden upon pain of death—one month given to Huguenot ministers, six to the people, within which they must abjure or emigrate.

When Henry of Navarre first heard the fatal tidings he bent his head upon his hand and was silent. For a moment he imagined that all was lost. "Unhappy France," he at last exclaimed, "I can then do nothing for you!" A courier from the Marshal Montmorency restored his courage. Traced hastily on the paper were the words, "Sire, I have seen the Treaty of Nemours. The King of France and the King of Spain wish to gain me; but I am yours, with my brothers and my army." The heart of Navarre revived. Knowing well where the heart and soul of the League lay, he sent off a cartel to the Duke of Guise, challenging him to single combat—a challenge that was courteously declined. The revenues of the kingdom of Navarre were but limited, ill-fitted to sustain such a war as seemed now impending; but Henry had other resources to draw upon. Coming out one day at Nérac from a meeting of his Council, in which his lack of funds had been brought fully out by Sully, taking his future great minister of finance aside, Henry said to him, "Baron of Rosny, it is not enough to speak well; we must act better. Are you not resolved that we shall die together? It is no time then to be frugal. All men of honor must venture now one-half of their estate to save the other." "No, no, Sire," said Rosny, "we shall not die together; we shall live together. I have still a wood that will produce 100,000 francs, and all shall be employed upon this occasion." At the close of the conversation, on parting with Sully, Henry said, "Well, my friend, return to your country, be diligent, bring as many friends with you as you can," with an arch smile adding, "and do not forget your forest of high trees." If Henry had the happy art of making others generous, he was as generous himself. The six months of grace at first allowed to the Huguenots, when it was seen that Montmorency and Navarre were resolved to have recourse to arms, was reduced to fifteen days. Many, whose goods were confiscated, and whose lives were in imminent peril, fled to Béarn. Henry gave them all he had to give. "As to us," said he gayly to his soldiers, "we shall go and find our living in the camp of the League."

But before he and the Leaguers met in arms Henry had to face another foe. Sixtus V. fulminated against him a Papal Bull, in which, as a relapsed heretic, he was declared incapable of all succession, excommunicated, and dethroned, his subjects released from all allegiance; all who recognized him in any way as a sovereign threatened with the heaviest penalties of the Church. One morning, soon after this Bull was promulgated, the eyes of the inhabitants of Rome were greeted with large placards, stuck upon the walls of their streets, on the doors of their Churches, one seen even fastened to the gateway of the Vatican. It was Henry's answer to the Papal Bull. One sentence tells the spirit of the whole. "And in that which touches the crime of heresy, of which the King of Navarre is falsely accused, he says and maintains, that Sixtus, calling himself Pope, hath falsely and maliciously lied, and that he is himself a heretic, as shall be made manifest in full council, freely and lawfully assembled." The Pope's first feeling on hearing of these placards was that of astonishment and rage. He could not however but secretly admire the vigor that gave stroke for stroke in such a way as this; this admiration grew as he followed Henry's after steps, so that he was heard one day to declare, that of all the monarchs of Europe there were but two whom, if they had not been heretics, he could entirely trust,—Elizabeth of England and Henry of Navarre.

To give time for the foreign succors to arrive, Henry resolved to attempt no great enterprise at first. He retained with himself in Gascony a small body of veteran soldiers, lightly armed, accustomed to fatigue, and wholly without baggage. Aware that he was so slenderly attended, Mayenne and Matignan, with two royal armies, closed upon and hemmed him in, till his position between the Garonne and the Pyrenees became perilous in the extreme; so much so, that Mayenne wrote to his friends in Paris that it was impossible he could escape. Henry however, in the mean time, was writing to his friends in quite a different strain. Having resolved to find or force a way through Mayenne's posts, he writes to De Batz, one of the friends he wished to join him in the enterprise, "Monsieur, they have surrounded me like a beast of the chase, and think that they will take me by the net. For my part, I intend to pass through them or over them. I have chosen my good men, and one of them is my mower. My mower, put wings to your best beast. I have told Montespan that he will have to break the wind of his—why? Thou shalt know at Nérac. Hurry, run, come, fly; such is the order of your master and the prayer of your friend, Henry." When he got his mower and other friends around him, Henry left Nérac, followed by about 200 horse. As they approached the enemy's lines he divided his little band into still smaller companies. Twenty chosen men he kept beside himself. Assigning to all a rendezvous on the opposite side of the Garonne, as the sun went down he took a by-path through the woods and heaths, well known to him by his having often hunted there, crossed the river, rode all night through the enemy's quarters, quite close to them at times, reached St. Foy, the appointed place of meeting, two hours before day had fully broken, and had the happiness to meet there all the rest of the 200, not a single mishap nor loss having occurred.

Henry now took up his head-quarters at Rochelle. Again and again the King of France, writhing under the heavy pressure of the League, had entreated him to change his faith, assuring him in that case of the succession. Henry steadily at this time resisted every proposal of the kind as one that it would be hurtful to his honor even to entertain. He consented, however, to have a personal interview with Catherine de Medicis, who came to St. Bris, December 15th, 1586, attended by her maids of honor,—that flying squadron, as it was called, by which so many of her intrigues were conducted, and not a few of her political conquests had so ingloriously been gained. No little alarm was felt among the Huguenots when it was known that this interview was to take place. The alarm turned out to be groundless. Henry knew thoroughly with whom he had to do. In serious argument Catherine found in him her match, in lighter repartee her superior. "Is all this trouble, then," said she to him at last, "to bear no fruit? will you give us no repose?" "Madame," said Henry, "I am not to blame. It is not I who keep you from sleeping in your bed. It is you who keep me from sleeping in mine." "Shall I always, then, be kept in trouble!" exclaimed the Queen; "I, who desire nothing so much as repose?" "Oh! Madame," said Henry gayly, "the trouble you take does you infinite good. You could not live if you were in repose." "What is there," at last said the Queen, somewhat petulantly, "what is it that you would have?" "Nothing that you have here," said Henry, casting a glance at the flying squadron,—a sarcasm coarse but merited. The conference came to nothing. The last effort of the arch intriguer failed. It was for the sword alone to decide the issue.

The war, called from the three leading actors in it the War of the Three Henrys, now opened in earnest. Seven powerful armies were marshalled on the part of the King of France and the League. The Huguenots were weak in numbers, but strong in the quality of their troops. An immense body of German *Reiter* had been enrolled to act as an auxiliary force, and for some time had been hovering on the frontiers. Hearing that at last they had entered France, Henry of Navarre set out from Rochelle to effect a junction with them. The Duke of Joyeuse, one of the French King's chief favorites, who had the charge of the army that occupied the midland counties, resolved to prevent their junction. By a rapid movement he succeeded in crossing the line of Henry's march and forcing him into action. The two armies came in front of each other on a plain near the village of Coutras, on the 19th of October 1587. The Royalist army numbered from 10,000 to 12,000, the Huguenot from 6000 to 7000—the usual disparity in numbers; but Henry's skilful disposition did more than compensate for his numerical inferiority. He had only three pieces of cannon, but they were planted so that when they opened fire upon the crowded ranks of the enemy, from twelve to twenty men were carried away by each discharge, while the heavy guns of the Royalists did little or no execution. A body of light cavalry was thrown out in advance to meet the first shock of the enemy's assault. Behind this, squadrons of heavy cavalry were drawn up, interspersed with companies of musketeers, five men deep, the front rank instructed to kneel, so that the whole might fire at once, the order issued being that no trigger was to be drawn till the enemy was within twenty yards. His ground well chosen, and his men well placed, Henry waited the approach of the Royal army. It was a dazzling sight that struck the eyes of the Huguenots, as, about eight o'clock on the morning of the 20th, that army spread itself out in battle-array before them,—glittering helmets, nodding plumes, doublets of silk and velvet, scarfs and bannerets of all brilliant colors, embroidered with gold and silver, floating from shoulder and from lance-head. As he stood gazing on a battalion of 1200 lances, the whole front rank of which consisted of nobles, some one called Henry's attention to the brilliancy of their arms. "We shall have all the better aim at them," said he, "when the fight begins." The Huguenots now fell upon their knees. There was stillness in the ranks as prayer was offered up. "What are they doing?" said Joyeuse to one of his officers, as he looked upon their cowering ranks of ill-clad, dingy-looking men. "They kneel—they are afraid." "Don't think so," said the officer, who had fought once in their ranks; "they are never so terrible as after prayer." At that moment the kneeling ranks all rose, and there pealed out the first verse of one of Marot's psalms. Henry now passed along the ranks, dropping words as he went by that fired all hearts. The first charge of the Royalists was now made. The shock was so severe that the light cavalry of the Huguenots gave way, and was driven back through the centre of the line upon the village of Coutras. Confident in his numbers, anticipating nothing but victory, thinking indeed that victory was already his, Joyeuse gave orders to his whole line to charge. The order was impetuously obeyed; but they had half a mile and more to cross before they closed with the enemy. Their horses got blown. Their ranks got into confusion as they so hurriedly advanced. An eagle eye was on them from the moment they began to move. Henry pressed the white-plumed helmet firmly on his head, waited till the distance between the ranks was scarce more than twenty yards, then at his command the deadly volley of the musketeers was given, and following the white plume as it dashed on in front, the veterans of Jarnac and Moncontour flung themselves upon the foe. The glittering but now divided ranks went down before them as the corn does at the stroke of the reaper. The struggle lasted but an hour, yet within that hour the Catholic army lost 3000 men, more than 400 of whom were members of the first families in the kingdom; 3000 men were made prisoners. Not more than a third part of their entire army escaped. The Huguenots lost only about 200 men. All through that bloody hour Henry was fighting hand to hand. Some of his attendants threw themselves before him at the very first to break the shock of the enemy. "Make way there!" cried Henry; "give room; you stifle me; I would be seen!" Not even in the thick of such a savage butchery as that hour at Coutras did Henry's unquenchable gayety forsake him. "Yield thee, Philistine, yield!" he shouted to a Roman Catholic officer he laid hold of, having just shot with his pistol another who had come to his rescue. And when the victory was clearly won, he did every thing he could to stop the carnage. When told that Joyeuse himself had fallen, he showed the tenderest concern at his fate, and had his body borne to a hall in the neighboring castle of Coutras. He went there himself to see it, and putting back the long fair hair, all dabbled with blood, with his own hand, that he might gaze upon the face of the dead, tears dropped upon the blood. He gave orders that the body should be embalmed and borne to Paris, to be delivered to the relatives of the deceased. His moderation of spirit was equally remarkable. He expressed no triumph as prisoner after prisoner of noble birth, as banner after banner, was brought into the hall where he sat at supper. Eighty-four ensigns taken from the enemy were floating around him. When some one asked him what terms of peace after a victory so signal he would demand, "The same," said he, "as at first." Before night fell he wrote a few lines to the French King, which run thus:—"Sire, my Lord and Brother,—Thank God, I have beaten your enemies and your army." It was but too true that the poor King's worst enemies were to be found in the very armies that were marshalled in his name.

Whilst Henry of Navarre gathered laurels from his victory at Coutras, scarce less renown, though won less worthily, accrued to Henry Duke of Guise from the victories obtained by him over the German confederates, whom he succeeded in chasing out of France. Birth, nature, education, surrounding circumstances, all conspired to mould the Duke of Guise into the great chief of a faction. He was the head of a family that in point of political position and power was inferior only to that of the Princes of the blood, and in point of wealth had added to its own patrimonial resources the revenues of fifteen bishoprics and of five provincial governments. His tall commanding figure, his light flowing hair, his lively piercing eyes, his face, which a wound got in battle marked without disfiguring (bestowing on him the epithet of le Balafré), were all gazed on with admiration by the multitude. In all military exercises he was unrivalled. He was seen once to swim against the current of a stream clad in complete armor. Without either the military genius of the one or the political talent of the other, he added the address of his uncle the Cardinal to the bravery of his father the Duke. Though never displaying the skill of a great commander, he was the dashing and gallant leader of many a military enterprise where prompt decision and unflinching courage were displayed. Ready to share with his soldiers all the perils of war, he was as ready to share with them its honors and rewards. An artist is represented as having painted his portrait, and on being asked why he had not planted a wreath of laurels on the brow—"Because," he said, "the Duke would have plucked them off and distributed them among his companions in arms." The courtesy of his manners, especially to his inferiors in rank, was complete. Reserved to those immediately around him, seldom indeed admitting them to his confidence, often alienated in this way from the members of his own family, he would cross the street hat in hand to hail some acquaintance of low degree. He had an eye that never failed in the most crowded companies to notice all whom it became him to salute, and the grace of his recognition and conversation was such that a'l felt delighted and honored by them. Old family alliances, the sincerity and zeal of his own attachment to the Roman Catholic religion, and his consistent devotedness to the interests of the Church, placed him now at the head of the Catholic party, and made him the idol and main pillar of the League. At Paris especially his popularity outran all bounds. The King had done really more to rid France of the Swiss and Germans, but in the eyes of the Parisians the Duke carried off the main share of glory. "Saul," they chanted through the streets, "has slain his thousands, but David his tens of thousands." Already he had obliged the King to issue the edict of Nemours, and now still further demands were made, the effect of granting which would be the virtual transfer of the chief authority in the State from the sovereign to the subject. The King felt bitterly the humiliation, but wanted the courage, perhaps the power, at once openly and peremptorily to refuse compliance. Whatever were the Duke's own ultimate designs, there can be no doubt that the bigoted Parisians, inflamed at this time almost to madness by all kinds of ecclesiastical stimulants, meant to dethrone Henry of Anjou and plant the crown on the Duke's brow. Three times in the course of this winter (1587–88) schemes were concocted for seizing the King's person, and consigning him for life to a monastery,—schemes that failed only in consequence of information conveyed secretly by Nicholas Poullain to the King. Alarmed at last as to his position, which grew daily more perilous, the King sent for 2000 Swiss, and had them stationed in the immediate neighborhood of Paris. The Leaguers, with Paris now thoroughly organized at their command, sent for the Duke of Guise. Henry heard of it, and despatched message after message interdicting his approach. In defiance the Duke entered the city (on Monday, the 9th of May 1588). Accompanied by the Queen-mother he went, in the first instance, unarmed and unattended, to pay his respects to Henry in the Louvre. They found the entrance to the Palace strictly guarded, and passed in through ranks of frowning soldiers, whose captain scarce returned the Duke's salute. The King had for the moment opened his ear to those councillors who advised that if Guise ventured into the royal presence he should not leave it alive. In the audience-chamber Catherine's quick eye soon saw that some deed of violence was meditated. She laid her hand, weakened now with age, but still strong enough to control him, upon her son, and, after a stormy interview, Guise was permitted to leave the palace untouched. Feeling the imminence of his peril he threw himself upon the city for protection. Paris was at this time filled with strangers, partisans of the League, many of them men of desperate fortune, fitted for any deed. Next day the King issued a royal edict, commanding all such to depart within twenty-four hours. Officers were despatched to make domiciliary visits throughout the city, and to see that this edict was carried out. These officers returned to the Palace with the information that they had been ill treated in the execution of their office by the citizens, and that the Royal edict had fallen powerless to the ground. Henry now resolved it should be obeyed, and the troops outside the town were ordered to enter. The intelligence of their coming spread like wildfire through the city. The wildest rumors were set afloat: Guise and others were to be beheaded—the city was to be sacked—Navarre and the Huguenots to be called in to the King's help. As the Swiss entered, and in scattered detachments marched to the different posts allotted to them, infuriated crowds followed and closed in upon them. At the ends of the streets and the openings of the squares they occupied, strong barricades began to rise, the first appearance of that powerful instrument of city warfare with which the streets of Paris were destined in after times to be so familiar. The troops were cut off thus in sections from one another. Their officers sent for orders to the Palace. If allowed to charge before these barricades were completed, and before the full force of the city was called out, the outbreak might still be quelled. The King sent strict orders to act solely on the defensive, and not to fire upon the people. There then for hours they stood, whilst thousands of well-armed men swarmed out from every purlieu of a city that was now in the full tide of revolution. Some of the more moderate Leaguers went to the palace, entreated the King to withdraw the troops. He would not consent. He vainly thought that their simple presence would awe the wild community into submission. It had just the opposite effect. It stirred them into intenser and intenser hate. It needed but a chance collision for the bloodshed to begin. The soldiers acting at such disadvantage had no chance against such odds. They were speedily overpowered. "I have defeated the Swiss," wrote the Duke in a circular he sent off by hundreds to the provinces, "cut to pieces the greater part of the King's guard, and I now hold the Louvre so closely besieged that you may be certain I will render good account of all whom it contains." Nevertheless the Duke had never appeared as the leader of the insurrection, but had kept quiet all the time within his own hotel, giving it to be understood at the Palace that it was not his doing. But now his triumph was complete. Had the street conflict continued much longer, every man of the Swiss must have perished. The King submitted to the humiliation of sending to Guise, requesting him to interfere and open a way for their retreat. And now the Duke went forth unarmed from his hotel. At his bidding the firing ceased; openings through the barricades were made for them; the Swiss were saved. But the King himself was still in danger. Barricade after barricade had been pushed on closer and closer to the Louvre, and the mob was in no mood to stop. It was the hand of the Duke alone that could hold them back. Would he do it? Henry would not stoop to ask the question, but the Queen-mother went to the Duke to learn upon what terms an accommodation between him and the King might be adjusted. They were too high, too haughtily insisted on, for even Catherine, friend as she was of Guise, to ask her son to accept. There was but one opening for Henry left—instant, though it were ignominious, flight. The gates of the city were guarded, all but one behind the Palace, which somehow or other the Leaguers had overlooked, though strangely enough the orders had been issued that it should be done that very night. Having arranged all with her son, the Queen-mother went a second time to see the Duke. She found him as inexorable as ever. Turning to an attendant, under pretext of sending him to obtain unlimited power from the King for her to treat with Guise, Catherine sent by him the preconcerted signal upon which Henry was instantly to act. Turning back again to the Duke, she took up in turn his proposals, dwelling at great length on each, arguing each point with the utmost coolness. Some hours had passed when a friend of the Duke rushed into the apartment and whispered a few hurried words into his ear. "Madame," exclaimed he, starting to his feet in the utmost excitement, "you have betrayed me. The King has quitted Paris. I am lost, for his Majesty will be more my enemy than ever." Catherine feigned surprise and incredulity. To ascertain, as she represented, whether there was any truth in the report, she hurried to the Palace. The King was gone. The day of the Barricades, as it was called, was over, and both the great actors in the drama had failed: the King in taking advantage of the opportunity, which he undoubtedly at first possessed, for preventing or crushing the outbreak; the Duke in suffering the King's escape, and with the chance of getting him wholly into his hands.

Burning with indignation, Henry fled to Chartres. Many an anxious glance was cast by him at that only quarter from which effective help could come; but he could not as yet bring his mind to enter into any compact or association with heretics. A fresh terror fell upon his spirit. Philip of Spain had some months before communicated privately to the Duke of Guise that the time for his breaking openly with his monarch had now come, and that if he did it promptly and vigorously all needful help in men and money would come from Spain. Guise was leaning upon that promise when he urged the Parisians to revolt, and Philip was leaning upon that revolt when he launched his great Armada against England; and those 150 stately ships, with their crowded crews, were coasting along the shores of France when Henry was invited once more to set himself right with the Leaguers. The Armada loosed from the ports of Spain on the 29th May 1588, and in the month of July, before its fate was sealed and England rescued, Henry signed an edict by which he placed himself once more at the head of the League—announcing it to be his purpose to prosecute to the last extremity the war against the Huguenots, and declared the King of Navarre, as a heretic, incapable of the succession. The Estates of the Kingdom were at the same time summoned to meet at Blois in October. The heavy price at which Guise's renewed friendship was thus purchased rendered the Duke more odious than ever in the King's eyes. The meeting of the States-General was opened by a speech from the Throne. Henry at last had risen to a full comprehension of his position, and resolved to make a final effort to save at once his person and his throne. He had a great talent for public speaking. That talent he now exerted to the uttermost. "I know not," says Ranke, "that ever a French King delivered a more remarkable discourse than that with which Henry opened these Estates." He went as far in his concessions as a monarch could be expected to go. But it was in vain. The League had packed the assembly. It was the Duke, not Henry, who was sovereign there. The whole assembly indeed united with the King in taking a solemn oath that the edict of Union lately issued from the throne should be obeyed. But that was the first and only act in which the King and the Estates agreed. He was willing to declare Henry of Navarre incapable of succession so long as he remained a heretic; but they demanded that he should be instantly, absolutely and forever excluded—and that upon the extreme and extraordinary ground that for a king even to tolerate heresy was to nullify his title.

Henry resisted a demand that would have cut away his own title from beneath his feet. He was ready to consent that every measure of the Government should in the first instance be submitted to the Estates, and after adoption by them, and approval of his Council, should be acted on. They demanded that their decisions should at once, and without right of revisal anywhere, become law. Henry desired that some adequate provision should be made for the maintenance of the Royal household. He was at the time in abject poverty—the wages of his servants, the pay of his guards, in large arrears. Confessing freely his former extravagances, he announced it to be his purpose to reduce his expenditure to the lowest point possible. He showed them the clothes he wore, and told them how long he meant to make them last. If two capons were too much for the royal table, he would be content, he said, with one. He stooped even to make a personal appeal on this matter to the generosity of the Duke. The States turned a deaf ear to all his entreaties, and resolved, instead of increasing, to reduce the royal revenue. The appeal to the Duke was equally fruitless. Hope and patience were exhausted, and now there burst forth the long and pent-up hate—the thirst intense for vengeance. The rebellious Duke must die.[1] It confirmed the

---

[1] The deed was done against the advice of Catherine, who died a few days afterwards, having seen three of her sons

King in his purpose when, from his faithful friend Epernon, from the Duchess d'Aumale, from Guise's own brother, there came to him no ambiguous notification that his own liberty and life were in danger from some new enterprise plotted by the Duke. Despairing of bringing him to justice by public trial, Henry resolved that Guise should be assassinated. The plan was coolly and skilfully contrived. A Council of State was summoned to meet at eight o'clock on the morning of the 23d December 1588. The hall in the Castle of Blois in which the members met communicated with the King's private cabinet; a small anteroom and then a bedchamber lay between them. It was in one or other of these two apartments that the deed was to be done. Closely as the secret was kept, a terrible suspicion that an attempt on the life of their chief was meditated took possession of Guise's friends. On the 22d several anonymous notes were thrown upon his table, one of them bearing—"Be on your guard; a dangerous attempt is about to be made upon your life." The Duke took a pencil and wrote beneath—"He dare not." A conference was held in his apartment. Some urged instant flight. The Duke demurred. "Affairs," said he, "are now in such a state, that if I saw death coming in by the window, I would not go out by the door." Schomberg, one of his truest friends, spoke

successively fill the throne, and a fourth, as she died, ready to lose it.

to him of the peril of his position. "I do not know the man on earth," replied the Duke, "who, hand to hand with me, would not have more reason to fear than I." Nevertheless he resolved to leave Blois the next forenoon. That night he supped in the apartments of Madame de Noirmoutiers. No less than five notes of warning were handed to him while at supper—he thrust them all beneath the couch, repeating always, "He dare not." On retiring to his own apartment at three o'clock in the morning, he was surprised to find his uncle there, who had crept into the room in the dark to give him his last warning. He turned it off with the accustomed speech—"He dare not." His contempt of Henry blinded him to the last. It was a cold, dark, dismal morning (on the 23d), the rain was pouring in torrents, when, between five and six o'clock, the King's body-guard of forty-five—whose captain was alone privy to what was to be done—stole gently, man by man, up a secret staircase, and found themselves in the presence of the King. A few nobles, whom he could entirely trust, assembled at the same time in the royal cabinet. To both Henry addressed a few emphatic words. "This day," said he to the members of his guard, "is destined to be the last of my life or that of the Duke of Guise. It is for you to decide whether he shall perish or your master be the victim." The answer was all that Henry could have wished. Eight out of the forty-five, who had daggers as well as swords, were then stationed in the antechamber, and to them the execution of the deed of blood was committed. So soon as he learned that Guise was in the Hall of Council, Henry sent his valet to summon him to a private interview in the royal cabinet. The Duke, who was standing warming himself at the fire, on getting the message hastily gathered his cloak around him, and, with a gracious salute to the other members of the Council, passed into the anteroom. The dark and lowering countenances of the men stationed there startled him as he crossed the floor; he had turned round to look at them, and was lifting the tapestry to pass into the bedroom, when the eight flung themselves upon him. Arms and legs were grasped, and swords and daggers pierced him in different parts of his body. He was encumbered with his cloak, and could do nothing to defend himself. Yet such was his extraordinary strength, that he dragged the men that clung to him and were still stabbing at him, from one end of the chamber to the other, falling at last at the foot of the King's bed, where in a few minutes he expired.

The news of the assassination reached Paris on the afternoon of the 24th December 1588. It was Christmas eve, and the people were gathered in the churches for the nocturnal services of the great Christian festival. A night consecrated by the traditions of Christendom to cheerful joy was turned into one of gloom and mourning. The midnight and the morning masses were recited in the midst of a silence broken only by sobs and muffled imprecations. Grief quickly gave place to rage. The people rushed tumultuously from the churches, demanding vengeance on the murderer of the Duke. The statues of Henry III., the pictures of him in the churches, the royal arms suspended in different parts of the city, were cut down, were torn in pieces, were trampled under foot, or cast into the gutters. A fanatical priesthood guided and ruled the populace; all kinds of means were taken to kindle into fury its enmity to the King. His name was dropped out of the public prayers. By day and by night, under priestly marshalling, vast processions paraded through the streets; 100,000 youths, each holding a lighted taper in his hand, assembled in the Cemetery of the Innocents, marched to the ancient Abby of Ste. Geneviève,—stopped as they reached its portals, and dashing their tapers to the ground, exclaimed, as they quenched the flame, "So perish the race of Valois!" Preaching to a great multitude, Lincestre, one of the chief orators of the League, called upon his audience to take upon the spot a solemn oath that they would avenge to the last drop of their blood the death of their favorite. "Lift up your right hands," he said, "and swear." One man only hesitated. It was Harlay, the first President of the Parliament. "Lift up your hand, Monsieur le Président," cried the excited preacher. Harlay hesitated, but partially obeyed. "Lift it still higher; lift it so high that every man may see it." The frightened President had to do as he was told. Paris, in fact, was for a time wholly under the dominion of that faction which had adopted the strange politico-ecclesiastical theory woven for the use of the League by the expert hands of the Jesuits, according to which the sovereign civil power (subject, however, always to the Papacy) lay in the people, to whom pertained the right of electing and dethroning kings. And Paris acted now, as it has so often done, as the representative of the people of France. The Sorbonne issued its declaration that Henry had forfeited the throne, and that his subjects were released from their allegiance. The Parliament of Paris adopted and ratified the declaration. The Council of Sixteen, under whom the general community was organized, proceeded as if the throne were vacant, and called upon the Duke of Mayenne to assume the supreme power, under the title of Lieutenant-Governor of France. The Duke, after some hesitation, for he was a slow and cautious man, accepted the office. The spirit of Paris spread over the country. Henry had counted on the death of their chief quenching the spirit of the Leaguers; instead of that, he heard only of new forms of opposition, new instances of resistance to his authority. In the north of France, town after town followed the lead of Paris, till at last a few cities upon the Loire were all that he could count upon. Week by week his position became more perilous. It was evident that his best, if not indeed his only, chance lay in effecting an alliance with Henry of Navarre, still in arms with his Huguenots in the south of France, bravely and successfully battling there against both Royalists and Leaguers. It was not an easy thing for the chief counsellor of the massacre of St. Bartholomew to make up his mind to this alliance. He tried, in fact, all that he could to avoid it. He made overture after overture to Mayenne; but they were all indignantly repelled. The Duke was too confident, trusting to the support of all true Catholics in France, and encouraged to do so by the approving judgment of the Pope. Henry at last yielded to the advice of his wisest counsellors, and consented to receive Duplessis-Mornay as envoy from the King of Navarre. The Béarnese threw himself heartily and chivalrously into the King's cause. By a treaty signed 26th April 1589 he bound himself to employ the whole force at his command in his service. Leaving his army a day or two's march behind, he hastened forward, but slenderly attended, accepting an invitation from the King to visit him at Plessis-les-Tours. After years of separation and hostility the cousins met in the park of the Château. So great a crowd had filled the grounds, and so eagerly did they press in to witness the important interview, that for nearly half-an-hour the two Kings, though within a short distance of one another, were unable to effect a meeting. The way at last was opened, and Henry of Bourbon bent the knee before Henry of Valois. The latter hastened to raise and to embrace him. The two Princes retired to the château for an interview, equally satisfactory to both. On retiring to his quarters that evening on the other side the Loire, Navarre wrote to his friend and counsellor Duplessis-Mornay:—"At last the ice is broken, not without many warnings that if I came here I came to die. I have passed the water commending myself to God." "Sire," wrote Mornay in reply, "you have done what you ought to have done, but what none of us ought to have ventured to advise." Next morning at six o'clock, without mentioning his purpose to any one, on foot, and attended by a single page, the King of Navarre crossed the river, entered the château, and surprised the French King in his bed. The frankness, the heartiness, the confidingness of the Béarnese Prince dispelled all clouds of doubt from Henry's mind. All was concerted for the campaign as projected by the warrior-Prince. Navarre returned to his army, but he had scarce reached the camp when intelligence was brought of a bold attempt of Mayenne's to surprise and seize upon the King. Navarre hurried instantly to the scene. But he came too late. A band of his own gallant Huguenots under Chatillon had rendered good service in repelling the night assault of the Leaguers, and, alarmed at the very sight of the white scarfs, Mayenne had given up the attempt and had retired. "Ventre St. Gris!" exclaimed the King of Navarre, as, booted and spurred, and covered with mud, having been on horseback from daybreak, he burst into the royal presence, "had I been here he would have decamped after a different fashion. The armies of the two Kings united and advanced upon Paris. On their route they learned that the Pope had fulminated the thunders of an excommunication against the French monarch. The weak spirit of Henry of Valois quailed for the time beneath the stroke. For two days he refused all nourishment; he fancied for the moment that all good Catholics would shun him as one suspected with the leprosy. However, Navarre was beside to cheer him up. "My brother," said he gayly, "the bolts of Rome don't touch Kings when they conquer. I know an asylum where you will be safe enough from their stroke—in Paris. To-morrow from St. Cloud I will show you that ungrateful city, and will crush it with bolts of even greater power than those of Rome." On the evening of Saturday the 30th July the allied army, swelled to the number of from 35,000 to 40,000, sat down before the capital. Mayenne had sent more than 9000 regular troops with which to conduct the defence. The assault was fixed for Tuesday the 2d August. The doom of the capital seemed sealed. Its only hope lay in the fanatical courage of its inhabitants. The Pope's recent Bull had put into the hands of the priestly haranguers a new instrument of excitement. The wildest projects were openly announced and encouraged. In the course of one of his frantic tirades from the pulpit, Lincestre held up to the people a little chandelier that had once, he said, been the King's, around which there were moulded figures of satyrs. "See," said he, pointing to these strange figures, "these are the demons of the King, these are the gods he worships, the instruments of his enchantment. Would it be lawful to kill such a tyrant? For myself, I would be quite ready to do it at any moment of my life, save that in which I am consecrating the Body of the Lord." Among those whom harangues like this excited was a Dominican monk, Jacques Clement, —young, ignorant, superstitious, imaginative, passionate,—who had been a soldier before he became a monk, who as a monk had been guilty of a scandal that brought disgrace upon his convent, and who had been taught that so great a sin as his could be expiated alone by some great act of service rendered to the Church. The idea seized him that that great act would be the ridding France and the world of Henry of Valois. His only scruple was about his office. He asked the superior of his convent if it would be a mortal sin in a priest to kill a tyrant. He was told it would only be an irregularity. The Duchess of Montpensier, the sister of the murdered Duke of Guise, heard of and sent for the young Dominican. He told her that for three nights running an angel had appeared to him, and said, "Brother Jacques, I am a messenger from the Almighty come to assure you that by your hands the tyrant of France must be put to death. The crown of martyrdom is prepared for you." The blandishments and promises of the beautiful Duchess were not less powerful than the words of the angel. The monk bought a knife and bathed it in what he believed to be a decoction of poisonous herbs. Getting access to the Bastile where many of the Royalists lay imprisoned, he introduced himself to the brother-in-law of Epernon, the King's great favorite, and by playing the part of a Royalist got a passport to carry him through the Royal army. A letter in his favor to the King, in which the handwriting of the first President of the Parliament was so well imitated that, after the keenest scrutiny, it escaped detection, was put into his hands. Prepared thus, he set forth from the city on the forenoon of Sunday the 31st, the very day that the King reached St. Cloud. On the way he was overtaken by the King's Attorney-General, M. La Guesle, to whom he showed his credentials, stating that he had a communication of the utmost moment to make to the King from his friends in the city. La Guesle offered to be the medium of its conveyance. Jacques quietly but resolutely declined. He must see the King himself. The Attorney-General carefully inspected the credentials; he could detect no flaw. The severest cross-examination of Jacques himself afforded no ground of suspicion. Taking him to his own residence, La Guesle went instantly on his arrival at St. Cloud to Henry himself, and told him of the young monk and his errand. The King commanded him to be brought to him next morning. Jacques supped with the servants of the Attorney-General, cutting his bread with the knife that he carried, and gibed by them for knowing the use of his knife better than that of his breviary. He slept so soundly that they had to waken him next morning to take him to the King. Henry was sitting half-dressed in his closet when it was told him that the young monk stood without waiting an audience. The King looked over the credentials he had brought, and desired him to be introduced. "My brother," said Henry to him as he entered, "you are welcome. What is the news in Paris?" Clement craved permission to speak to him alone. The officers of the bed-chamber resented the proposal, and bade the monk go on and say out all he had to say, for none but the friends of the King were in the room. Clement hesitated. The King then ordered those around him to retire for a moment or two. Clement put a letter into his hand. The King's eye was fixed upon the page, when, snatching his knife out from his sleeve, the monk plunged it to its hilt into the body of the King. Henry seized the handle, which the assassin had let go, drew out the knife, and struck Clement with it on the face. "Ah, my God," he cried, "that wicked monk has killed me!" At the cry the attendants rushed into the apartment. Seeing at once how the matter stood, they passed their swords through the assassin, leaving only a mutilated corpse to be dealt with by the public executioner. The bleeding monarch was laid back upon his bed. At first but little pain was felt, and it was thought he might recover. The hope had soon to be relinquished. At the first tidings of the disaster Henry hurried to the lodgings of the King. He was most affectionately received. The King spoke to him as the legitimate heir to the Crown; but exhorted him, as he regarded his safety in the next world and his position in this, to change his religion. Addressing himself to the courtiers, many of them in high office, who filled the chamber,—"I entreat you as my friends," he said, "and as your King I command, that after my death you recognize my brother here as my successor." He then invited them to take the oath of allegiance to Navarre in his presence, which they did. The rest of the day was given up to the exercises of devotion. Between two and three o'clock next morning the King expired—the last of a family which gave thirteen Kings to France, whose reigns extended over a period of 261 years.

CHAPTER VII.

HENRY IV., 1589–1593.

Acknowledgment of title.—Arrangement with the Catholic Lords.—Their desertion.—The battle of Arques.—Siege of Paris.—Relief of the city.—Siege of Rouen.—Adventure of the King.—Triumph of Parma.—Abjuration of Henry IV.

A SHORT time after the King breathed his last, Henry of Navarre entered the chamber of the dead. An ominous reception was given to him. Hats that should have been raised were pressed down upon the brow, hands that should have been held out were drawn back, voices that should have saluted him as King he heard muttering "rather die a thousand deaths!" It was a critical moment in the history of this great Prince. The slightest hesitation on his part might have proved fatal. But he assumed at once, and exercised, all the prerogatives of royalty. The Catholic nobles and courtiers retired to deliberate. They were all ready to acknowledge the legitimacy of his title as next by birth in the order of succession; but in the opinion of nearly all of them his faith as a Calvinist disqualified for the occupancy of the throne. It was resolved that they should tender their allegiance to him on condition of his immediate adoption of the Roman Catholic religion. Henry had always resisted the attempt to force upon him a change of faith. "I have been often summoned," he had said in a manifesto addressed to the Estates of France, and published three months before this time, "to change my religion; but how? —the dagger at my throat. If I had no respect to my conscience, my honor would have hindered it. What would the best Catholics say of me if, after having lived thirty years in one way, they saw me suddenly change my religion in hope of a kingdom; and what would they say who have seen and tried my courage if I quitted basely through fear the form in which I have served God from the day of my birth? No, gentlemen; it will never be the King of Navarre who will do that, though he had thirty crowns to gain." His answer now to these Catholic lords was to the same effect. To expect from him, he said, so sudden a change of faith, was virtually to say he had no faith to change. He was ready, as he had always been, to abide by the decisions of a General Council; and he was ready to give all possible guarantees that the rights and freedom of his Roman Catholic subjects should be protected, as indeed they had always been wherever his sway had extended. But he would go no further. Within an hour after Henry's death, he had directed that instant measures should be taken to gain the adhesion of the large body of Swiss auxiliaries which formed part of the royal army. While he was yet disputing with the nobles and courtiers, the welcome intelligence arrived that the Swiss had engaged to remain in the new King's service. "Sire," said the gallant officer who brought the happy news to him, "you are the King of the brave, and none but cowards will abandon you." A night's reflection brought both parties a little nearer to one another, and the next day (Wednesday, August 3) the terms were settled upon which Henry's accession to the throne should be publicly recognized by the Catholic Royalists. Henry engaged to allow no further innovation in religion—to preserve entire all the existing possessions and privileges of the Roman Catholic Church—to withdraw the prohibition of its worship wherever it had been attempted to be enforced—to commit the government of all such towns, fortresses, or provinces as should be conquered, or should become vacant, except those expressly reserved by former treaties, into the hands of Roman Catholics—to call a meeting of the Estates-General within six months—to submit to the decision of either a General or National Council in the matters of debate between the two religions, and meanwhile to offer himself for further instruction as to the tenets of the Church of Rome:—as good a bargain as these Roman Catholic lords could well have hoped to make—one indeed which trenched not a little upon the position which Henry hitherto had taken, and the principles of religious liberty and general toleration which he had professed. But though willing to go so far as to acknowledge in words the validity of Henry's title, these Catholic Royalists were not prepared to assist him in the deadly struggle with the Leaguers that lay before him ere that title was firmly and securely established. Two days after the decision of the King, the Duke d'Epernon asked leave to retire from the camp; the example was followed by many others. In five days half of the Royal army was gone. Henry saw at once that the siege of Paris must be given up.

Before retiring from its walls, he issued an address to the nation, in which, referring to those who had deserted him, he said—"Such persons doubtless hope by their conduct to compel me to abjure my religion. Let every man however assure himself that I esteem not the realm of France, nor even the empire of the whole world, sufficient to renounce my religion; nor will I ever accept any other doctrine in lieu, unless such shall be confirmed and proposed by a General Council as I have before explained. You know that I am a good Frenchman, and that I have a sincere and true heart. I have been King of Navarre for seventeen years, and during that period I believe that I have never violated my word. Consider, I pray you, how hard and unjust a thing it must appear to me this attempt on your part to coerce me on religious matters, when I, who am your King and master, permit you to enjoy perfect freedom of conscience. I appeal to you and to the nation. Meantime, I beg that each one of you will pray that Almighty God will enlighten my conscience, direct my council, and bless my endeavors."

Breaking up that part of the army which still remained true to him into three divisions, Henry retired with one of them, not into the south of France, which would have been a giving up of the entire north into the hands of his enemies, but into Normandy. Learning this, and flushed with the advantages that the late change in the state of affairs had brought with it to his party, Mayenne imagined that the hour had come for driving Henry from the French soil as an exile, or forcing him to surrender. So confident was he of success that the officers were named who were to post to Paris with the news of the capture. The windows were taken at a fabulous price in the Rue St. Antoine, along which the captive Huguenot was to be conducted. Lying in the neighborhood of Dieppe, Henry learned that an army of 30,000 men was on its march to hem him in. He had not more than 8000 soldiers with him. It looked a desperate venture to meet such odds. Many of his best friends counselled him to retire for a time to Germany, or to cross over to the friendly shores of England. But, true to the motto he had early adopted, to conquer or die, Henry resolved to face the danger. He made the most skilful preparations to meet it. The town of Dieppe lies in a depression between two ranges of hills enclosing the valley through which the river Arques flows into the sea. A few miles up the valley this river is joined by another stream, the Bethune. On a height near the junction of the two rivers stood the castle of Arques. Instead of shutting himself up in the town and standing a siege there, Henry formed an entrenched camp in the neighborhood of the castle, placing his little army so that its right was covered by the castle guns, and its left by the river. A thick wood lay in front, close to which there stood an hospital for lepers, called the Maladreric. Taking in this building, running between it and the wood, Henry had a trench dug eight feet wide, which he carried all round the camp. Earthworks fortified by cannon were thrown up within this trench. These works were carried on with extraordinary activity, the King himself working heartily in the trenches. The cloud that was rolling on to cover him looked thick and dark enough, but nothing could quench the gayety of that gayest of spirits. "Here I am," he said of himself at this time, "a king without a kingdom, a husband without a wife, a general without an army." "My heart," he writes to the Countess de Grammont, "it's a marvel I'm living under such toil as I have. God have pity on me and bless my labors, as He has done in the face of not a few. I am well myself, and my affairs go well.

My enemies think sure to trap me here, but I am waiting for them in a camp that I have fortified. I expect to see them to-morrow, and if they attack me, I trust that, with God's blessing, it will be a bad bargain for them. The bearer of this goes by the sea, and the wind and my affairs oblige me to conclude." [1] Having failed in his first attempt to turn Henry's position and to cut off the communication with Dieppe, Mayenne at last (on the morning of the 21st September 1589) resolved to attack the Maladrerie with his entire force. A thick fog favored the approach. A German legion under Collato crossed the trench, waving their caps and giving it to be understood that they were deserters coming in to join the King. As they were mercenary troops, known to have no strong affection to the party on whose side they were fighting, the snare succeeded. The Swiss troops who occupied the Maladrerie received them with cheers and helped them to mount the earth-work. The entrance thus effected, the Germans turned upon the Swiss, while two French regiments that had been placed in ambuscade rushed across the trench. The Swiss were over-

---

[1] *Collection de Documents Inédits sur l'Histoire de France.* Publiés par ordre du Roi et par les soins du Ministre de l'Instruction Publique.

Recueil des Lettres Missives de Henri IV. Publié par M. Berger de Xivrey, Membre de l'Institut de France. Paris: Imprimerie Royale, 7 tom. 4to, 1843–1858. Tome iii. pp. 40, 41.

borne, the building so important for the defence of the King's position was occupied. Elated by this first success, Mayenne ordered a general charge. Battalion after battalion poured down upon the small beleaguered band. Henry, as always, was in the midst of the *mêlée;* his spirit got joyous in the strife. "Keep a pike for me there," he called out to Galato, the leader of the Swiss, whom he was trying to rally, "for I mean to fight at the head of your battalion." Montpensier's division had now advanced to support the King, but it was falling back under the heavy assault of the enemy. Henry felt that its repulse would be fatal. "Can it be," he exclaimed, as he dashed forward to rally the retreating column, "can it be that in all France there are not fifty cavaliers courageous enough to die with their King?" It had fared ill with him at this moment of the fight had not the fog which hitherto hung heavy over the field cleared up. The guns of the castle opened a murderous fire upon the assailants, while at the same time Chatillon, with a company of 500 Huguenot veterans, appeared upon the field. "Sire," said the youthful leader, as he rode up to Henry's side, "here we are; we will die with you." Above the noise of battle there rose for a few moments the notes of that war-song of the Huguenots, the 38th Psalm: "Let God arise, and his enemies shall be scattered." That gallant company then plunged into the strife with such a dash of impetuous valor that the enemy at once gave way. The tide of battle turned. All on Henry's side took heart again. Marshal Biron, who had been wounded and unhorsed early in the fight, mounted once more, and with the young Coligni by his side attacked and retook the Maladrerie. There and everywhere the assailants were driven back, and after an hour or so of desperate fighting, a victory complete and decisive crowned the arms of the King.

This brilliant success brought more than fame with it. It brought large succors to Henry, both home and foreign. At the head of an army more than 20,000 strong, he advanced rapidly on Paris. The faubourgs on the left side of the river were taken by assault and given up to pillage. The attempt, however, to take the city by storm failed, and Henry retired for winter-quarters to Tours.

The campaign of 1590 opened by the siege of Honfleur on the part of the Royalists, and that of Meulan on the part of the Leaguers. The two armies, marching to the relief of the two places so threatened, met on the 14th March in the plain of Ivry. The advantage in point of numbers still lay with the Leaguers. It was 16,000 against 10,000. Notwithstanding that superiority, Mayenne would not have crossed swords again so soon with the victor of Coutras and Arques, had not the young Count Egmont brought with him into France 6000 infantry and 1200 Walloon lances, a part of Parma's well-drilled troops, boasting that with them alone he would undertake to meet the Béarnese on the field. Mayenne yielded to Egmont's importunity and risked another battle. The two armies, drawn up in each other's presence, prepared for the encounter in the usual fashion. Along the ranks of the Leaguers a cordelier, with crucifix in hand, invoked the aid of Heaven, and doomed the heretics to destruction. Henry called upon his minister D'Amours to do as he had done at Coutras, Henry and all the Huguenot soldiers going down upon their knees, while D'Amours poured forth his fervid prayer. One other preparation for the combat Henry made. A day or two before the battle Schomberg, a German officer, had asked pay for himself and for his men. In a pique of the moment the King had said to him that no man of honor ever asked for money on the eve of a battle. He now called the German to his side. "Schomberg," he said, "I have done you wrong. To-day may be the last of my life. I don't want to sully the honor of a gentleman. I know your valor and your merit, pardon me and embrace me." "Your Majesty," said Schomberg, "wounded me the other day, but to-day you kill me. The honor you have done me will oblige me to die in your service," and he kept his word. After the battle he was found dead upon the field. The action that followed was essentially a cavalry engagement. Though the foot-soldiers on either side were three times more numerous than the horse, they never encountered each other till the fate of the battle was fixed. When drawn up to face the enemy, Henry's cavalry regiments, mustering not more than half the number of their antagonists, looked otherwise ill-fitted to meet the shock. His troopers were all, for that age, lightly armed. The heavy lance of the cavalier, too costly for the poor Huguenot gentlemen, had been universally laid aside, the sword and the pistol being alone employed in action. What was lost in momentum was found to be more than made up by the greater mobility. Henry, as he planted himself at the head of his troopers, had put a plume of white feathers in his crest and on his horse's head. "My friends." said he, ere he gave the signal for the charge, "If to-day you run my fortune, I run yours. I am resolved to die or to conquer with you. Keep your ranks, I beseech you; if you break them in the heat of battle rally immediately, and if you lose sight of your standards then rally round my white plume; you will find it the road to victory and honor." The two lines of cavalry dashed upon each other. At first it looked as if by the sheer force of weight and numbers the Leaguers were to overbear the Royalists. Further and further back the white plume was seen to move. At last, calling out that those who did not wish to fight might at least turn and see him die, Henry, accompanied by not more than a dozen followers, plunged into the thick of the enemy. The white plume was lost to sight, and for a short space it was not known whether its bearer was dead or living, but again it waved on high. The words and action of the King sent a fresh fire through the ranks of the Royalists. Once more well-trained and high-spirited valor carried it over numbers. One short but terrible struggle, and the Leaguers everywhere gave way—hopelessly gave way,—all attempt to rally them quite vain. Egmont fell. Mayenne, Nemours, and D'Aumale fled, and left their army to its fate. Many companies of the Swiss laid down their arms, having never fired a shot. The Germans cried for mercy, but the treachery of Arques was too fresh in the memory; they were pitilessly massacred. As many perished in flight as in the battle-field. Mayenne had taken down the bridge of the Eure behind him to prevent pursuit. He left there hundreds of his own men to be shot down on the banks, or drowned in the river. "Spare the French," cried Henry, as he gazed on the bloody work that the sword of the pursuers was doing, "but down with the foreigners!" Scarce a man of the Spaniards and Walloons got quarter. 1500 of them were slain. Never was victory more complete. The Leaguer army was gone: a fourth part of it slain, a fourth part of it captured, the rest scattered and irretrievably disorganized. How finely has Lord Macaulay caught the spirit and seized upon the chief incidents of this decisive battle—

" Oh! how our hearts were beating, when, at the dawn of day,
We saw the army of the League drawn out in long array,
With all its priest-led citizens, and all its rebel peers;
And Appenzel's stout infantry, and Egmont's Flemish spears.
There rode the brood of false Lorraine, the curses of our land;
And dark Mayenne was in the midst, a truncheon in his hand.

The King is come to marshal us, in all his armor drest,
And he has bound a snow-white plume upon his gallant crest;
He looked upon his people, and a tear was in his eye,
He looked upon the traitors, and his glance was stern and high,
Right graciously he smiled on us, as rolled from wing to wing,
Down all our line a deafening shout—' God save our Lord the King!'
'And if my standard-bearer fall, as fall full well he may,
For never saw I promise yet of such a bloody day,
Press where ye see my white plume shine amid the ranks of war,
And be your oriflamme to-day the helmet of Navarre.'

Hurrah! the foes are moving! Hark to the mingled din
Of fife, and steed, and tramp, and drum, and roaring culverin!
The fiery Duke is pricking fast across St. André's plain,
With all the hireling chivalry of Guelders and Almayne.
'Now, by the lips of those ye love, fair gentlemen of France,
Charge for the golden lilies—upon them with the lance.'
A thousand spears are striking deep—a thousand spears in rest,
A thousand knights are pressing close behind the snow-white crest;

And in they burst, and on they rushed, while, like a guid-
 ing star,
Amidst the thickest carnage blazed the helmet of Navarre.

Now, God be praised, the day is ours! Mayenne hath turned
 his rein,
D'Aumale hath cried for quarter, the Flemish Count is
 slain;
Their ranks are breaking like thin clouds before a Biscay
 gale;
The field is heaped with bleeding steeds, and flags and
 cloven mail.
And then we thought on vengeance, and all along our van—
'Remember St. Batholomew,' was passed from man to man;
But out spake gallant Henry, 'No Frenchman is my foe,
Down, down with every foreigner, but let your brethren go.'
Oh! was there ever such a knight in friendship or in war
As our Sovereign Lord King Henry, the soldier of
 Navarre!"

Four letters of Henry are extant, written on the evening of this eventful day of his life. One of these runs thus:—"MONSIEUR LA NOUE,—God has blessed us. To-day the battle came off. It has been fought well. God has shown that he loves right better than might. Our victory is entire. The enemy totally broken. The *Reiter* fairly destroyed. The infantry surrounded. The foreigners badly handled. The whole cornets and the cannon taken. The pursuit carried to the gates of Mantes. From the camp at Rosny, within a league of Mantes, at ten o'clock of the evening of the 14th day of March 1590."[1] Next forenoon saw him in the tennis-

---

[1] *Recueil*, etc., tome iii. pp. 171-2.

court at Mantes, as eager in the game as he had been in the fight. The bakers of the town beat him, won money from him, and refused to give him his revenge. The King got hold of some ovens, set them a-baking all the night, and next morning had bread offered all through the town at half the common price. The bakers in their turn were beaten, and were too glad to give in. Two days' quick march would have carried Henry's victorious army to the gates of Paris; and such was the panic created there, that had the advice of La Noue been taken, and the capital at once attacked, there can be little doubt that it would have fallen into Henry's hands, and, that heart of the League crushed, Henry would have been King of France without needing to abjure. But as after Coutras he let fifteen days go idly by before he again placed himself at the head of his army, so it was not until the 7th May that he appeared before Paris. The Parisians had made good use of the respite. The fortifications were repaired; chains thrown across the river. There were not more than 5000 regular soldiers in the garrison, but 30,000 well-armed men enrolled themselves as the city militia. The royal army, relinquishing the idea of assault, drew its iron cordon round and round the city; every avenue was blocked up by which food of any kind could enter. The city was to be starved into surrender. So soon as the first pressure of this blockade was felt within the walls, an accurate count was taken of the number of inhabitants and of the amount of provisions of all kinds. It was found that there were about 200,000 to be fed, and but food enough, on short allowance, to last a month. Though poorly supplied with viands, the city was richly enough provided with priests, and on them lay the burden, one willingly and nobly borne, to keep the spirit of " no surrender " up among the people. They did so by deed as well as word. On the 14th May (seven days after the siege had commenced) 1300 priests and monks, with the Bishop of Senlis at their head as their colonel, marched through the streets with casque and corselet over their priestly vestments, crucifix in one hand, musket or halberd in the other—a new order of city guard improvised to assist in the defence of the city. Charmed with the chivalry of his order, the Papal Legate goes forth to meet the procession. Four abreast, they defile before him; he rises in his carriage to hail them as a very band of Maccabees. He must receive the due military salute, but unhappily one of these clerical volunteers had forgotten that he had charged his arquebus with ball, and in the height of his excitement, not looking, perhaps not caring, how he held his piece, he shot the secretary of the Legate dead in the carriage by his master's side. Though awkwardly handled, however, there were some of these arquebuses that did good service in the siege, and many of their awkward handlers gallantly gave up their lives.

The month passed, and the ordinary stores were all exhausted. The rumor ran that the religious houses had stores of food laid up. They were inspected by the city police, and in more than one of them food enough to keep its inmates for a year and more was found. An order was issued that for fifteen days the conventual establishments should undertake to supply the wants of the entire population. To execute this order the clergy were obliged at last to erect large copper vessels, out of which a broth of abominable meat, composed of dogs' flesh, bran, and pease—a kind of food soon to be remembered with regret—was served out daily. June and July ran their course; gaunt famine grew gaunter and gaunter. It was now only on the table of the wealthiest, and then as a rarity, purchased at an exorbitant price, that horse-flesh appeared. Dogs, rats, mice, all kinds of living creatures, were hunted, snared, devoured undressed. A lean and hungry dog, and a lean and hungry man, fought with each other for each other's bodies in the street, and the dog got the better of the man. All kinds of vegetable food were sought for everywhere,—the grass that grew in deserted streets torn up with greedy hands. August came, and outside the city walls the ripe grain was seen waving in the fields. Hundreds of famishing creatures rushed out, and attempted, under the fire and the sabre-stroke, to snatch a few bloody handfuls. And now at last the horrors within the city reached their height. The last and best historian of France tells us that the history of that country presents nothing that can be compared with them.¹ One by one all kinds of flesh, and grain, and herbs had been eaten up. To soothe the raging hunger they pounded slates down to mix with a little bran and water. The Papal Legate chanced to remember hearing that in a city of the East, besieged by the Persians, they had made bread of pounded bones. The cemeteries were rifled, and of human bones was made that inhuman bread. And they had the flesh as well as the bones of the dead. Children who had died through sheer want of nourishment were salted and kept for their own mothers' food. Two hundred corpses daily of those who dropped down by the way strewed the streets. Henry had been early touched with what he saw and heard, and had allowed 3000 old men, women, and children to pass out through his lines. He had some food conveyed into the city to supply the tables of the Princesses within the walls, and he winked at the practice of some of his officers who made large gains by a secret traffic in eatables. But though the most favorable terms were offered, the famine-stricken city still held out, clinging to the hope given by Mayenne, that a Spanish army was on its way for their relief.

And the relief did come at last. On the morning of the 30th August the haggard sentinels on

---

¹ *Histoire de France*, par Henri Martin, vol. x. p. 219.

the city walls looked out, and no besiegers were to be seen. During the night Henry and his army had disappeared. It was not a day too soon. The Duke of Parma had entered France, united his forces with those of the Duke of Mayenne, and was already at Meaux. It seemed to Henry that the opportunity would be given him of measuring swords with the greatest general of Christendom. He hastened to the encounter. Marching at once to the heights of Chelles he placed himself in Parma's front. In point of numbers the two armies were about equal. In discipline, indeed, the well-paid, well-fed, well-drilled troops of Farnese had all the advantage; but Henry had 4000 French gentlemen in his camp, who longed once more to follow the white plume on another such field as Ivry. On the evening of the day on which the two armies came in sight of one another, Parma ascended a neighboring height. Having slowly reconnoitred the camp of the enemy, he turned eagerly to Mayenne, and said, "I do not see here that assemblage of 10,000 squalid adventurers you spoke of; instead, I see a numerous and well-trained army of 25,000 men, with artillery." Henry's own burning wish was to close the struggle by one other decisive blow. "I write this word to you," such were the terms of a note despatched by him at this time, "on the eve of a battle. The issue is in the hands of God. If I lose it, you will never see me more; for I am not the man to retreat or fly. And if I die, my last thought but one will be given to you; my last to God, to whom I commend us both."[1] But the wily Italian, as cautious as his antagonist was bold, had resolved not to fight. He saw how he could gain the end he came for without running such a risk. Next day, seeing his adversary remain unmoved within his lines, Henry sent a herald to Parma inviting him to battle. "Tell your master," said Parma in reply, "that I am come by command of the King, my master, to raise the siege of Paris; if I find that the shortest way to this is by a battle, I will give it; but that I have not come so far to take his advice as to what it is best for me to do." For five days the two armies remained in presence of each other, but nothing could tempt the Farnese out of his entrenchments. On the morning, however, of the 6th September the Spanish cavalry was seen deploying on the heights. Henry fancied that the longed-for hour had come. It was but a skilful manœuvre to cover the movement of a body of troops, thrown rapidly by a bridge of boats across the river Marne, by which the town of Lagni was taken by assault, and the threat of Parma, that he would relieve Paris by uncorking one of the supplying rivers that Henry had so carefully sealed up, was adroitly executed, almost under

---

[1] This letter was addressed to Madame de la Roche Guyon, Marquise de Guercherille. See *Recueil*, etc., vol. iii. p. 244.

Henry's eyes. Baffled by the great military tactician, after an unsuccessful attempt to take Paris by escalade, Henry broke up his army. Early in November Parma left the neighborhood of Paris to carry his army back into the Netherlands. No sooner was Henry informed of a movement which he had all along anticipated, than he summoned to his side the Royalist nobles of the north, hung upon Parma's retreat himself day and night in the saddle, appearing now on the rear, now on the flank, sometimes even in the front of the enemy. And it was during this same hot pursuit of the Spaniard that Henry found himself at La Fère, within twenty-four miles of the castle of Cœuvres, to which the fair Gabrielle d'Estrées had retired to avoid the impetuosity of his affection. The castle was close to Soissons, then held by a garrison of the Leaguers. Nevertheless Henry resolved to visit it. At early dawn he set off to take a road that it would have been perilous for any common Royalist soldier to traverse. When nine miles from the castle, he sent young Biron to announce his approaching visit, then entering a little village hostelry he threw off his dress, put on a peasant's, and, to make his incognito all the more complete, he threw a sack of straw upon his back, and, burdened thus, the Royal wooer trudged along. The sack indeed was thrown off before he presented himself to Gabrielle; but he was still in the rustic garb, and she scarce could retain her laughter at the sight. This singular mark of attention made, however, the impression he desired. "I have good heart," he said, "regarding it, and that after this interview nothing will go wrong with me." The King was back at the camp by nightfall, and next day was in the saddle again, pursuing the harassed and enfeebled enemy, whom he finally, on the 1st December, saw safely across the border.

Great military preparations marked the opening of the year 1591. Turenne had been despatched to England and Germany, and in both countries had been eminently successful. The niggard hand of Elizabeth had been somehow opened, and 5000 English infantry and 500 English horse, under Essex, were sent across the Channel. Our English Queen, with her accustomed prudence (that we may use no harsher term), had sought to impose it upon Henry, as a condition of her aid, that Calais should be delivered as hostage into her hands. There is no nobler letter of this King than that in which, in great straits though he was, he rightly and patriotically refuses compliance with this demand. Elizabeth, however, prevailed so far that Henry consented that the first great enterprise attempted should be the reduction of Rouen. A German auxiliary force of 10,000 infantry and 6000 cavalry was organized under the Prince of Anhalt. Before, however, the combined forces had sat down before Rouen, events had transpired in Paris which revealed in characters of blood the intestine divisions of the League. The extreme party there had quarrelled with the Parliament and with Mayenne, whose measures were too slow and too moderate for their taste. Irritated at the manner in which memorial after memorial, each containing more extravagant demands than its predecessor, had been received, they had recourse to open violence. One morning, as he was on his way to the Palace of Justice, Brisson, the first President of the Parliament, was seized and conducted to one of the city prisons. A self-constituted and illegal tribunal passed speedy judgment on him, and condemned him to immediate death. In vain the President protested against the lawlessness of the deed; in vain he asked for trial before any competent court; in vain he asked for a few days' delay—to be shut up where they liked, and fed on bread and water, if only time were given him to finish a book for the instruction of the young that he was engaged in preparing. He was hurried down to a vault of the prison, a rude kind of gallows was constructed, and he was hanged upon the spot. Two other magistrates of the city shared his fate. The perpetrators of this deed had counted upon a popular *émeute* in their favor. They were disappointed. Paris lay motionless, struck dumb. Fearing to face the people by day, they bore the three bodies in the night to the Place de Grève, and there the morning saw three gibbets, with the corpses of the three magistrates hung on them, with large placards on each, denouncing them as traitors and favorers of heresy But neither did that sight do any thing to rouse the passions of the populace. They had outrun all public sympathy; the tide had begun to set the other way—in favor of peace, if possible of some compromise. Mayenne was at Laon when he heard of this affair. He immediately returned to Paris, and a day or two afterwards four of the ringleaders were arrested, and, with as little respect to the forms of justice as they themselves had shown, were hanged in a hall of the Louvre. A futile attempt at resistance was speedily quelled, and the Duke's triumph was complete. The rule of the Council of Sixteen was over.

Rouen was completely invested. Every preparation, however, had been made for its defence. Its gallant commander, Villars, had sent away all strangers, all old and infirm persons, from the city; had strengthened its fortifications and laid in ample stores of provisions. Parma besides, who had received his master's orders to do for Rouen what he had done the year before for Paris, once more entered France. So soon as he heard of this, leaving the main body of his own troops to continue the close investment of the city, Henry took with him some squadrons of cavalry, and set off to watch the motions of the enemy. One day, riding forward with a few hundred horse, the rest being left behind under the command of the Duke of Nevers, Henry found himself suddenly in front of the entire

Spanish army. His little band, composed principally of the noblemen and gentlemen in immediate attendance upon him, was instantly attacked. Instead of ordering a retreat, Henry dashed forward to meet the charge. But meanwhile large companies of the enemy's light cavalry came in upon him on either flank. It was no longer a question of victory, but of escape. Henry signalled his companions to make for a little bridge that lay on his way back to where Nevers was lying. But the white plume had been seen. The cry that it was Navarre himself ran through the Spanish lines. There needed but the order from Parma, and such a force would be launched upon the little band that was fighting its way back slowly to the bridge, as must have cut off all possibility of retreat. Henry must either have been cut down or have yielded himself a prisoner. But Parma hesitated—he suspected stratagem; he could not believe that so good a soldier as Henry would advance so far without having adequate supports at hand. He held back his troops and gave positive orders against any thing like a general advance. Even as it was, Henry was fighting against tremendous odds. His friends were falling fast around him—a full half of the entire number of them was cut off. He was himself the last to pass the bridge, and just as he was crossing, a gun-shot struck him in the loins. At last his retreat was covered by the advancing troopers of Nevers. It was a day of wild excitement, when hand to hand each man was fighting for his life—full too of changeful incident. The survivors met in the evening in the chamber of the King, whose wound, though weakening him for the time by the loss of blood it occasioned, turned out not to be dangerous. "And I have to observe," says Sully, "as singular, that of all those assembled who had been present at the combat not two individuals could agree in the recital." Both generals were loudly blamed in their respective camps—Henry for his rashness, Parma for his caution. The one scarcely took the trouble to excuse himself for a fault which he knew would be so readily forgiven. The other only haughtily said that he thought that he had to contend with a general of a great army, and not with a captain of dragoons.

The Spanish army advanced to within seven leagues of Rouen. Parma now wished to fight, but Mayenne and his French counsellors had as little desire to see the Spaniard triumph, as Biron and many of the Catholic royalists had to see Henry do the same. They would not risk all on the fate of an engagement, and so Parma had to content himself with the raising of the siege, which he effected with his usual skill. On retiring from Rouen, he again yielded to French counsel, and undertook the reduction of Caudebec, a small town in the neighborhood. It was here, while engaged in examining its defences, that a musket-shot hit him in the arm about the elbow, the ball running down and lodging at the wrist. He gave no token that he was struck—continued his survey as if nothing had happened—and it was the sight of the blood flowing down upon his cloak that first told what had occurred. The ball was clumsily extracted, and the weakness that followed unfitted the great officer for much active duty. The command fell mainly into the hands of Mayenne, who conducted the allied army from Caudœbec to Yvetôt, an almost peninsular projection of land running into the Seine. The eagle eye of Henry saw at once the mistake that had been committed. Gathering up all the troops he had beside him, and sending off his officers in all directions to summon back those who had but just left the camp; he advanced to within a mile of the Spanish lines, occupying the only ground along which they could either advance or retreat. Parma must now either risk a battle, and that in a position most unfavorable to him for such a combat, or he must capitulate. "Now," said he exultingly, as he contemplated the advantage he had gotten, "Now for the stroke that shall win for me my crown." But Parma had no sooner discovered the perils of his position, than he had hastened to provide for his deliverance. Secret orders were at once despatched to Rouen to have a sufficient number of boats and rafts prepared and sent down quietly to Yvetôt by the reflux of an evening tide. Henry went to rest believing that he was on the eve of another Coutras or Ivry, but the first sight the morning showed him was full one-half of the Spanish army safe on the opposite bank of the Seine, the other half on its way, so protected by cannon and cavalry that he could do nothing to hinder, little even to mar, the passage. It was the last great triumph of the Farnese. He led his army back again as he had done before, to the Netherlands, and a few months afterwards he died at Spa.

Hostilities languished in France as soon as Parma had retired. Henry saw his English, Dutch, and German auxiliaries depart. Two years of heroic struggle had left him nothing but the sterile glories of Arques and Ivry. He was as far from the throne as ever. It was not upon the battle-field, it would seem, that the great question of the succession was to be decided. In one respect he had been latterly making way with the nation. The monarchical principle and that of hereditary succession represented in his person had been becoming more and more allied with the spirit of national independence. This was owing to the form which Spanish intrigue had been taking. The intervention of Philip II. in French affairs had sprung originally from his dread that French aid would be given to the Netherlanders in their great revolt against his authority. By degrees, however, as he got his hand more fully in, and felt at once the weakness of the Guises and of the democratic and priestly party in Paris and elsewhere, his aims expanded till at last the Crown of France itself seemed within his grasp, and the reduction of France to the condition of a mere dependency on the Spanish monarchy formed part of that vast scheme of universal European empire which his counsellors had mapped out for him. The evidence of this being now the end and aim of all his meddling with French affairs was too direct and too copious to be any longer questioned, and in proportion as the knowledge of the fact spread among the people the repugnance to Spanish intervention grew broader and deeper.

The peril from that quarter Henry did not fear so much to face, but a new peril had sprung up nearer at hand. Impatient of his long delay in fulfilling the promise he had made at the death of his predecessor, dissatisfied with the favor that he continued to extend to the Huguenots, irritated at the strong sayings of the King that the Calvinists were constantly circulating, that he would live and die in their faith, offended at the sight of English, Dutch, and German Protestants taking so large a share in all military operations,—the Dukes of Montpensier, De Nevers, De Longueville, D'Epernon, the Marshal D'Aumont, the superintendent Francis d'O, the great chiefs of the Catholic royalists, were gradually drawing off from him, and approximating to those Bourbon Catholic Princes, the sons of his uncle Condé, one or other of whom had been often named in connection with the succession to the throne. The old Cardinal of Bourbon, Henry's uncle, had been actually proclaimed King under the title of

Charles X. by the League. He was now dead, and a meeting of the Estates-General of the kingdom had been summoned by the Duke of Mayenne to meet in Paris in January 1593, to deliberate as to the selection of a successor to the throne. The legal authority of any such body, so called, Navarre utterly repudiated. Its authority however was acknowledged by Philip of Spain, who sent the Duke of Feria to be present as Ambassador-Extraordinary from Spain. It was countenanced by the Papal Legate, who, exerting all his influence, ordered it to take instant steps for filling the throne of France with a Prince devoted to the Papacy. In either way, whether through the success of Spanish and Papal diplomacy, or through a union with the more moderate Leaguers and the *tiers parti*, composed of the Catholic royalists, should an actual election be come to and another King proclaimed, a new and very serious obstacle would be placed in Henry's way to the throne. A thousand voices kept now repeating it in Henry's ears that the only way for him at once to save the monarchy and secure for himself the throne was his return into the bosom of the Roman Catholic Church. His pride had hitherto revolted at the idea of a change of faith forced on him from without. His sense of honor revolted equally at the idea of confessing with the lip what in his heart he did not believe. But against these came now the strong pleadings of self-interest and of public duty. Was a crown to be lost, a kingdom ruined, for a difference about creeds and churches,—matters that in themselves he had never cared much about? Was that France, which from his youth he had so dearly loved, which it had been the day-dream of his ambition that he was the destined instrument to save and to regenerate, to be torn in pieces or thrown enslaved into the arms of the stranger? He consulted his ablest advisers. With few exceptions they agreed as to the course that he should take. Sully has told us without reserve how he presented the matter to his royal master. "I can find," he said to Henry, "but two ways to any good issue out of your present embarrassments. By the one you must put forth strong resolutions, practise severities and rigor that are quite contrary to your humor and inclination; you must pass through a million of difficulties, fatigues, pains, perils, and labors, have your body always on the saddle, the corselet always on your back, the helmet on your head, the pistol in your finger, and the sword in your hand; nay, what is more, farewell to repose, to pleasure, to love, to mistresses, to games, to dogs, to hawking, to buildings,—for you cannot come out through these affairs but by multitudes of combats, taking of cities, great victories, and a great shedding of blood. Instead of all this, by the other way,—which is for you to accommodate yourself in the matter of religion to the will of the majority of your subjects—you escape all these pains and difficulties in *this world;* but as for the other world," said the courtier, smiling, and the King laughed with him as he said it, " I *cannot answer for it.*"

It became urgent that Henry should not only come to a decision, but announce it. After three months wasted in idle debate, the Estates-General were informed that the Duke of Feria had a communication to make to them from his Royal master. Without circumlocution or disguise, Philip demanded that his daughter should be at once proclaimed Queen of France in her own right, as granddaughter of Henry II. The Duke might have guessed what the temper of many of the Leaguers was when one of the most violent of them, the Bishop of Senlis, sprang up upon his feet as soon as this proposition was made to the Estates, and at the pitch of his voice exclaimed, " Heaven punishes us for our faults. The proposition of the ambassador is the greatest evil that could have befallen the League; it confirms all that the *Politiques* have said, that interest and ambition have had more to do with this war than zeal for religion; it lets us know that in thinking to serve the Church we have been the blind instruments of a foreign King. To break the Salic Law is to destroy this kingdom." Uninstructed by this effusion, when the ambassador was asked to whom his master meant that his daughter should be married, he answered, " To the Arch-Duke Ernest." He was soon taught to know that the idea of filling up the French throne in such a way as that never could be entertained. He yielded so far as to consent that it should be a French Prince who should be chosen; and, pressed at once to name him, he announced that it would be the young Duke of Guise upon whom the honor of this alliance should devolve.

The time for prompt action on Henry's part had come. He announced to the Estates-General that he had resolved to conform to the Roman Catholic religion. This announcement and the proposals of the Spanish monarch came at the same time before the notice of the Estates. The slow and cautious Mayenne distrusted Philip, and shrinking from taking the last and irrevocable step, induced them to declare that they could not proceed to the election and proclamation of the Infanta till they saw the means provided and secured for maintaining her upon the throne. A like dilatory policy dictated the answer given to Navarre's announcement. It was to the effect that the Estates thanked God for the conversion of the King; but as that conversion was a purely spiritual act, the recognition of it lay alone with the Pope; and that till his Holiness had absolved Henry and received him back again into the Church, no action could be taken by the Estates. Henry however had resolved not to subject himself to the delays and risks attendant upon an application to a Pope who was acting as an ally of Spain. Preparatory to his public act of abjuration, he invited five Catholic Bishops to hold a private conference with him at St. Denis. Early in the morning of the day fixed for this conference (Friday, July 23) he wrote thus to Gabrielle d'Estrées, "I arrived here early last night, and was importuned by God-fearers till bed-time. The hope I have of seeing you to-morrow keeps back my hand from making a long discourse. On Sunday I am to take the perilous leap. Even now, when I am writing to you, I have a hundred distractions upon my shoulders, that make me hate St. Denis as much as you do Nantes. Good-by, my heart; come early to-morrow, for it seems a year since I saw you." The Bishops were admitted immediately after this epistle had been despatched. Seven hours were spent in going over all the topics in dispute between the Calvinists and Romanists, with the view of removing any remaining doubts or scruples on the part of the King. The merry monarch took a malicious pleasure in puzzling his instructors with passages of Scripture and arguments which it gave them no little trouble to answer. One or two of the points were lightly enough disposed of. "Well," said the King, when they came to Prayers for the Dead, "we may pass by the requiem; I'm not dead yet, and have no wish to be so. The doctrine of Purgatory came before them: "As to that," he said, "I will receive it, not as an article of faith but as a belief of the Church, and also," he added bowing to the Bishops, "to please you, knowing that it is the bread of priests." At last the weary hours were over. "You have not satisfied me," such were the King's parting words, spoken not in levity,—"you have not satisfied me as much as I had desired; but I put my soul into your hands to-day, and do, I pray you, have a care; for the way in which you now make me enter I leave only by death. That I protest and swear." Tears stood in the King's eyes as he spoke these parting words. The Bishops declared themselves satisfied.

At eight o'clock the next Sunday morning, attended by an imposing escort, Henry made his way to the ancient church beneath which lay the ashes of so many of his predecessors. Arrived in front of it, the doors were closed. The King knocked; the doors were folded back; and in the grand entrance, seated upon his episcopal throne, and surrounded by a throng of surpliced ecclesiastics, the Archbishop of Bourges appeared. "Who are you?" said the Archbishop to the advancing monarch. "I am the King." "What is that you ask?" "I ask to be received into the bosom of the Roman Catholic Apostolic Church." Henry knelt then at the Prelate's feet and said, "I promise and make oath to live and die in the Catholic religion; to protect and defend it against all enemies, at peril of my blood and life, renouncing all heresies contrary thereto." He then handed to the Prelate a paper signed by him containing his recantation, kissing the Prelate's hand and ring. The Archbishop then rose, and laying his hands upon the head of the King, pronounced the words of absolution and reception into the Church. Peals of artillery and the plaudits of assembled thousands rent the air; the King's attendants plucked their swords from their scabbards and waved them in the air; the soldiers of his body-guard shouted for gladness. The procession entered the Church. Again, before the high altar, Henry knelt, and kissing the sacred volume, and then laying hand upon it, repeated the oath of abjuration. He then retired to make confession to the Archbishop. On his reappearing, High Mass was celebrated. At the elevation of the Host, t'e King bent till his brow touched the pavement. The organ pealed, and the notes of the *Te Deum Laudamus* filled the arches of the ancient edifice. The act was done. The two principles that had been at war with each other—the monarchical and the Catholic—were at peace again. The bond between Church and State that had been severed was renewed.

It was not with unmingled satisfaction that all the Roman Catholic prelates looked on as that great ecclesiastical drama was performed. "I am a Catholic," said one of them, "by life and profession, and a faithful subject and servant of the King, I shall live and die such. Yet I think it would have been better had the King remained in his religion than changed as he has done; for there is a God above who judges us, respect to whom alone should sway the consciences of kings, and not a regard to crowns and kingdoms. I expect nothing but evil from it."

With that truth-loving Bishop every right-thinking man will now cordially agree; for, let us do all the justice that we can to Henry in the difficult position that he occupied,—let us believe of him that it was love of country more than love of self, his patriotism even more than his ambition that prompted him,—let us believe that no deep religious belief on his part stood in the way, and had to be belied,—let us acknowledge the weight of the political considerations that presented themselves, and the immense benefits—the unity—the peace—the great national recovery that ensued. Still, however much we may try to excuse, as we cannot believe it to have been one of sincere and honest conviction, we cannot but condemn the deed. Nor have we been able to persuade ourselves that it was not one which finally entailed upon France far greater evils than those which it averted. A fearful picture has been drawn of all the consequences that must have attended his continuing to be a Protestant. The prolongation of the civil and religious wars—the final defeat of the Huguenots—the dismemberment of France, or reduction under a foreign yoke. But with a sixth of the entire population of France still Protestant—with that Huguenot army so trained to war and so thoroughly devoted to him—with that growing number of the Catholic aristocracy, and especially of the middle classes, ready to attach themselves to him despite of his Calvinism—with that strong spirit of nationality rising to support his claim—with the League before him divided and distracted with councils—with Philip weakened in all his resources, no second Parma left to supply by military genius the decline of his military power—with the aid that England and the Netherlands and Germany would have been ready to extend, who can readily believe that any common French or Spanish General would have been a match for the conqueror of Arques and Ivry, or that any political party that could then have been organized in France would have been able to pluck the crown from the strong hand which grasped it? Doubtless, as Sully told, in that way of it he might have had a long enough and hard enough battle to fight, but it would have been as honorable as arduous. Even had he failed, or had he perished in the conflict, then, still readier than now, would we have hailed him as Henry the Great. But had he succeeded, as we believe he would, had religious liberty been at that time established in France, unpurchased by the price of royal perfidy, had truth and honor unimpeached sat down in his person upon the throne, what a different future had there been for France and for Europe! for it is impossible to forget that though the immediate and proximate results seemed to justify the course he took, yet that finally and in the long-run his policy was a failure—that he himself at last sank beneath the knife of the assassin—that the religious toleration which he had been at such pains to establish was, in the reign of his grandson, trampled to the ground in that unhappy year that saw a million of the thriftiest and most virtuous of the French population driven into exile—that the monarchy grounded on his abjuration perished amid the horrors of anarchy, and that the last of his line who filled the throne fell under the stroke of the public executioner.

CHAPTER VIII.

HENRY IV., 1593–1610.

Entrance into Paris.—Attempt at assassinating the King.—Affair of Fontaine Française.—Absolution by the Pope.—Reception at Amiens.—Siege of Le Fère.—Submission of Mayenne.—Sully.—Assembly of Notables.—Taking of Amiens.—Recapture of the city.—Close of the civil wars.—Edict of Nantes.—Peace of Vervins.—Death of Marshal Biron.—Ten years of peace.—Their fruitful labors.—Assassination of the King.

HENRY lost no time in trying to get the absolution of the French Episcopate ratified by the Holy See. To give the greater weight to his application he not only wrote himself in submissive enough terms to the Pope, but despatched the Duke of Nevers, who was accompanied by some eminent ecclesiastics, as his ambassador to Rome. Clement, however, had made up his mind not to listen to this application. Nevers was not recognized in his official character at the Papal Court. He was denied all public audience by his Holiness Clement refused to submit the matter for consideration to the Sacred College. He never would believe in the sincerity of Henry's abjuration of the Reformed faith ; no, not though an angel from heaven were to vouch for it. He never would absolve the relapsed heretic of Navarre. But he would not state the grounds of his refusal; he would not even put that refusal down in writing, nor condescend to inform the French Ambassador what Henry ought to do in order to establish the genuineness of his conversion. He went so far as to have it not obscurely hinted to Nevers that the ecclesiastics who accompanied him, by the part that they had taken in the French absolution, had rendered themselves amenable to the Holy Inquisition, before whose tribunal it was possible they might be called. Dreading some act of violence directed against the Bishops, Nevers had them brought to his own lodgings, and gave it distinctly to be understood that he would let himself be cut to pieces before one of them was touched. Exasperated at the treatment he had received, Nevers at last quitted Rome. The rumor ran that the agents of the Inquisition were to arrest the Bishops on their way out of the city. The Duke took them beside him in his own coach, declaring that he would cut down with his own hand whoever dared to molest them. No one who knew Nevers doubted that he would make good his word. The carriage with all its freight passed out of the Estates of the Church untouched.

The Pope's refusal to grant absolution furnished to Mayenne and to the zealots of the League the ground or the excuse upon which they maintained an attitude of continued hostility to Henry. But the rude and insulting manner in which the refusal had been conveyed stirred up on the part of a large body both of the clergy and laity the spirit of Gallican independence, so that it may be doubted whether upon the whole the gain to the King was not greater than the loss. Despite the obstinacy of the Pope, Henry resolved to proceed with his coronation and consecration. Rheims, the ordinary place for this great ceremonial, being in the hands of the Leaguers, Chartres was fixed upon in its stead. The vial of holy oil with which Clovis and his successors had been anointed was also in the hands of the enemy, but it was remembered that another flask of oil of almost equal antiquity and holiness, which it was believed that an angel had of old brought down from heaven for the healing of St. Martin, was preserved in the Abbey of Marmontiers at Tours. This was sent for, and escorted with all the pomp of a solemn procession to Chartres. The costliest preparations had been made; the order of all preceding coronations was carefully observed, and never on any like occasion had there been a more magnificent pageant than that which graced the day (27th February 1594) when, within the Cathedral of Chartres, the King, magnificently attired, sat down upon the throne that had been erected before the altar, and upon that brow, which Pope Sixtus V. had declared was especially made for it, the crown of Charlemagne was set. There was but one thing to tarnish the splendor of the spectacle. It was when Henry placed his hand upon the Holy Evangel, and adopting the old coronation oath, swore to root out from the land placed under his jurisdiction all heretics denounced by the church;—an oath he never meant to keep, that he had in fact resolved to violate. All of outward form that ancient usage had prescribed to mark the assumption of royal power having been completed by the hands and under the sanction of the Gallic hierarchy—the popular and practical recognition of Henry's sovereignty rapidly extended. In the eyes of a great majority of the nation his adoption of the Roman Catholic religion had removed the only obstacle that lay in the way of that recognition. Immediately after that event a truce for three months was agreed to between the Leaguers and Henry; and so tired was the community of its thirty years of intestine strife, that even in Paris (which Mayenne still held) the desire had become general that this truce should terminate in a general and lasting peace.

The old priestly agitators, thrown now into stricter alliance than ever with Spain, did their best to stir up the community to reject to the last, and in all circumstances, Henry's title to the crown. The pen, however, was lifted now against the pulpit. During the three months' truce, while the sword was idle, Paris was deluged with pamphlets; nor did the trenchant sword of Henry ever inflict a deeper wound upon the League than that now given by the stinging satire *Ménippée*. The truce however expired without any settlement of affairs. Henry, whose eyes ever turned longingly towards it, approached the capital with his army. Feeling his position there insecure, Mayenne retired to Soissons, leaving Paris in the hands of the Spanish garrison and of the faction of the Leaguer demagogues. The governor of the city, suspected of loyalist leanings, was deposed, and Count Brissac, who had shown such zeal against Henry III. on the day of the Barricades, was installed in his stead. He had a brother-in-law, St. Luc, in Henry's camp, through whom he entered into secret correspondence with the King. Like many others, Brissac, who had got thoroughly tired of acting the part of a rebel, resolved to do an act that should at once place him among the most valued servants of the Crown. The two brothers-in-law had meetings outside the city walls, ostensibly to settle a painful pecuniary difference that existed between them. To avoid suspicion they never met alone, and parted always apparently in greater wrath than ever with one another. Nevertheless they contrived, under cover of their angry altercations, to concoct the plan and arrange all the terms upon which Brissac was to put Henry and his army in possession of the capital. The night of the 22d March 1594 was fixed upon for the great *coup d'état*. Late on the evening of that day, Brissac assembled the leading Royalists of the city, told them that he had confided the particulars of a plan, which was to be executed that night, to a few chosen friends then present, whom he named, and asked them whether they would follow their leader when the time for action came. They at once and unanimously consented. Without any further resolutions made to it, the meeting broke up, on the understanding that they were to hold themselves ready and armed all through the hours of the coming night. It was not possible, however, to prevent all treachery. The Duke of Feria, the Spanish Ambassador, got private notice that about midnight some great Royalist conspiracy was to explode. He despatched a messenger requesting the presence of the Governor at his hotel. The Governor at once complied. The Duke informed him of the report. Brissac made light of it, and proposed to make himself a round of the ramparts and see that all was safe. So satisfactory a proposal could not well be rejected, but a Spanish guard was sent along with the Governor, whose officers had private instructions given them, that on the least sign of treason on Brissac's part, they were to poniard him on the spot. Through the city, along and round the walls, they marched, Brissac conversing in the most unembarrassed way with the Spaniards. All was silent and secure. The dreaded midnight hour went by. It was two o'clock in the morning before the Governor got quit of his suspicious attendants. They parted however from him at last, the Spaniards satisfied that all for that night at least was safe. Brissac lost no time in perfecting his plans and issuing his orders. As the clock struck four, two strong companies seized upon and threw open the Porte Neuve and the Porte St. Denis, and so silently, so rapidly, with such admirable preconcerted order did the royal troops pour into the city, that in half-an-hour all the most important positions in it were occupied. The King himself, who had been waiting for the appointed signal outside the Tuileries, entered unarmed, and was received by Brissac at that same gate which, six years before, he had shut against Henry III. in his flight from the capital. The inhabitants of Paris awoke that morning to see the King, surrounded by a brilliant staff, riding quietly along the Rue St. Honoré, his army in full possession of the city. A company of Germans had, in the first instance, resisted, and about sixty of them had been cut down, but that was nearly all the blood that the occupation of Paris had cost. The Spanish garrison, composed of about 4000 men, lay motionless in its quarters. Henry let the Duke of Feria know that they were at liberty to depart with all the honors of war and a safe conduct to the frontier, provided they left Paris that afternoon,—an offer too generous to be refused. Preserving still his Spanish dignity, the Duke made answer that he had been sent by his master to protect this people from the King, and since they had submitted he would except the offer that had been made. The people had more than submitted.

At first the crowds that filled the streets had gazed upon the unexpected scene with silent astonishment, but as the King proceeded, before going to the Louvre, to give thanks for his success in the cathedral of Notre Dame, the liveliest acclamations of "Vive le Roi!" broke out on every side. And when he alighted to enter the sacred edifice, the pressure around him became so great that the captain of the guard had to drive the people back and open a passage for the King. "No, no," said Henry, in great good-humor, "I am quite content to be knocked about a little that they may see me all the better; they're starving to see a king." "An old woman of about eighty," he wrote afterwards, when himself describing the scene, "took hold of me by the head to kiss me. I was not the last to laugh at it." The *Te Deum* duly celebrated, Henry returned to the Louvre, where all had been prepared for the mid-day repast, according to the old royal custom. It was like a dream to him to seat himself at the head of that table at which, in his earlier years, he had so often sat a guest, while Catherine de Medicis and one or other of her sons did the royal honors. By this time all the shops had been opened; complete order reigned. Faithful to the orders given, the soldiery had abstained from committing a single act of violence. Two citizens only had fallen in the first confusion of the morning entrance. "Were it in my power," said Henry, "I would buy back those two lives with 50,000 crowns,—to have the satisfaction of saying that I had taken Paris without a single drop of French blood being shed." At two o'clock Henry repaired to a window that overlooked the Porte St. Denis, through which the Spanish garrison was to defile in taking its departure. The Duke of Feria, seeing the King, raised his hat and made a slight and somewhat haughty salute in passing. Too happy to stand upon any ceremony, Henry waved his hat to him in reply, and said, "Present my best respects to your master, but do not trouble yourselves, gentlemen, to come back here again." The King's clemency was unbounded. It was a saying of his, "The satisfaction that one gets from revenge lasts but a moment; that which clemency yields is eternal." All was now to be forgiven, forgotten. From the public records, from all public places, every unpleasant memorial of the past was erased. A general amnesty was proclaimed. With the exception of dismissing from the city a few of the most turbulent partisans, Henry received all back into his favor as if no offence had been committed. All hastened to take the oath of allegiance to the King. The Sorbonne itself issued its allocution, declaring that, as the legitimate heir of the throne, Henry should be acknowledged and obeyed, notwithstanding the Pope's refusal to absolve—an allocution directly in the teeth of one which, five years before, the same body had given forth. One party only in all the city refused to follow the general example. The Jesuits would not take the oath of allegiance, nor would they pray for Henry as their lawful King till he had been acknowledged as such by the head of the Church. In the name of the University a process against them that had been suspended for thirty years was revived, and a petition praying for their expulsion from the kingdom, as enemies of the States and spies and allies of Spain, was laid before the Parliament. That Court, however, was not prepared to take at once so extreme a course, and after many heated debates the discussion on this petition was indefinitely adjourned. The Jesuits were exulting in what they regarded as a victory. A tragic incident turned that victory into a defeat. One evening in December (1594), the King had returned to Paris from a short tour in the provinces; a crowd of courtiers awaited his entrance into the reception-room. Henry was in the act of stooping to raise a gentleman who had bent the knee on being presented, when a youth who had glided into the company unperceived, and had made his way close up to the King, struck at him with a knife. The blow was aimed at the throat, but owing to the movement made by Henry at the moment it fell upon the mouth, cutting through the upper lip. The youth was instantly arrested, gave his name as Jean Chastel, acknowledged that he was a pupil of the Jesuits, and that it was from them that he had learned that it would be not only a lawful but a meritorious act to kill the King. At first, as being but little injured, Henry was for letting him escape; but when he heard his confession about his connection with the Jesuits, the recent process against that Order rushed into his memory, and, unable even at such a moment to restrain his pleasantry, "Ah!" said he, "other lips have told me that these Jesuits hate me, but now I feel it in my own. It's by my mouth then that they are to be convicted." I was even so, for not only did the poor youth whom they had initiated into their doctrine of regicide pay the terrible penalty of his attempt by being torn to pieces by horses, but such a storm of public indignation was raised that the Parliament no longer hesitated, but banished the whole Order from France. The King, ever quick to catch at such opportunities, took advantage of the excitement thus created, to get the Parliament to re-establish the edict of 1577 in favor of the Huguenots—a measure unsatisfactory to them, as coming so much short of their demands and expectations, and offensive to those Catholic lords who saw in it a violation of the promise that Henry made on the demise of the late monarch, yet running in the line of that policy which in religious matters Henry had wisely resolved to pursue.

The submission of Paris was followed by that of Rouen, Meaux, Orleans, Toulouse, Amiens, and other leading towns of the kingdom. "Paris is well worth a Mass," the King had said, and the Mass won for him many cities besides the capital. Many, too, of the leading Leaguer chiefs, Vitri, Villars, La Chastre, Villeroi, passed over, or were bought over, to the King's side. Thirty-two millions of livres were spent by Henry in this way. "Well," said he one day in the Louvre, to one of his old antagonists who had made a very profitable transfer of his services to him, "What do you think of seeing me in Paris as I now am?" "Sire," said the ex-Secretary Nicholas, "I say it is the giving to Cæsar the things that are Cæsar's," "Ventre St. Gris!" exclaimed the King, turning to Brissac; "he did not give the things to Cæsar—he sold them, and made a good bargain of it too." The terms, indeed, were so favorable upon which the King entertained every offer of reconciliation, and so little prospect now remained of any thing like successful resistance to his authority, that before the end of the year 1594 the young Duke of Guise and the Duke of Lorraine had both been received as servants of the Crown. Mayenne, however, and his brother, the Duke of Mercœur, still held out, in the hope that the success of Spanish arms or of Spanish diplomacy might raise them to some higher and more independent position than any which, as subjects of the French monarchy, they could reach. Philip, indeed, had now given up the hope of placing his daughter on the throne of France; but he had done so only to fall back upon his earlier project of fomenting divisions in France, and trying to dismember that kingdom. Many towns in the north and west of France were still garrisoned by Spanish troops, and Mayenne and Mercœur had still a considerable French following. Henry, however, was so successful in the summer campaign of 1594, having taken Laon after a protracted siege, and notwithstanding the utmost efforts of the Spaniards under Count Mansfield to relieve it, that, contrary to the advice of his wisest counsellors, he published in January 1595 a declaration of war against Spain. Philip gave immediate and peremptory order to his lieutenants to punish the audacity of the Bourbon. Henry was at Dijon when he learned that a formidable Spanish army under Velasco, the Constable of Castile, had marched to invade France, and was already close upon the frontier. He set off with a few hundred horse to make a reconnaissance of the army. In the neighborhood of Fontaine Française the scouts whom he had sent forward came suddenly in front of the entire Spanish force, and were driven back upon the King. Henry was so taken by surprise that he had not time to put on his armor. Those near him, looking at the overwhelming force that was driving the fugitives before it, advised him at once to fly, pointing to a swift Turkish horse that stood at hand. "It is not your advice," exclaimed the King, "it is your assistance that I need," as he threw himself among the fugitives. He rallied them, charged back upon the enemy, scattered in turn three or four squadrons of their cavalry, each three or four times more numerous than his own; ending one of the closest, deadliest conflicts in which he ever had been engaged, by drawing off his men in safety from the field. "Elsewhere," he said himself, "it was for victory that I fought, but there for life." "Haranbure," he wrote, "hang yourself that you were not found at my side in a combat that we have had with the enemy which we fought like madmen."[1] The result was extraordinary. In a letter to De Mornay describing the conflict, Henry says, "Less than 200 horse have put to flight 2000, and hindered an army of 10,000 foot and 2000 horse from entering my kingdom."[2] It was on Henry's part the folly of D'Aumale acted over again, and Velasco acted over again the part of Parma. Early in the fight Mayenne had recognized the King, and urged it on the Constable to order a general advance of the whole army. Velasco, overcome by caution, not only resisted all the Duke's importunity, but, under the impression that the entire French army was at hand to support the King, he hastily re-crossed the Saône, and, without striking another blow, left Franche Comté open to the King's army. Mayenne in disgust parted from the Spanish camp.

The success which crowned Henry's efforts in the field, and the growing accessions to the number of his adherents, were not perhaps without their influence upon the pope. Clement besides had got alarmed at the independent attitude assumed by

[1] *Recueil*, etc., vol. iv p. 875.   [2] Ib., p. 872.

the Gallican Church, which it was not impossible might throw off the Papal yoke. Whatever were his motives, the Pope began now to show no less eagerness to be reconciled with the French monarch than he had shown obstinacy in remaining alienated from him. The negotiations, opened at his suggestion, were brought to a satisfactory conclusion; and on the 17th April 1595, in a ceremonial which all that Papal skill and experience in that department could do to render imposing was done, Clement publicly absolved Henry, and received him as an accepted and beloved son of the Church. The conditions of the reception were mainly these—the restoration of Catholicism in Béarn, the education of the Prince of Condé, the heir-presumptive to the throne, in the Romish faith, the restoration to the Church of Rome of all its property, and the preference of Catholics in the distribution of all the honors and offices of the State. Henry would not consent as the Pope wished—that his absolution by the French prelates should be declared null and void. He would not acknowledge that the Papal excommunication from which he had been relieved carried any other than an exclusively spiritual character and effect. He would neither ask nor take any investiture with royal rights from the hands of the Holy Father, and he would not engage to violate or reverse the edict passed in favor of the Huguenots. Clement yielded in all these points to the resolution of the king, and in so doing made it clear how much lower ground the Papacy consented to occupy compared with that which it had occupied in the palmy days of Gregory VII. and Innocent III.

All the fresh spirit and strength that this public reconciliation with Rome could give was needed to sustain the King under the reverses that happened to his arms in Picardy. Fuentes, the ablest Spanish general that had risen to take the place of Parma, had defeated the French army opposed to him. Villars and d'Humèires, two of the bravest of Henry's officers, had fallen, and the towns of Le Chatelet, Dourlens, and Cambrai had been taken by the Spaniards. Henry heard of these disasters at Lyons, and hastened northward to repair them. He reached Paris in October. The Parliament deputed some of its leading members to wait upon him. The King replied to their condolences and congratulations in very animated terms. "You admonish me," he said, "that I hazard my life too freely; but, gentlemen, unless I lead, I perceive that nobody follows. If I had money to pay an extra regiment or two of regulars, my life would not be so often in peril. What I want, therefore, is money; and this want the edicts that will be presented to you tomorrow must supply. If you accept them willingly I shall be infinitely obliged to you: first, for your ready concession to my wishes; secondly, because my life will not be so often in danger. I am in excellent health. I came here at a trot, and I mean to go off at a gallop. I want nothing but money. Help me, therefore, and you will soon have the assurance that never have you had a better King than myself." With such help of this kind as he could extract from the pockets of its good citizens, Henry set off from Paris. He reached Amiens, not a little fatigued at the galloping pace at which he travelled. At the gate of the town he found a city orator waiting to inflict upon him a harangue in the shape of an address from the municipality. "O King!" said the orator, "so very great, so very clement, so very magnanimous—" "Ay," said Henry, interrupting him, "and just add, 'so very tired.' I am going to rest at present, and will hear the remainder from you some other time." The authorities escorted the King to the house that had been fitted up for his reception. The dinner stood upon the table, and the King, as hungry as he was tired, was just sitting down to the repast, when another deputation entered to bid him welcome to the city. "Sire," said this new haranguer, "Hannibal, when parting from Carthage—" "O ventre St. Gris!" said Henry, "Hannibal parting from Carthage had dined, and I have that yet to do." And so that piece of eloquence also was cut short.

The winter campaign of 1595–96 began by the siege of La Fère, a small but strongly fortified town which served as an advanced post to the Spaniards in Picardy. This siege began in November, and the place was not reduced till March. It was during its course that Mayenne at last accepted the generous offers of Henry, and in attaching himself to the King linked himself to the fortunes of his country in its conflict with Spain. It was in January 1596, while the King was living at Monceaux en Brie, that Mayenne arrived to make his submission in person. Henry was walking in the grounds of the château when the Duke presented himself. Mayenne bent the knee, and was beginning in very formal terms to thank his Majesty for his bounty, and for having delivered him from the arrogance of the Spaniard, when Henry embraced him with the greatest cordiality, grasped his hand, and set off with him at a rapid pace to show him all the improvements that he was making in the gardens. The poor Duke, who was exceedingly fat and fond of ease—spending more time, as the pope used to say, at his dinner than Henry spent in his bed— was hurried along, limping, panting, blowing. "Tell the truth, cousin," said the King to him at last, after he had given him a thorough heat, "don't I go somewhat too fast for you?" "Indeed, Sire," said the duke, "you do; and if you go any further with me at this rate I'll expire." Bursting into a hearty laugh, and holding out his hand to Mayenne, "There's my hand for you; take it, my cousin, and believe me that's the only punishment it ever will inflict on you." And it was the only revenge taken for all the wrongs done him by the last head of the League.

Early in the spring of 1596 one of the largest Spanish armies that had ever crossed the French frontier mustered under the command of the new governor of the Pays Bas, the Cardinal Archduke Albert. The declared object of its movements was to raise the siege of La Fère. Henry gathered all the forces he could command at St. Quentin and prepared to meet the danger. A battle under the walls of La Fère appeared inevitable. Suddenly, however, the Spanish army, leaving La Fère to its fate, wheeled westward, and by a rapid and unlooked-for march threw itself upon Calais, which in a week or two it forced to surrender. The loss of this important seaport, taken before his eyes and notwithstanding every effort on his part to succor it, fell heavy upon the heart of the King. That heart, however, was not one to sink beneath any such calamity. "Well, my friends," he said upon this occasion, "Calais is taken; but we must not lose courage, since it is in the midst of afflictions that brave men become braver, and strengthen themselves with new hopes. It is the fortune of war to lost at one time and gain at another. Our enemies have had their turn, and, by God's help, we shall have ours. Let us not then give way to murmuring or complaint, nor cast blame on any one. Rather let us do honor to the memory of the dead, and let us apply ourselves to find out the means that this place may remain in the hands of the Spaniards only as many days as our ancestors left it years in the hands of the English." Knowing how much the passing of Calais into the hands of her greatest enemy would annoy Elizabeth, Henry despatched an ambassador to her, asking her aid in the retaking of it. Elizabeth ventured to propose, as a condition of that aid being given, that Calais should be garrisoned by her troops. "Madame," wrote Henry to her, "I have received our letter, delivered by M. de Sidney, and have also listened to the proposals which he was charged by you to make. These demands I deem so unseemly, and so contrary to the sincere friendship which I have ever met with from your Majesty, that I would fain persuade myself that they have been inspired by those who understand not the promptings of your spirit. . . . Permit me, Madame, to believe, despite the communication which I have received, that you disdain to measure your friendship by the standard of your self-interest and gain, even on this supreme occasion, when the urgency of affairs is so great that no time may be lost in negotiation."[1] Elizabeth felt the dignified rebuke, professed to have been misunderstood, and, overcoming the ill-humor she had manifested at Henry's abjuration, concluded along with the United Provinces, a new and closer treaty with France, in which the contracting parties bound themselves to mutual succor against the common enemy. Calais, however, was not retaken. The Spaniards not only continued to hold it, but succeeded in reducing and retaining Guesnes and Arras.

[1] *Recueil*, etc., vol. iv. p. 573.

It was but a poor compensation to Henry when La Fère at last capitulated (16th May 1596). Famine and pestilence now broke up his army, and hindered him from making any further effort to retrieve his losses. The military chest had got exhausted, and he had tried in vain to replenish it. On asking his Council for a very moderate sum with which to undertake the siege of Arras, he was told it was absolutely impossible to get it. The condition to which the King himself was reduced at this time was pitiable. "I am near the enemy," he writes, "and I have scarcely a horse to ride or a suit of armor to put on. My shirts are all torn; my coat is out at the elbows; my pot is often empty,—these last few days I have dined with one or other of my friends, my purveyors telling me that they had no longer the means of supplying my table."

It was full time for Henry to look into the state of the public finances. They were in a truly deplorable condition. Besides the ordinary expenditure, heightened by such constant war, the vast sums paid to Leaguer chiefs and Leaguer towns to win back their allegiance had utterly drained the treasury. All this however it might have stood, had it not been for the enormous abuses that had crept into the administration of the public funds. Such an extensive and complicated system of peculation had been carried on that not a half, in some instances not a third, in some not even a fourth, part of the sums actually levied reached their destination. The prompters of these peculations were so many, and of such high rank and power, that it seemed difficult to touch the evil or apply any effective remedy. Nevertheless, if the Monarchy was to be upheld that must be done, and Henry resolved to do it. The task was committed to Rosny, and never was hand better fitted for such a task than his. Clear-headed, cool-hearted, quick to detect abuse, prompt in devising the remedy, constant and indomitable in the application of it; short, and dry, and reserved in his address, yet with enough of the courtier about him to give no needless offence; imperturbable, impenetrable, incorruptible, inaccessible to flattery; deaf to the voice of emotions; with an inborn taste and talent for calculation, a wonderful capacity for work, and a quiet, steady, unwearying and unbending energy,—there met in Sully all the qualities required in the man who was to deal successfully with such a thick and tangled forest of financial abuses,—that incarnate genius of economy that was in him obeying but one spirit higher and greater than itself, the one great ruling passion of a sincere and unbounded attachment to the King. It was Henry's good fortune that there was a man so qualified for the work that had to be done within his reach. It proved his own possession of a kindred capacity, that he soon discovered and so entirely trusted him, and it redounds to the honor both of monarch and of minister, that the one gave himself up with such a thorough devotedness to the service of his royal master, and that that master so fully understood and so thoroughly appreciated the service that was rendered.

Sully's first trial of his hand in the executive department—for it was by slow degrees he rose to power—was when a preliminary inquiry into the state of matters all over the realm was resolved upon, and the inspection of four districts of the country was assigned to him. He returned from his financial tour with 500,000 crowns in solid cash, four times the amount the King had asked for carrying on the siege of Arras—these 500,000 crowns not extorted from the taxpayers, not the produce of the taxation, but the amount of detected and admitted defalcations in the payment of those by whom the taxes had been farmed. The evidence that this single instance supplied convinced the King that many radical reforms were needed; but how were these to be carried out? It might have been by convoking the Estates-General of the kingdom, and committing to them a function like to that now exercised by our own House of Commons—by putting the imposition and administration of all the public funds into the hands of the representatives of the people. Henry was not prepared to take such a step—to initiate in such a way free representative institutions in France. Afraid to call together the Estates-General lest some invasion might be attempted by them on the royal prerogatives, he satisfied himself with summoning to Rouen about 150 persons of distinction, to constitute, along with the ordinary counsellors of the Crown, what was designated as the Assembly of Notables. The Assembly met in October 1596. Henry in opening it said, "If I wished to earn the title of an orator I should have learned by heart some fine and showy harangue, the which I should have pronounced with becoming gravity. My ambition soars to a higher distinction. I covet the glorious titles of Liberator and Restorer of this realm. In order to attain this end I have assembled you. You know to your cost, as I know to mine, that when God called me to this Crown I found France not only half ruined, but also quite lost to Frenchmen. By Divine favor, by the prayers and counsels of those among my good servants not called to the profession of arms, by the swords of my valiant and generous noblesse, and by my own incredible toils and labors, I have saved France from outward enemies. Let us now save this France of ours from financial ruin. Participate with me, my dear subjects, in this second triumph, as you have already shared in the first. I have not assembled you after the fashion of my predecessors to confirm my fiats, but I have called you to listen to your counsels, to follow your advice; in short, to place myself under your tutelage, a resolve which has seldom actuated kings who like myself had gray beards and were conquerors."

The Assembly proceeded to acquit itself of the task thus generously assigned to it. Estimating the revenue required for all purposes of State at thirty million of livres, it proposed that the raising and application of one half of this sum should be committed to the King and his Council to meet the expenses of the royal house and of the army and navy, and that the raising and application of the other half should be committed to a new Council to be chosen, in the first instance, by this Assembly of Notables, and afterwards by the great courts of the kingdom. As the current income fell short of the required one, to meet the deficiency they proposed that a new tax of a sou per pound on all articles of merchandise indiscriminately should be levied. Sully advised the King to adopt the measure; choosing for his half of the revenue the one most easily raised, and committing the administration of the other half, and especially the levying of this new impost, which he foresaw would be both unpopular and unproductive, to the newly established Council. Henry adopted the advice, and it ended as the sagacious counsellor had foreseen. The affair became speedily unmanageable, the new tax had to be given up, the new Council dissolved, and the entire control of the public revenue returned into the hands of the King, to be lodged by him in the hands of Sully himself.

From Rouen Henry returned to Paris, and gave himself up to the festivities of the capital. A luxurious entertainment, described minutely by L'Étoile, was given by the Constable De Montmorency to celebrate the baptism of his son and heir 12th March 1597). The day was dawning before the King returned from the banquet to the Louvre. He had retired to unrobe when a courier with a despatch from the Governor of Picardy was ushered into his chamber. The despatch bore that the town of Amiens had been taken, and was in possession of the Spaniard. The way from the frontier to the capital lay open to the enemy. The blow fell like a thunderbolt upon the King. "Those miserable men of Amiens," he said to Sully, as, half-dressed, with his hands behind his back, he paced impatiently up and down his chamber, " have ruined themselves and me, but by the help of God we will yet prevail. I have played too long the King of France; it is time to play once more the King of Navarre. Five hours afterwards, the Louvre, Gabrielle d'Estrées, and all the fascinations of the capital were forsaken, and the hero of Navarre was on his way to meet the enemy. It had been by an ingenious stratagem that has been often practised that the Spanish Governor of Dourlens, Portocarrero, had got possession of Amiens. A wagon of straw, behind which a number of soldiers disguised as peasants with bags of walnuts on their backs, driving into the city, stopped under the portcullis. One of the peasants let fall the sack he carried, so that its contents were poured upon the ground. While the city guard were scrambling for the scattered walnuts, a pistol-shot was fired, the peasants threw off their disguise, and an ambuscade that awaited the signal rushed to their support. In vain the sentinel let fall the portcullis; the wagon with its high load was then beneath it; in vain the citizens flew to arms: an overpowering force swarmed through the gate into the city, and Amiens was taken. The King sprang to recapture it. His military ardor communicated itself to the nation.

A splendid army, in which we find 4000 English soldiers, sat down before the city. The siege lasted all the summer months. It was not till September that the Archduke attempted the relief. He brought with him a force greatly superior to that under Henry's command. The King resolved to do as he had done at Arques—to keep within the entrenchments that he had thrown up. A single attempt to force his position was made by the Spaniards. The effect was such that, without striking a second stroke, in haste and fear, as before a victorious and pursuing foe, the vast army of the Archduke retreated and left Amiens to its fate. It was in the height of his triumph that the King wrote the note misquoted and misdated by Voltaire:—
"Hang yourself, brave Crillon, for not having been near me on Monday last at the finest encounter which has ever been seen, or perhaps will ever be witnessed again. Believe me, I longed much for you. The Cardinal came on very furiously, but he has gone off very sneakingly. I hope on

Thursday next to be in Amiens. I shall not stay long inactive, as I have now one of the finest armies imaginable. Nothing is wanting but the presence of the brave Crillon, who will always be welcome. Adieu.—From the camp before Amiens, 20th September 1597." [1]

Amiens capitulated on the 25th, and the King instantly turned the fine army of which he was so proud against the only Leaguer chief who was still in arms against him. So long as Henry had other and more powerful enemies to contend with, he had left the war in Brittany with the Duke of Mercœur to be conducted by one or other of his lieutenants. But when the Duke saw the royal army led on by the King in person now ready to be launched at him, it appeared very clear to him that his time for submission had come. And he had a clever wife, who saw even clearer and further than he did. Since they could not, as it now appeared, even with Spanish aid, acquire the independent sovereignty of Sedan, why not marry their only daughter and heiress to the King's eldest son by Gabrielle d'Estrées, and so protect the family inheritance from royal grasp? The proposal was grateful to Gabrielle, who at this time was full of hope that on Marguérite de Valois being divorced she would be acknowledged as Queen. Henry heartily acquiesced, as it gave his son, whom he had already placed in the first order of the peerage, a

[1] *Recueil*, etc., vol. iv. p. 848.

heritage to sustain his title. The articles of contract were drawn up and the treaty signed which left Henry without an enemy in arms, and closed the long and bloody civil wars by which France during the course of nearly forty years had been desolated.

While the laurels won at Amiens were yet fresh upon his brow, Henry resolved to accomplish another work, which has gained him a more imperishable renown. At his accession, the Huguenots, over whom the oppressive Edicts of 1585 and 1588 were still legally impending, besought his interference on their behalf. He revoked the obnoxious Edicts, but in the way of legal enactment did nothing more on their behalf. It was doing but little for those by whose help he had mounted to the throne, and who had been so prodigal of their lives in his service, to make their position in the State as good but no better than it had been under the reign of any of his predecessors. Still however he had it at first to say to them that they did not need enactments in their favor when a Prince of their own faith was upon the throne. But his abjuration changed that state of matters. It turned the confidence of the Huguenots into jealousy and suspicion. The public oaths that he took to exterminate them filled them not unnaturally with alarm. They met both in synod and political assembly, and organized themselves as perfectly as they could. Prepared to find in their former chief a foe, they showed the same determined front they had ever shown. Henry in his turn was annoyed at their suspicions, and irritated at the self-protective measures they took. He had really no intention to interfere with their existing liberties, he was ready even legally to ratify and extend them; but he had to proceed cautiously; he was watched by those who were ready to interpret every thing that he did in favor of his former friends into the evidence that he meant to prove false to the Catholicism he had professed. For some time after his abjuration he did not feel his position strong enough to do more than re-establish the Edict of 1579. It was but a scant security and a limited freedom that this measure gave to the Huguenots. Even such as it was they did not get the full benefit of it. By other and separate treaties which Henry had made with Leaguer chiefs and towns, the Reformed faith was prohibited in districts where, under the edict, it should have been allowed. In many parts of the country, in open violation of the edict, the Huguenots were treated with the greatest harshness. Their books were burned, their children torn from them in infancy to be educated in the Roman Catholic faith, their testamentary dispositions in favor of their families disputed and invalidated, their refusal to salute the Host punished as a civil offence, their very dead torn up out of the public burying-grounds and cast away as carrion. Year after year they carried their complaints to Henry, but year after year they had to listen to the same reply—the assurance of his personal friendship and his resolution to do his utmost for them so soon as his position was secure. In their impatience the Huguenots did injustice to the King; and when at last his time of weakness and of danger came—while it pleases us to hear of them shutting their ears as they did to those counsellors—the chief men, too, of their party in rank and power, the Dukes of Bouillon and Tremouille—who advised them to take up arms on their account and extract by force what they had failed to get by entreaty; it pains us to see that at the siege of Amiens not a white scarf was to be seen. They should not have deserted their monarch in his hour of need. But Henry was not resentful. He knew what good reason they had to complain of the treatment they were receiving, what good right they had to expect protection at his hands. No sooner therefore did victory crown his arms than one of the first exercises of that freedom and power it gave was to sign at Nantes, on the 15th April 1598, that celebrated Edict which for eighty-seven years covered and protected the liberties of Protestantism in France.[1]

By this celebrated Edict, full liberty of conscience was guaranteed to all—*i. e.*, no man was any more to be persecuted or punished for his individual belief. Liberty of public worship was granted to the Reformed in all places where it had been previously

---

[1] The Edict is fully given in Drion's *Histoire Chronologique*, pp. 208-258.

practised. Both the higher and lower nobility attached to the Reformed faith were allowed to have private chapels in their residences; but the lower were not to admit more than thirty persons to the service. The Reformed were held to be admissible to all offices and employments under the State—all their civil disabilities were removed. The public schools, colleges, and hospitals were opened to them. Their children were to be protected, their testamentary dispositions held valid, disabilities on account of religious connection were prohibited, separate places of sepulture allowed. Mixed chambers, or courts composed in equal numbers of Catholics and Protestants, were instituted to try all cases in which Protestant interests were involved. As material guarantees, a number of fortified towns, amounting finally to about 200, were put into the hands of the Huguenots, and a yearly subsidy was granted for the maintenance of the Protestant ministry—a large and liberal measure, entitling Henry to be called the inaugurator of the reign of religious toleration in France; a larger and more liberal measure than any of the great Protestant kingdoms had at this time granted to their Roman Catholic subjects. The honorable precedence that France thus took was not owing to the greater advance of her population in the spirit of toleration, but to the determination of her King. Neither was that determination grounded on any profound and enlightened regard on Henry's part for the rights of the individual conscience. It was policy not principle; it was his past experience of the evils of intolerance on both sides; it was his desire to put an end to these evils and secure for his country the blessings of peace and concord, that regulated his conduct in this matter.

He had the greatest difficulty in effecting this object. The Parliament of Paris refused to register the edict. The Parliaments of Bordeaux, Toulouse, Rouen followed its example. Rouen sent deputies to remonstrate with the King. They found him upon the floor of the room into which they were introduced, romping and rollicking with his children on his back. "I'm playing the fool," said he as they approached, "here with my children; but I'm quite ready to play the wise man with you;" and rising, he conducted them to an adjoining chamber. Their President made a long story of it—quite too long for his hearer. The reply was brief: "I am your lawful sovereign. I am the head, my kingdom is the body, and you have the honor to be members. It is the office of the head to command and of the members to obey. I have made an edict; I wish to see it executed, and however it be I must be obeyed." So spake he, in effect, to the deputies from all the Parliaments. He knew that nothing short of this would do, and he was thoroughly resolved that the provisions of this edict should be executed. It was in favor of that very kind of liberty that we prize the most that the high hand of absolute and arbitrary power was thus employed.

We cannot however but regret that a measure in itself so wise and good owed its establishment to the exercise of such despotic authority. Henry no doubt succeeded when otherwise he might have failed; but he did so by perfecting and putting into the hands of his successors the instrument which one of them employed in overturning that very edifice of religious toleration he had raised; he did so, by planting the monarchy itself on that slippery edge over which at last it fell to be broken into fragments.

So needful to France did entire repose appear, that Henry hailed these overtures now made to him through the Papal Legate. Philip II., foiled in all his efforts, failing in strength, within a few months of death, at last was willing to lay down the sword. He found as great a willingness to do so on the part of the French monarch. The terms were not difficult of settlement when both parties were so bent on peace, and on the 2d of May 1598 that Treaty was signed at Vervins which restored to France all the late Spanish conquests. "By the stroke of a pen," said Henry, "I have conquered more towns than I could have captured with the best swords of my realm in a long campaign." Within the short space of three months, the Treaty with the Duke of Mercœur, the Edict of Nantes, and the Peace of Vervins, three of the most important measures of Henry's reign, were accomplished. The civil and religious strifes were closed, the foreign yoke finally and fully thrown off, and an honorable peace established, which gave twelve years of tranquillity to France.

One thing only the peace of Vervins left unsettled. In the preceding troubles a small Italian appanage, the Marquisate of Saluces, had been seized by Charles Emmanuel, Duke of Savoy, and remained still in his possession. The right of France to it was not disputed, did not admit indeed of dispute; but the Duke was unwilling to part with what constituted one of the keys of Italy. He came to Paris in December 1599 to negotiate the affair in person. Henry offered to exchange the Italian Marquisate for a much larger territory, embracing districts both on the northern and southern sides of the Alps, but the Duke was reluctant to make a transfer which would give the French a footing upon the Italian soil. After a two months' residence in it he left Paris, having signed an engagement that within three months he would either accept the French proposal or restore the Marquisate to its rightful owner. During his stay in the French capital he had contrived to sow the seeds of disaffection in the breast of more than one of the chief nobles. The overweening vanity, the haughty pride, the insatiable ambition of the Duke of Biron aid him particularly open to the wiles of the Savoyard. Charles Emmanuel, as son-in-law to Philip II., brother-in-law to the then reigning King of Spain, was in strict alliance with the Spanish Court. The offer of the hand of one of the Duke of Savoy's daughters, and of the support of Spain in erecting Burgundy, of which he was governor, into a separate and independent principality, was too tempting for Biron, and he entered into treasonable correspondence with the Duke. Meanwhile the three months given to the Duke to decide expired, but he still kept hold of the Marquisate. Wearied with delays, whose object was transparent, Henry at last had recourse to arms. Savoy was speedily overrun with French troops, and its chief strongholds taken. Spain was not prepared to back her ally, and the affair terminated by Henry's accepting in lieu of the Marquisate that part of Savoy which now constitutes the Department of Aisne in France. The King had been made aware of Biron's traffickings with the Duke and with Fuentes, the Governor of Milan, one of France's bitterest enemies. The clue had been obtained through Lafin, a Frenchman whom Biron had employed as his confidential agent, and Renaze, Lafin's associate. Unwilling to believe the worst of his early friend and companion in arms, Henry sent for Biron, told him of the suspicions of his fidelity that had been excited, advised him to have no more to do with Lafin, and warned him in the most solemn manner that crimes committed against the State private friendship could not overlook. Biron denied all, and heedless of this first warning renewed the correspondence with Fuentes. Again the King was informed of his infidelity, but this time Biron threw himself on the clemency of the King, and made partial acknowledgment of his guilt. Henry was moved to tears by the avowal, and readily forgave. It was not long however till Biron was again seduced, and became party to a treaty, the object of which was to renew the troubles in France and dethrone the reigning monarch. The Duke of Bouillon and the Count d'Auvergne, half brother of the Marquise de Verneuille, were more or less involved with him in the plot, but managed to keep their participation in it less open to detection. Biron was at this time (the summer of 1601) sent as Ambassador to England. He was received with the most distinguished honors at the English Court, and admitted to many interviews with Elizabeth. In one of these, at an open window from which the gibbet could be seen on which the head of Essex was impaled, the conversation turned upon the fate of the unfortunate Earl. Biron dropped some words indicating that in his judgment the sentence executed had been too severe. Elizabeth fired up at the implied censure of her conduct. "He suffered righteously," she said to Biron, "and the King, my brother, would do well to act in Paris as I have done in London. He should deliver up to condign punishment every traitor and rebel of his realm. I pray Heaven that the clemency of your Prince may not be fatal to him. For myself, I never pardon any one who dares to disturb the peace of my realm." Ominous words, spoken in full knowledge of the rumors about Biron then rife at the French Court. The full evidence of the Marshal's guilt was at last placed in Henry's hand. Renaze had been thrown into prison in Italy, Lafin had solicited Biron's intervention to have him delivered, the Duke had refused, and Lafin had turned traitor and revealed the whole. Remembering perhaps the early warning of his sovereign, Biron had commanded his agent to burn all the papers which in any way committed him. Lafin pretended to do so in Biron's presence, but carefully concealed them all. There was one peculiarly criminatory document, in Biron's own handwriting, which he had in his own possession: Lafin suggested that it too should be consumed. The fatal paper was handed to him for this purpose; dexterously hiding it, he crumbled up another piece of paper in its stead, which he flung into the fire. Lafin presented all the letters and papers to Henry. The Marshal was summoned to Fontainebleau. He arrived there early in the morning of the 12th of January 1602. As he entered the palace Lafin saluted him, and whispered in his ear as he passed, "Courage, my master, speak boldly." Biron had been previously assured by letter from himself that Lafin had made no discoveries. He found the King walking in the garden. Henry passed his arm round the Marshal's neck, and embracing him said, "You have done well, my friend, to confide in me." The King at once told him why he had been sent for, and entreated him frankly to confess. The

Marshal would confess nothing, had nothing to confess, was there not to justify himself, but to learn who were his accusers. That was the sole object of his journey. He dined with Epernon. The Duke told him of Lafin's treachery, and entreated him to throw himself upon the King's mercy. The Marshal was unmoved. Afterwards he was sent for by the King, who, going back upon all the scenes of their early intimacy, conjured him to be open and to tell all. Under the fatal delusion that Henry, in absence of other evidence, was trying to entrap him into a confession, Biron was as haughty and inflexible as ever. At the King's instance the Count de Soissons invited Biron to supper, and assuring him that his Majesty was perfectly informed of his proceedings besought him to acknowledge his guilt. Next morning Henry asked him to join him in his walk. He had no other answer to give the King than that he had given the day before. As a last chance given Sully was despatched to wait upon Biron. "Tell him," said Henry, "that if he disguises nothing, I give you my royal word that I will, with all my heart, grant him a free pardon." Sully's entreaties were as fruitless as had been those of Epernon and Soissons. Biron by this time had got alarmed and given secret orders to have his horses saddled and sent out to meet him in the woods at midnight, that after quitting the royal circle, which he was to join at supper, he might effect his flight. As he ascended the staircase of the Palace, a note was put into his hand; it told him that within three hours he would be arrested. He showed the note to his companion and laughed, as he passed on to the Queen's saloon. The King was playing at cards with her Majesty, and they invited Biron to join them in the game. As the clock struck eleven, Henry rose and led the Marshal aside. "My friend," said he, "you know that I have loved you; confess your errors with your own lips, and, on the word of a king, whatever they may be, I will forgive; but force me to prove your guilt publicly, and I will not, I swear to you, interfere with the award of justice." Stubborn to the last, Biron demanded only that the names of his slanderers should be given up to him. "Well, Marshal," said Henry, "I see I can make nothing of you." He passed into his cabinet and closed the door. Vitry, the captain of the guard, who had been told to have all in readiness, was instantly sent for, and directed to arrest the Marshal as he left the room. In a few minutes the court, the corridor, the staircase, the antechamber were filled with soldiers. Henry re-entered the saloon and dismissed the circle. "Adieu, Baron Biron," he said, the title given telling ominously of coming degradation, "remember what I said." In the antechamber the Marshal was arrested, and conveyed the next day to the Bastile. He remained sullenly defiant, till his own letters and papers were put into his hands, and he was confronted with Lafin. Then his spirit broke, but broke only to vent itself in frantic tirades against the wretch who had sworn such solemn oaths to be faithful to him. "The testimony of so perfidious a villain was not," he said, "to be trusted for a moment, and that if only Renaze were there, he could convict Lafin of many falsehoods in the testimony he had given." Unfortunately for the Marshal, Renaze, having escaped somehow from prison, was there waiting to be brought in as a witness. His testimony confirmed all that Lafin had stated. Biron's defence of himself before the Parliament still remains, and is referred to as one of the finest pieces of judicial eloquence in the French tongue. It could not avail against the evidence that was adduced. On Monday, the 29th of July, he was doomed to be beheaded. The King was besieged with entreaties to spare his life; but his resolution had been taken: justice must take its course. On Wednesday morning (the 31st), the Chancellor and other officials proceeded to the Bastile to inform the Marshal that the sentence would be executed that afternoon at five o'clock. He lost all self-possession at the idea of dying such a degrading death. Now he raved at the Chancellor and his associates, charging them with the guilt of his condemnation, and summoning them all to appear before God one year thereafter to answer for their deed. Then he grasped Bellièvre by the arm, pitiably exclaiming, "Must I die? Is there no way of escape?" Afterwards, when somewhat calmed, one of his attendants asked him how it came that he who had so often and so fearlessly faced death on the battle-field now trembled at his approach? "My friend," said he, "then I looked at death, but now death looks at me." For an hour or so he walked up and down through the chapel of the Bastile in unbroken silence. Then the paroxysm again came on him: he laughed, he wept, he prayed, he swore. At length the fatal hour arrived. A scaffold had been erected in the court of the Bastile. The Chancellor presented himself at the door of the chapel. Biron followed him mechanically to the foot of the scaffold. His eye wandered over the soldiers that were drawn up around. "Won't you oblige me," he said to them, "by sending a musket-ball through my body? Oh, to die so miserably, by such a shameful stroke!" His eye fell upon the executioner. "Don't touch me!" he exclaimed, "I won't be bound. I will die free." He was told that he must kneel. "No," he said, "I will die standing, as Vespasian counselled. If you can't cut me down in one stroke, take thirty; I will stand as quiet as an owl." He ascended the scaffold; a handkerchief was handed him; he bound it round his eyes, and bent. Then springing up, he tore the covering from his eyes. Then he asked Barenton. one of his own servants, to bind the handkerchief; across his eyes once more. Once more he tore it off, exclaiming, "O Heaven, let me gaze upon the sky once more!" The headsman spoke to him.

He glared at him and his attendants with fury in his eyes. "Don't touch me while there's life in my body; if you provoke me, I'll strangle the half of you, and force the other half to kill me." A third time the handkerchief was re-adjusted, and he knelt. "Quick, quick!" he said, and again was rising, when the sword-stroke fell. The head rebounded from the scaffold and rolled out among the horrified spectators.

It was a warning that many of the great nobles needed, and it spared Henry the necessity of giving another of the kind during the remainder of his reign. The ten years from 1600 to 1610 were years of tranquillity, and gave to Henry the opportunity he had so ardently longed for of restoring and regenerating France. In doing so difficulties had to be faced, and labors undergone, requiring greater courage and greater talent than were called for in the most arduous campaigns; and it gives one no slight idea of the far-sightedness, the versatility, the many-sidedness, the boundless activity of Henry of Navarre, that he, to whom from the age of fifteen the stir and strife of war had been as the breath of life, the battle-plain the field of glory, who had been present at 300 sieges, taken part in nearly 200 lesser combats, been commander-in-chief in three great pitched battles, should now, at the age of forty-six, have turned himself to the task of the reformer, the administrator, the legislator, and the politician, and should, in that new field of effort, have won for himself a higher place among those monarchs of France who have conferred great civil and social benefits on their country, than his sword had won for him among her warrior-kings. The Memoirs of Sully had already supplied large evidence of this, bearing, however, the impression that it was to the great minister more than to the great monarch that the result was due. Recent researches,[1] and the publication of his own letters, have presented this side of Henry's character in new and fuller light, and taught us to regard him as one of the wisest legislators and ablest politicians who ever filled an European throne, understanding far better than even Sully did what were the true and permanent foundations on which the peace and prosperity of this country should be based.

I can do little more now than allude to the important services which during these years of peace Henry rendered to France. The first thing that the King and his Ministers took in hand was the regulation of the public revenue. The yearly expenditure had been exceeding the yearly income, till at last the returns showed an annual deficit of about 7,000,000

---

[1] *Histoire du Règne de Henri IV.* Par M. A. Poirson, Ancien Proviseur des Lycées Saint Louis et Charlemagne, Conseiller honoraire de l'Université. Paris, 1856. 3 vols.

Henri IV. et sa Politique. Par Charles Mercier de Lacombe. Paris, 1860.

Histoire de France. Par Henri Martin. Tome x. Paris, 1857.

of livres, while the national debt had risen from 43,000,000 to 368,000,000. In the course of these ten years that debt was reduced by 327,000,000 having been paid off. Without any new burdens being imposed, and while many old ones had been lightened, the annual receipts were increased, and the annual expenditure diminished, so as to throw the balance on the other side, and instead of a deficit to show a clear annual surplus of 8,000,000. Of still greater importance than a mere right handling of the existing financial resources, was the stimulus given by the Government to agriculture, trade and commerce, the perennial and permanent sources of national wealth. Impoverished, loaded with debt, exposed to all kinds of oppression and extortion, liable to have their persons, their cattle, their implements of husbandry arrested, the peasantry of France had sunk into a wretched condition in the course of the civil wars. One-third of the land was out of cultivation, and such cultivation as there was, of the rudest and most ineffective kind. In the midst of this general depression and neglect of the art of husbandry, a gentleman of Languedoc had for years given his attention to the theory and practice of agriculture. Henry heard of Oliver de Serres, and of his model farm at Pradel. He sent for him to Paris, encouraged him to embody the results of his experience in a volume dedicated to the King, and entitled *Théâtre d'Agriculture.* For three or four months after its publication the King devoted half-an-hour each day after dinner to the reading of this book, and did every thing he could to have it widely circulated throughout the country. Vigorous measures were taken to protect the tillers of the soil; the existing arrears of taxes were remitted, the arrest for debt of their cattle and instruments of husbandry prohibited, the land-tax, which lay heavy upon them, was lightened, the legal rate of interest was lowered, and every encouragement was given to capital being advanced to them. Blessed with peace, protected in their labor, eased in imposts, directed to new and better methods of cultivation, the farmers of France set themselves heartily to work, and in a few years so added to the annual produce of the country that it became at last more than equal to meet all home demands. Watching with an intelligent eye this movement, Henry at last threw open the ports, and proclaimed a free traffic outwards both for the grain and wines of France. Another volume on the regeneration of manufactures in France had been dedicated to Henry by Barthelemy Laffemas. Among other proposals of its author was the introduction of the silk manufacture into France, hitherto confined to warmer climates. It was said that there were many districts in France in which the mulberry-tree, which furnished the food of the silkworm, would flourish. To test the statement, Henry ordered 20,000 young mulberry-trees to be sent to Paris, and had them planted in the gardens of the

Tuileries and of Fontainebleau. Houses were built in the royal gardens for the feeding of the silk-worms, and skilful hands were brought from Italy to teach the Frenchmen how to extract the silk. The experiment was eminently successful. The raw material thus produced was found equal to the finest foreign silk. A royal ordinance was issued that in every diocese of the land a nursery of 50,000 young mulberry-trees should be formed. Every inducement was held out to capitalists and skilled workmen engaging in the silk manufacture, and so the first impulse was given to a branch of industry that now yields above 300,000,000 francs annually to France. Other manufactures were not overlooked. It is to Henry that the Gobelin manufactory at Paris owes its origin. The greatest attention was bestowed on roads and bridges, tolls and pontages, so as to increase the facilities of inland transit. The idea that the North Sea and the Mediterranean might be connected by a series of canals uniting some of the chief rivers of France, had been broached in the reign of Francis I., but nothing had been done to realize it. Henry took the idea up, and set about its accomplishment, calling on the pen of the great scholar, Joseph Scaliger, one of his literary protégés, to write a learned discourse upon the junction of the seas. As compared with Holland, England, and Spain, France was weak upon the ocean, and had few colonies abroad. Her foreign commerce was but limited. It was one of the great objects of Henry's ambition to make her as powerful at sea as upon land. The first steps were taken to create a powerful navy. Commercial treaties were negotiated with England, Spain, and other foreign lands. In 1604, letters-patent were issued incorporating a company for trading with the East Indies, similar to those established at Amsterdam in 1594, and in London in 1600. Expeditions for maritime discovery and for colonization were fitted up. The great lakes of North America were for the first time made known to Europe. A French colony settled in Canada, and laid the foundation there of the cities of Quebec and Montreal.

For all that Henry did in remodelling the military establishments of France, his introduction of the modern system of warfare, his establishment of military schools and military hospitals, the progress in the art of fortification that he effected,— for all that he did in fostering those institutions devoted to the protection of life and promotion of public health, his abolition of the practice of duelling, his widening and improving the streets of Paris, his reconstruction and enlargement of L'Hôtel Dieu, his founding of the hospitals of St. Marcel, St. Louis, and De la Charité—his quadrupling, in fact, the number of such hospitals in France,—for all he did to encourage literature, science, and the fine arts, his remodelling of the University of Paris, his establishment and endowment of new professorships, his placing in the chairs so instituted such men as Joseph Scaliger and Isaac Casaubon, his foundation of the Bibliothèque Royale, one of the first libraries in Europe,—for all, in fact, that during these ten years this great Prince did to develop the resources, to stimulate the industries, to increase the commerce, to reform the institutions, to enlighten and refine and so elevate the condition of the people of France,—we refer the reader to the second and third volumes of Poirson's exhaustive work; enough to say that in no other ten years of her history did France make so large a stride onward in the path of prosperity and civilization—a stride that she was mainly helped and encouraged to take by the genius and example of her ruler.

It was however in the domain of foreign politics that Henry exhibited the acuteness and comprehensiveness of his genius, and his marvellous powers of contrivance, combination, execution. The house of Austria, embracing both its German and Spanish branches, had lapsed into comparative inaction on the death of Philip II. It had not renounced however its great and cherished scheme of a universal monarchy, involving the destruction of the national independence and the religious liberties of all the other nations of Europe. It waited but the time when, released from its existing difficulties, with its resources recruited, it might arm once more that half of Europe which was under its control, and employ it in the execution of this enterprise. The great political project, to the maturing of which Henry IV. devoted his untiring energies for the last years of his life, was the bringing of the other half of Europe into close political alliance, and arming it against the house of Austria, and striking when the fit time came such a blow at the ambition and intolerance of that house that it might never be able to recover. After innumerable negotiations, in which the greatest diplomatic skill was displayed by the king himself, and the many ambassadors and political agents whom he employed, he had succeeded in forming a coalition of twenty separate States, embracing England, the united Provinces, Denmark, Sweden, Northern Germany, Switzerland. At last the time for action came. The Duke of Cleves died, 25th March 1609. The succession was disputed. One of the claimants of the Dukedom was supported by the Emperor, another by the Protestant Princes of Germany. The contest about a small German Duchy presented the opportunity for bringing into action that alliance which Henry had planned and perfected. In the great military movements that were projected he was himself to take the lead. Four French armies, numbering 100,000, were to be launched against the great enemy of European liberty. One of these Henry was to command; even our young Prince of Wales was to bring 6000 English with him, and make his first essay in arms under the French King. By the end of April 1610, 35,000 men and 50 pieces of cannon had assembled at Chalons. The 20th May was fixed as the day on which Henry was to place himself at its head. The fire of earlier days was once more kindled in his heart. He had long had a presentiment, however, that his life was not to be a long one; and on the eve of every important crisis his fears revived. "I don't know how it is," he said to Bassompiere, "but I can't persuade myself that I shall ever get to Germany." He longed to be in the midst of his gallant soldiers, where he knew that all these fears would be scattered to the winds One thing alone detained him—the consecration of the Queen.[1] She was urgent that the ceremony should be gone through before he left. Henry exceedingly disliked the idea. "Ah, my friend," he said to Sully, "how this consecration galls; accursed consecration, you will be the cause of my death!" The idea somehow had struck him that he would never get out of Paris, and that he would die in a carriage. Sully advised him to put off the ceremony, and to leave Paris immediately on horseback. He yielded to the entreaties of the Queen. On Thursday, the 13th of May, she was consecrated at St. Denis. Her public entry into Paris was fixed for the 16th, and on the 18th Henry was to depart for Chalons. On the morning of the 16th he went to mass. Coming out of the church, he was joined by some of his courtiers, with whom he was

---

[1] Marie de Medicis.

talking with his usual sprightliness. One of them
happened to compliment Henry on the grace of
his pleasantry. A deep sadness at once succeeded
to the mirth. "Ah!" said he, "you don't know
me as I am; but I shall die one of these days, and
when you have lost me you will then know my
worth, and the difference that there is between me
and other men." Bassompiere remonstrated with
him about vexing his faithful subjects by speaking
about dying when surrounded with such prosperity.
"My friend," said Henry, sighing, "we must leave
all that." All forenoon he was sad and restless.
After dinner he retired to his cabinet, but he could
not write. He threw himself on his bed, but he
could not sleep. He rose and went forward to the
window, striking his hand upon his forehead, saying,
"My God! there is something within that troubles
me sadly." He walked up and down the room, then
threw himself again upon the bed, and was heard to
be engaged in prayer. Rising quickly, he inquired
what hour it was. He was told it was four o'clock.
"Sire," said the person who told him, "you are sad,
would you not be the better of going out and enjoy-
ing a little of the fresh air?" The King caught at
the idea, and ordered his carriage. Twice, when it
was at the door, he went back to the Queen: "Ma
mie, shall I go or shall I not go?" She entreated
him to remain; but he went. Five or six noblemen
went with him in the carriage; but when Vitry, the
captain of the guard, asked whether he should attend

him with a company of his men—"No," said the King, "I will guard myself." The carriage was an open one. Henry sat next to its left hand door, having the Duke of Épernon sitting beside him on his right hand, and the Duke of Montbazon sitting immediately opposite. They drove down the Rue St. Honoré, and turned into the narrow street La Ferronnerie. They met two conveyances in this street, and the royal carriage had to draw up for a few moments close in upon some shops erected against the walls of the church of St. Innocent. The King had turned round, and was speaking to the Duke of Épernon, having his left hand upon the shoulder of the Duke of Montbazon, leaving thus his left side exposed, when a man, who unnoticed had been watching and following the carriage since it left the Louvre, glided between the shops and the carriage, raised himself quickly by putting one foot on the curb-stone and the other on a spoke of the carriage-wheel, and with a sharp two-edged knife struck twice at the King in the region of the heart. He uttered a feeble cry. "What is it, Sire?" said Montbazon. "Nothing—nothing," was the answer, and Henry sank dead upon the seat. They buried him amid a nation's tears. And France might truly weep over his grave. For if ever she had a sovereign to whom her well-being was dear, and who lived and labored to promote it—if ever she had a monarch upon her throne that was every inch a Frenchman—if ever king of hers incarnated that love of gayety and glory for which as a nation she is so distinguished, it was Henry IV. Two centuries and a half have passed since they buried him, yet it is said that even now were he to rise from the grave there is not a village in France in which he would not instantly be recognized. The light and springy figure, the loose and easy gait, the oval countenance, the beaming blue eye, the ruddy sunburned cheek, the long peaked nose, the salient chin, the curly gray beard, the bushy eyebrow, the arched and lofty forehead, would tell them who he was.

It has been the chief events in Henry's reign rather than the features of his personal character, or the incidents of his private and domestic life, that I have endeavored in these lectures to trace. As a soldier and as a ruler we can think of him with unmingled admiration. As soldier he is perfect. Not a great tactician like Parma, nor a great military genius like Marlborough, nor a great general like Napoleon, but above them in that fiery dash of fearless, gay, impetuous valor, which passed like an electric flash into the ranks he led, and guided them to victory. In a land where military courage was so common, and carried to such a height, he wore and deserved the title of the bravest of the brave. As humane as he was courageous, his military renown is unstained with a single deed of cruelty.

It is but seldom that a soldier of Henry's type is as great in the cabinet as on the battle-field. But it was so with him. The result of all recent researches into the domestic and foreign administration of his reign is to place him in the very highest rank as a wise and able ruler—a subtle and expert politician. Many of those speculations about the future political ordering of Europe, in which, during his later years, he was so fond of indulging, were certainly Utopian; but many, indeed the most important, of them have since been realized; nor was any man so capable of and so fond of speculation as he proved himself to be, ever less under the influence of theory in the field of action—the same eye that wandered over the region of the conceivable being so quick to discern what alone should be attempted and what could actually be carried out. He died on the very eve of the execution of that great design that for years he had been maturing. There can be but little doubt that had he lived a few years longer Europe would have been saved that Thirty Years' War through which she afterwards had to pass. Her movement onwards toward that condition of a well-regulated equilibrium among the great powers, in which were guarded the liberties of individual States, would by a century at least have been accelerated.

It is as a man that we have the greatest difficulty in adjusting our estimate of Henry. There is such a fascination, such a seductiveness about his irrepressible vitality and humanity—his sparkling wit, his ready repartee, his piquant but genial raillery, his imperturbable, inexhaustible, glorious good-humor, that we forget that these laughing eyes are never off the watch, that behind that free and easy, most *dégagé* mien and manner, there is a subtlety and a selfishness that keeps in constant view the ends he is pursuing, and never loses the opportunity of advancing them. By that jovial bonhommie, in itself so natural and so true, he lays a spell on the hearts of men, he wins them to him and makes them all his own. He keeps too as well as he wins—most affectionate and generous in all his intercourse with them; but he turns them all to his own uses, and if any of them cease to be serviceable, or should begin to thwart him, he contents himself with discarding them; incapable of revenge, but as devoid, perhaps as incapable, of any deep and lasting gratitude; the pleasantest of all companions, but not the truest of all friends. Strange mixture here, but one not altogether so rare, of that free outgoing sociality and amiability of disposition which delights in being happy for the time with others, and in making others happy, in pleasing and being pleased, with a refined and concentrated, a cool, a calculating, often a heartless self-regard. The only shrine at which we see Henry sacrificing his self-interest was the shrine of self-indulgence. There it was, in that unbridled taste for self-gratification, that his great weakness lay. He knew it so well himself, was so ready to acknowledge it, that we find ourselves more than half disarmed in censuring. We cannot help liking even when we condemn; for there wanted but in this man the power of self-restraint, the deep conviction of duty, a conscience toward God, to have made him not only one of the greatest of sovereigns, but one of the greatest and most lovable of men.

THE END.

www.ingramcontent.com/pod-product-compliance
Lightning Source LLC
Chambersburg PA
CBHW031857220426
43663CB00006B/655